Old and Middle English Words for 'Disgrace' and 'Dishonour'

BY
INGEGERD LOHMANDER

Inaugural dissertation
by due permission of the Philological Section of the Arts Faculty
of Göteborg University to be publicly discussed in English at the
Department of English, Lundgrensgatan 7, Room 237, on
November 9, 1981, at 10 a.m., for the degree of Doctor of
Philosophy.

For an abstract of the thesis, see overleaf.

ABSTRACT

<u>Old and Middle English Words for 'disgrace' and 'dishonour'</u>, Ingegerd
Lohmander, University of Göteborg, Department of English, 1981.

This study aims to investigate some structural changes in the English
lexicon. It deals with vocabulary in translations from chiefly three
periods of the English language. The first period, which is the initial
stage of Old English prose writing, embraces the late ninth and the early
tenth centuries; the second, which is the so-called classical Old English
period, the time from ca. 950 to ca. 1100; finally, the third, the late
Middle English period, a time-span from ca. 1350 to ca. 1500. The
twelfth, thirteenth, and early fourteenth centuries are also represented
in the material, though only to a small extent.

The semantic field has been delimited by means of the Old English word
<u>bismer</u> 'shame', 'disgrace', 'insult', etc., and its derivatives and com-
pounds. In the Old English translations these "<u>bismer</u>-words" render
several Latin words. The Latin words which have been translated by a
<u>bismer</u>-word at least twice form the basis of the present collection. The
collection includes all the Old and Middle English words used to render
those Latin words in the excerpted sources.

Important sources from the early Old English period are King Alfred's
translations into West Saxon. A conspicuous feature of King Alfred's
vocabulary is the great variety it shows in the renderings of a Latin
word. New compounds and derivatives were often formed to render Latin
words. Alfred's vocabulary can be said to reflect his endeavour to adapt
the old native word material to new use. In the classical period Alfred's
dialect, West Saxon, prevailed, but very few of the words he used in the
semantic field in question continued to be used in the same way. Towards
the end of the fourteenth century all the words which covered the relevant
semantic field in the classical Old English period, except three, had disappeared completely or almost completely. They had been replaced by
French loan words, one Scandinavian word, and two new English formations
which did not survive in Modern English.

In the Old English period translative activities resulted in a richly
varied literary vocabulary of native origin. However, the results of the
thesis lend support to the theory that the thorough restructuring of the
English vocabulary, again often initiated by translators, which took place
in the Middle English period produced a somewhat less varied vocabulary of
largely French origin.

Key words: translations, Latin, Old English, Middle English, vocabulary,
           semantic field, shame, restructuring

PREFACE

On the completion of the present work I would like to express my indebtedness to my supervisor, **Göran Kjellmer**, who has devoted many hours to it. It owes a great deal to his constructive criticism and advice. I also wish to thank Professor Alvar Ellegård for his encouragement, and for advice, especially on matters of presentation. Professor Åke Fridh was kind enough to supply valuable information concerning the Latin texts and word material. My thanks are also due to Ronald Paul, who kindly undertook to revise my English. Finally I want to mention how much help I have got from my husband, Carl-Johan Lohmander, on all levels of my work, endless proof-reading alternating with discussions about the logic of individual passages.

Göteborg, October 1981

Ingegerd Lohmander

ABSTRACT

Old and Middle English Words for 'disgrace' and 'dishonour', Ingegerd
Lohmander, University of Göteborg, Department of English, 1981.

This study aims to investigate some structural changes in the English
lexicon. It deals with vocabulary in translations from chiefly three
periods of the English language. The first period, which is the initial
stage of Old English prose writing, embraces the late ninth and the early
tenth centuries; the second, which is the so-called classical Old English
period, the time from ca. 950 to ca. 1100; finally, the third, the late
Middle English period, a time-span from ca. 1350 to ca. 1500. The
twelfth, thirteenth, and early fourteenth centuries are also represented
in the material, though only to a small extent.

The semantic field has been delimited by means of the Old English word
bismer 'shame', 'disgrace', 'insult', etc., and its derivatives and compounds. In the Old English translations these "bismer-words" render
several Latin words. The Latin words which have been translated by a
bismer-word at least twice form the basis of the present collection. The
collection includes all the Old and Middle English words used to render
those Latin words in the excerpted sources.

Important sources from the early Old English period are King Alfred's
translations into West Saxon. A conspicuous feature of King Alfred's
vocabulary is the great variety it shows in the renderings of a Latin
word. New compounds and derivatives were often formed to render Latin
words. Alfred's vocabulary can be said to reflect his endeavour to adapt
the old native word material to new use. In the classical period Alfred's
dialect, West Saxon, prevailed, but very few of the words he used in the
semantic field in question continued to be used in the same way. Towards
the end of the fourteenth century all the words which covered the relevant
semantic field in the classical Old English period, except three, had disappeared completely or almost completely. They had been replaced by
French loan words, one Scandinavian word, and two new English formations
which did not survive in Modern English.

In the Old English period translative activities resulted in a richly
varied literary vocabulary of native origin. However, the results of the
thesis lend support to the theory that the thorough restructuring of the
English vocabulary, again often initiated by translators, which took place
in the Middle English period produced a somewhat less varied vocabulary of
largely French origin.

Key words: translations, Latin, Old English, Middle English, vocabulary,
semantic field, shame, restructuring

TABLE OF CONTENTS

I.   INTRODUCTION 5

II. MATERIAL 8
     1. Selection and Delimitation of Semantic Field 8
     2. Periods 12
     3. Regions 15
     4. Maps of Old and Middle English Dialect Areas 16
          4.1. The Dialects of Old English 17
          4.2. The Dialects of Middle English 18
     5. Nature of the Sources 19
          5.1. Bible Texts 19
          5.2. Non-Bible Texts 21
     6. Arrangement of Collected Material 25
     7. Delimitation 27

III. INTERPRETATION OF MEANING 29
     1. Meaning of Latin Words According to Current Dictionaries 29
     2. Information from the Context 35
          2.1. Qualification in the Form of Adjunct Words, Prepo-
               sitional Phrases or Relative Clauses 35
          2.2. Contrast 36
          2.3. Variation 36
          2.4. Passages outside the Immediate Context 36
     3. Parallel Versions 37
     4. Deviations from the Original 37

IV. SEMANTIC CLASSIFICATION 41
     1. The Two Main Sense Groups A:Activity and B:State 41
     2. Sense Group A:Activity and Its Division into Subgroups   43
          2.1. Subgroup A I:Devil-Men 43
          2.2. Subgroup A II:Men-God 44
          2.3. Subgroup A III:Men-Men 44
     3. Sense Group B:State and Its Division into Subgroups 48
          3.1. Subgroup B I:Misfortunes 50
          3.2. Subgroup B II:Unchastity 50
          3.3. Subgroup B III:Misbehaviour 51

4. Expressions from A III b:Men-Men-TS Compared with Expressions from B:State 51

5. List of Division into Sense Groups 55

V. VOCABULARY OF DIFFERENT SENSE GROUPS 56

1. Lists OE 3-5 and ME 3-4 56

2. The Words Discussed Individually and in Relation to Each Other within the Sense Groups 56

   2.1. Sense Group A:Activity 56

      2.1.1. Subgroup A I:Devil-Men and the Minor Group A III 1:Men-Men-Derision 56

         2.1.1.1. The Old English Bismer-Words 57

         2.1.1.2. The Old English Non-Bismer-Words 58

         2.1.1.3. The Middle English Words 58

      2.1.2. Subgroup A II:Men-God 59

      2.1.3. The Minor Group A III 2:Men-Men-Calumny 61

      2.1.4. The Minor Group A III 3:Men-Men-Insult 63

         2.1.4.1. The Old English Bismer-Words 63

         2.1.4.2. Old English Edwīt and Hosp 63

         2.1.4.3. Old English Tēona 63

         2.1.4.4. Old English Words Other than Tēona Used to Render Contumelia and Injuria 65

         2.1.4.5. Middle English Wrong 66

         2.1.4.6. Middle English Repref/etc. 66

         2.1.4.7. Middle English Shenship/etc. 66

         2.1.4.8. Middle English Words Other than Wrong, Repref/etc., and Shenship/etc. 68

      2.1.5. Summary of Sense Group A:Activity 70

   2.2. Sense Group B:State 71

      2.2.1. Special Features of Latin Words in B:State ... 71

         2.2.1.1. Confusio 72

         2.2.1.2. Verecundia and Pudor 73

         2.2.1.3. Reverentia 74

         2.2.1.4. Ignominia 76

      2.2.2. Subgroup B I:Misfortunes 77

         2.2.2.1. Old English Words 77

         2.2.2.2. Middle English Words 77

      2.2.3. Subgroup B II:Unchastity 78

         2.2.3.1. Old English Words 78

         2.2.3.2. Middle English Words 78

            2.2.4. Subgroup B III:Misbehaviour 79
                   2.2.4.1. Old English Words 79
                   2.2.4.2. Middle English Words 79
            2.2.5. Summary of Sense Group B:State 80
      3. Words Occurring in Both Main Sense Groups, A and B 81
         3.1. Old English Words 81
            3.1.1. The Bismer-Words 81
            3.1.2. Teona 81
            3.1.3. Orwyrd/Orwurd 82
            3.1.4. Scomu/Sceomu - Scamu/Sceamu 83
            3.1.5. Scand/Scond 84
            3.1.6. Yfel 84
         3.2. Middle English Words 84

VI. VOCABULARY OF DIFFERENT PERIODS 87
    1. The Early Old English Period 87
       1.1. The Vocabulary of the Different Sense Groups 87
          1.1.1. The Bismer-Words 87
          1.1.2. The Non-Bismer-Words 88
                 1.1.2.1. King Alfred's Vocabulary 88
                 1.1.2.2. The Anglian Vocabulary of the Early
                          Old English Period 92
    2. The Classical Old English Period 93
       2.1. The Vocabulary of the Different Sense Groups 93
          2.1.1. The Bismer-Words 93
          2.1.2. The Non-Bismer-Words 94
    3. The Late Middle English Period 97
       3.1. The Vocabulary of the Different Sense Groups 98
       3.2. Native Words 99
          3.2.1. Shame 99
          3.2.2. Harm 99
          3.2.3. Filth 100
          3.2.4. Shenship and Filthhed 100
       3.3. Scandinavian Words 100
          3.3.1. Wrong 100
          3.3.2. Ill 101
       3.4. French Words 101

VII. REASONS FOR CHANGES IN SEMANTIC FIELD 101

      1. Loan Word Prestige 103

      2. Influence of Latin Originals 104

VIII. SUMMARY 108

APPENDIX A. TEXTS 113

     I. REGIONAL AND CHRONOLOGICAL ARRANGEMENT OF TEXTS 115

       1. Old English Texts 115

       2. Middle English Texts 117

     II. DESCRIPTION OF TEXTS 118

       1. Old English Bible Texts 119

       2. Old English Non-Bible Texts 124

       3. Middle English Bible Texts 130

       4. Middle English Non-Bible Texts 132

APPENDIX B. LISTS 135

     List OE 1. Distribution of Old English Material over
              Latin Words 136

     List OE 2. Recorded Variants of Old English Head-
              Words 140

     List OE 3. Distribution of Old English Material over
              Sense Groups 143

     List OE 4. Distribution of Old English Material over
              Sense Groups and Centuries 145

     List OE 5. Distribution of Old English Material over
              Dialects and Centuries 148

     List ME 1. Distribution of Middle English Material
              over Latin Words 155

     List ME 2. Recorded Variants of Middle English Head-
              Words 159

     List ME 3. Distribution of Middle English Material
              over Sense Groups 162

     List ME 4. Distribution of Middle English Material
              over Sense Groups and Centuries 164

APPENDIX C. TEXT MATERIAL 173

APPENDIX D. BIBLIOGRAPHY 213

APPENDIX E. INDEX 217

      1. Old English Words 219

      2. Middle English Words 224

      3. Latin Words 227

I. INTRODUCTION

The object of this study is the vocabulary of a limited lexical "field" in Old and Middle English.

The idea of "field" in semantics began to appear half a century ago. One of the most important of the so-called "field-semanticists" is the German linguist Jost Trier, whose work in the 1930´s was very influential. He assumes that there are regions, or "fields", in a language in such a way that the words in each region of a language are dependent on each other for their meaning. Semantically related words delimit and influence the meaning of each other. They should therefore not be treated as isolated items but as pieces of a complex whole. The fields join to form in turn fields of a higher order. Thus the vocabulary of a language forms a complete semantic structure in the manner of a mosaic which covers an underlying conceptual field without gaps and overlapping. The synchronic (descriptive) method was given preference over the diachronic (historic) method, which had predominated in the nineteenth century. Semanticists began to study sets of related words at various stages of a language instead of the changes in the meaning of individual words over the centuries.

There are linguists who doubt that the descriptive method can ever be fully applied to vocabulary in the same way as it has been to phonemics and grammar. Waldron (1967), p. 169, maintains that "those [descriptive] techniques rest upon the heuristic construction of an état de langue, a synchronic section through the language enabling the observer to view the linguistic system in a fixed state in which every part has a determined function in relation to the whole. But where vocabulary is concerned change is too rapid for the concept of a fixed state to carry much weight ...". It may in any case sometimes be expedient to widen the concept of "synchronic" to embrace many decades or even whole centuries, where the vocabularies of linguistic systems in the remote past are concerned, as in the case of parts of the Old English and Early Middle English periods, from which only a small number of documents remain (see pp. 12-14).

The metaphor of a mosaic for the semantic structure of a vocabulary has been criticized by many linguists. Waldron (1967) holds that overlapping is the rule rather than the exception. Lehrer (1974) prefers for the analysis of semantic fields the model of focal points, which

"allows for fuzzy borders among lexical items ..." (Lehrer, 1974, p.
16).   The expression "Feld", English "field", is misleading, says
Leisi (1973), p. 100. He prefers "Bezirk", "Bereich", or English
"semantic area". "Feld", he says, implies something more sharply delimited than "Bezirk", "Bereich", or "semantic area". To determine
what semantic fields there are and which lexical items belong to each
field is clearly a problem of the field approach. Lehrer (1974) makes
the following statement at the end of her book (p. 201), "The problem
of determining the inventory of lexical items in a field remains." My
method of selecting lexical items for this study, which is an attempt
to investigate a limited semantic field in Old and Middle English (see
p. 5), is explained in Chapter II. The items (words) can be said to
have the concept of shame/disgrace as a common denominator.

My material, chiefly taken from three periods of the English language, shows the vocabulary of the chosen field in translations of Latin texts (see p. 11). The first period, which is the initial stage of
Old English prose writing, embraces the late ninth and the early tenth
centuries; the second, which is the so-called classical Old English
period, the time from ca. 950 to ca. 1100. Finally, the third is late
Middle English embracing a time-span from ca. 1350 to ca. 1500. The
twelfth, thirteenth, and early fourteenth centuries are also represented in my collection. The number of manuscripts from these centuries,
however, is small. See p. 14.

To compare vocabularies from the Old and the Middle English periods
can, in many cases, only to a lesser extent be a matter of studying
changes in the sounds and meanings of individual words. Often the
words in semantically equivalent sets are not the same. The strong
French political and cultural influence during the Middle English period brought about great changes in English vocabulary. Large groups of
abstract Old English nouns, for instance, have almost completely disappeared. Out of those Old English words that in Hall & Meritt (1970)
(henceforth quoted as HM) have been rendered by any of the Modern English words shame, disgrace, and dishonour, only one has survived, viz.
Old English scamu. The words I refer to are given below in alphabetical order: ablysung, aefwyrd/-u, aepsenes, arscamu, aewisc, aswarnung,
bismer, edwit, edwitscipe, edwitstaef, forwandung, fracod/-cud, gescendnes, orwyrd/-u, scamu, scamung, scand, scandlicnes, tael, unar, unge-
risnu, ungewiss, unhlisa, unweordscipe, unweordnes, unwlite, and wamm/

<u>wem</u>. The Old English vocabulary of the opposite concept, that of <u>honour/</u>
<u>glory</u>, seems to have the same rate of survival. Only one of the words
rendered by <u>honour</u> or <u>glory</u> in HM has survived in Modern English (see p.
104).

I have carried out this investigation in the hope of showing how and
when this restructuring of the English vocabulary for the semantic field
of <u>shame/disgrace</u> took place. The following questions will give an in-
dication of the aims of my study: How did the early translators use the
Old English vocabulary? How did they apply it to the new shades of
meaning which they had to render (see pp. 9 and 91)? What changes took
place in the relevant field in the course of the Old English period, i.e.
what are the differences between the Old English vocabulary of the early
and that of the later, so-called Classical, period? What happened to
the vocabulary of this particular field in the Middle English period?
How could words from a foreign vocabulary oust whole groups of old well-
established words?

II. MATERIAL

1. Selection and Delimitation of Semantic Field

There are no objective criteria by which the vocabulary of a language
can be divided into semantic fields. The delimitation of a field is
therefore more or less arbitrary or rather dependent on the sphere of
interest chosen in each individual case. The most common method of delimitation has been to proceed from a general notion or concept. Trier
(see p. 5), for instance, investigated the field of the intellect at
various stages of medieval German. During the last few decades a number
of German semanticists have carried out studies of sets of abstract
nouns in the Old English vocabulary. The following works are of special
interest here as they deal with words closely related to those dealt
with in this investigation (see pp. 6-7): Käsmann (1951), " 'Tugend
und Laster' im Alt- und Mittelenglischen"; Fetzlaff (1954), "Bezeichnungen für die sieben Todsünden in der altenglischen Prosa"; Schabram
(1965), Superbia I. These semanticists have more or less consistently
used the relevant Latin words as a basis of their collections. Others
have settled upon certain conceptually related words, e.g. Büchner
(1968), "Vier altenglische Bezeichnungen für Vergehen und Verbrechen
(firen, gylt, man, scyld)".

Several approaches are possible when studying semantic fields. The
intuitive approach, which amounts to including the words that somehow
seem relevant, is arbitrary and depends on the knowledge and amount of
reading of the research worker. The dictionary approach, which I have
exemplified on pp. 6-7, is less arbitrary but implies all the same
that relevant items may be missing. My example on p. 6 gives the Old
English words rendered by shame, disgrace, and dishonour in HM. It includes the Anglian word edwit, but not its West Saxon counterpart hosp
(see p. 70); it also includes scand and its derivatives, which are the
most frequent words in one of my main Sense groups, B:State, but not
gedroefnis/etc., which is the third most frequent word in the Sense
group (see List OE 3). Bismer is there but none of its derivatives or
compounds (see List OE 2). I have chosen a third approach. My semantic field was at first delimited by means of one word, namely bismer
'disgrace, shame, insult', a word which renders several conceptually related Latin words in the Old English translations. The Latin words in
question form the basis of my collection, which includes all the Old

and Middle English words used to render those Latin words in my texts.
About drawbacks see below, p. 11.

To proceed from the Latin words in a semantic study of Old English
vocabulary seems suitable for many reasons. As far as we know, prose
writers in England before the time of King Alfred wrote in Latin only.
King Alfred, devoted to the education of his people, the West Saxons,
"hit upon the simple but revolutionary idea of using his mother tongue
rather than Latin as a basic medium of instruction, both in the schools
and in adult education." (Baugh, 1967, pp. 96-97.) Old English prose
from Alfred's time (late ninth century) consists mainly in translations
of Latin texts. An obvious consequence of the prominent position of
Latin at this initial stage of Old English prose writing was that the
Latin vocabulary exerted great influence on the formation of the Old
English literary vocabulary, which to a great extent was formed or
transformed by the translators. When Alfred and his assistants (see p.
12) set out to translate the works of the Church Fathers as well as
other important theological, philosophical and historical works (App. A
II, pp. 124-126), they had to find words for new concepts (see p. 91).
Loan words were not as readily adopted in this period as they were later,
especially in the Middle English period. Instead of borrowing foreign
words the early translators tried to manage with the native stock. Often
new compounds and derivatives were formed for the purpose of rendering
certain Latin words. Examples of such formations occurring only in
Alfred's texts are woruldbismer:contumelia, unār:injuria, and unweord-
scipe:indignatio/dedecus (see p. 90). Compare also woruldgielp:gloria
temporalis/laus humana and lēasgielp:(inanis) gloria, one of the seven
deadly sins (Fetzlaff, 1954, pp. 33-36). As a result of the endeavours
to adapt the old native word material to new use many old words acquired
new shades of meaning, i.e. they adopted or "borrowed" the meanings of
the Latin words which they rendered. An often quoted example of such a
"semantic borrowing" is gōd spel (modern gospel):evangelium. Gōd spel
'good message' is a literal translation of bonum nuntium (or bona adnuntiatio[1]), which was used as an explanation of the etymological sense
of evangelium (Greek euangélion). In a glossary from ca. 1050 (WW X,
314,8), for instance, we find "Euuangelium, id est, bonum nuntium, gōd-

[1]The OED (s.v. gospel) records an instance of gōd spel rendering Latin bona adnuntiatio from the Corpus Glossary (App. A II, p. 129). I
have not been able to find the instance in the Corpus Glossary.

spel". Cf. translations such as bismer-spraec and ebolsung/yfelsang/
etc., which were used for just one Latin word, viz. blasphemia (pp. 60-
61). Only one of the Old English words relevant to this investigation
is of Latin origin (see p. 89, footnote 2). About Latin influence on
Old English before Alfred's time see Baugh (1959), p. 93 f. Latin
borrowings of a learned character, which owe their introduction to the
religious revival of the Benedictine Reform in the latter part of the
tenth century (see p. 13) have been dealt with in Baugh (1959), p. 102 f.

During my preliminary investigations, when I tried to find a suitable group of words to settle upon for my study, I worked with King
Alfred's translations. As they represent an initial stage of Old English prose writing (see above) they seemed appropriate to start with.
What I wanted was a group of abstract nouns which had not been the object of an earlier investigation. Words denoting sins and vices as well
as virtues had been studied by the German scholars mentioned above, p.
8. Others have written about Old English words for joy[1], happiness,
success, luck[2]. Also honour/glory[3] has been investigated to some extent. It occurred to me that the opposite of honour/glory, i.e. shame/
disgrace, seemed not to have been dealt with so far. I found that the
word bismer in King Alfred's translations was used for a large number
of Latin nouns in my general semantic field, no less than 12, meaning
'disgrace', 'insult', 'reproach', 'shame', etc. As all the Latin words
which bismer rendered in these translations showed a certain degree of
semantic relationship, bismer was obviously not a strongly polysemantic
word. This made it appropriate as a basis for selecting Latin words,
and I decided to collect, from the Latin originals and the Old English
translations, all the instances of those Latin nouns that had been rendered, at least once, by a bismer-word. The definition of "bismer-word"
is to be found on p. 25.

As my work proceeded, the number of Latin nouns rendered by bismer-
words increased to 26. Of course these Latin nouns were not rendered
everywhere by bismer-words. In the great majority of instances they
were rendered by other words. Thus, my collection of Old English words

---

[1]Reuning (1941)
[2]Winter (1955)
[3]Freudenthal (1959)

grew to a very large number. In order to avoid including a lot of Old
and Middle English words which have little or no meaning in common with
bismer I decided to exclude all Latin nouns that had not been rendered
by a bismer-word "at least twice". By means of this delimitation I
could exclude nine Latin nouns (see p. 27). One more Latin word (expression), viz. nenias/naenias (vanitates), which has been rendered by
a bismer-word more than once, was excluded because of its low frequency
in the excerpted texts. The instances recorded for it are to be found
on p. 28.

To sum up, my Old and Middle English material consists of the English
words that were used to translate those 16 Latin nouns that had been
translated at least twice by Old English bismer-words.

With such a method, of course, it is not entirely possible to avoid
including English words which have only little meaning in common with
bismer. Examples of such words are Old English gewrixle ´turn, change´,
duolma ´chaos´, and Middle English confusion/confusioun in the sense of
´disorder, mixture´. The words render Latin confusio (see pp. 72-73).
However, none of the 16 Latin words referred to are strongly polysemantic or have spellings representing different words. Consequently my
material contains very few instances of words which lie entirely outside
the limits of the relevant semantic field.

Six of the Old English words which have been rendered by shame, disgrace, or dishonour in HM (see pp. 6 and 8:"dictionary approach") are
missing in my material. They are aefwyrd, āewisc[1], ārscamu[2], āswārnung[3],
edwītscipe[4], and wamm/wemm. Wamm/wemm usually renders Latin macula,
one of those nine Latin words that were excluded on account of the fact
that they had been rendered by a bismer-word only once (see above).

---

[1]Cf. āwescnis/āewiscnes/āewiscnys, which renders reverentia in the
Vespasian, the Junius, and the Cambridger Psalters, Ps. 34,26 (p. 74).

[2]In HM ārscamu ´shame, modesty´ has a reference to PPs 68[19] (= the
Paris Psalter, Ps. 68,19). Such references are given in the case of words
occurring only once or very rarely (HM, p. vii). In the passage referred
to the word renders verecundia or possibly reverentia (p. 71). In
Krapp´s edition (App. A, p. 121) the word arscamu has been explained as
the result of a misinterpretation.

[3]In HM āswārnung ´shame, confusion´ has a reference to LPs 43[16] (= the
Lambeth Psalter, Ps. 43,16), where it renders Latin verecundia (p. 71).
References to particular passages are given in the case of rare words, -
more especially "hapax legomena" (HM, p.vi).

[4]Edwītscipe has a reference to a line in a poetical text (Wald 1[14]) in
HM, indicating that it occurs only once or very rarely (HM,p vii).

2. Periods

In my linguistic source material seven centuries (the ninth – the
fifteenth) are represented, i.e. the time from the beginning of King
Alfred's reign (871) when Old English began to be used in literary
prose, to the end of the Middle English period (here regarded as being
ca. 1500). However, the collection is not as large as might be ex-
pected considering the length of time which it embraces. Extant documents written in the English language are unevenly distributed over
the centuries. There are periods when learning decayed and when literary activity consequently was low. In the preface to his Pastoral
Care (App. A II, p. 124) Alfred tells us about the decay of learning
at the beginning of his reign. A Modern English version of the relevant passage reads as follows: " ... there are very few on this side
of the Humber who could understand their ritual in English, or translate a letter from Latin into English, and I believe not many beyond
the Humber. So few were there that I cannot remember a single one
south of the Thames when I came to the Kingship." (Baugh, 1959, p.
100). The decay was a result of the Scandinavian invasions which had
begun towards the end of the eighth century and which continued with
intermissions during the ninth century. The two famous monasteries
of Northumbria, Lindisfarne and Jarrow, were sacked for the first time
in 793/794. The great Danish invasions of 867-870 put an end to monastic life north of the Humber. Also the monasteries of Wessex and
Mercia were either extinguished during the wars or reduced to houses
where only a few priests or clerics lived together without any full
regular life. See Knowles (1941), pp. 24 and 32. However, parts of
Mercia seem to have been spared, Worcester in particular. We know
that King Alfred, though he wrote for his own people, the West Saxons,
and consequently translated into the West Saxon dialect (see p. 9),
was assisted in his work by four Mercian scholars, viz. Werfrith/Waer-
ferth, who was bishop of Worcester, Athelstan, a Worcester priest,
Plegmund and Werwulf, who were probably also of the Worcester school.
See Baugh (1967), p. 97, and Robinson (1923), p. 13.

The Early Old English period is here delimited to cover the late
ninth and early tenth centuries. King Alfred's Pastoral Care (see
above), the Anglian Vespasian Psalter (see p. 15), and a few vocabularies (see App. A II, p. 129) are the only translations of any impor-

tance that have been preserved to this day in manuscripts written during
the ninth century. Few documents exist from the first half of the tenth
century, the time between King Alfred's death (900/901) and the start of
the second, so-called classical, period. Three of the texts in my material derive from this time. They are the Junius Psalter, a text dependent on the Vespasian Psalter (p. 12), Alfred's Orosius in MS. L (the
Lauderdale MS.), and finally Bede's History in MS. T (MS. Tanner 10)[1], a
translation considered to have been made by one of King Alfred's Mercian
assistants (p. 12). These texts, all three of them copies of older documents, have been dated ca. 925 (Ker: "X[1]"). The Anglo-Saxon Chronicle,
which records contemporary events from the ninth, tenth, eleventh, and
twelfth centuries, does not tell us anything about the second quarter of
the tenth century. The Chronicle ends with the year 923, the year in
which the last of King Alfred's scholarly ecclesiastics, Archbishop Plegmund (p. 12), died, and was not taken up again until 955 (Robinson, 1923,
pp. 15, 25, and 41-42).

The classical period was initiated by the great monastic revival under
Dunstan and Aethelwold, the Benedictine Reform movement, in the latter
part of the tenth century (p. 10). Aethelwold himself translated Regula
S. Benedicti between 960 and 970 into West Saxon, the dialect which pre-
vailed in the classical period (Baugh, 1967, p. 100, Schabram, p. 56, and
App. A, p. 125). Aelfric, the leading prose writer of the period says:
"Until Dunstan and Aethelwold revived learning in the monastic life no
English priest could either write a letter in Latin or understand one."
(Baugh, 1959, p. 101.) The classical period is fairly well represented
by extant documents. The majority of them, however, as e.g. Aelfric's
most important works, are not literal translations and therefore of no
use for my investigation (p. 22). Many of the excerpted texts are based
on West Saxon copies of translations originally made in the early period.
Such copies are e.g. the extant MSS. of Gregory's Dialogues and two MSS.
of Bede's History (MSS. O and B)[1], translations considered to have been
made by two of King Alfred's assistants (App. A, pp. 125-126). Of course,
new translations were also made in the classical period, as for instance
the translations of the Gospels (App. A, p. 122) and the Rule of St.
Benedict (see above). However, very often we do not know for sure if a
manuscript is an original or a copy of an earlier document. About the

---

[1]MS. Tanner 10 (Bede's History) has been dated "end of the tenth century" in Miller's edition, in Ker, however, "X[1]", i.e. ca. 925.

Regius Psalter (dated ca. 950), for example, we can only say that it is
the oldest representative of the West Saxon Psalter glosses not dependent
on the Anglian Vespasian Psalter (App. A, pp. 119-120).

The Norman Conquest (1066) brought about a break in the literary tradition of the English language. For about two centuries after the in-
vasion French was the language of the ruling class in England, and, beside Latin, the language of learning and culture. French was the usual
language of the law courts and of parliament down to 1362. That year
parliament was opened by the chancellor with a speech in English for the
first time, and a statute which constitutes the official recognition of
English was enacted (Baugh, 1959, pp. 177-183). We know that after 1349
English began to be used in schools and also that this practice had become general by 1385 (Baugh, 1959, p. 179). The predominance of French
and Latin as literary languages in the twelfth and thirteenth centuries
accounts for the scarcity of Middle English documents from these centuries. In my lists the twelfth century is represented only by a few "Old
English" texts (App. A, p. 116). My Old English material also includes
a text written in the thirteenth century (see p. 22). Only three of my
Middle English sources have been written in the thirteenth century. They
are the Ancrene Riwle, St. Katherine, and the Surtees Psalter (App. A, pp.
131 and 133). The earliest text in my material from the fourteenth century is the Midland Prose Psalter, London MS., written 1340-50. All other
excerpted Middle English texts are based on manuscripts written during
the second half of the fourteenth or the first half of the fifteenth century.

Dates and origins of my sources are given in Appendix A.

3. Regions

The regional aspect has been considered only in relation to the Old English material, Appendix B. Appendix A I, however, contains regional and chronological arrangements of all the excerpted sources, the Old English (pp. 115-116) and the Middle English (p. 117).

Anglian (Mercian and Northumbrian) and West Saxon are the two main Old English dialects (App. B, List OE 5, pp. 148-154). West Saxon, Alfred's dialect, prevailed in the classical Old English period. Genuinely Anglian documents preserved to this day are very rare. The most important are the Vespasian Psalter (A) from the late ninth century, the Lindisfarne MS. (CND4), dated ca. 950, the Rushworth MS. (Ru[1] and Ru[2]) from the late tenth century, and the Durham Ritual (Dur. Ri.) also from the late tenth century.[1] All remaining texts classified as Anglian are actually West Saxon copies of Anglian originals, but such as are considered to have preserved Anglian characteristics in the vocabulary. See App. A, p. 120: Psalter glosses of A-type, App. A, p. 126: Gregory's Dialogues, MS. C, and App. A, p. 125: Bede's History, MS. T.

---

[1]The Vespasian Psalter and the first part of the Rushworth MS. (Ru[1]), which contains the Gospel of St. Matthew, are written in the Mercian dialect. The second part of the Rushworth MS. (Ru[2]), which contains the three latter Gospels in the Northumbrian dialect, is a copy of the Lindisfarne MS. (CND4). The Durham Ritual (Dur.Ri.) has been written by the same scribe as the Lindisfarne MS. (CND4). See App. A, pp. 122 and 127.

4. Maps of Old and Middle English Dialect Areas

I have not delimited the dialect areas as my intention is to give only a rough idea of the the extention of each area. For exact information I refer to the maps in Baugh (1959), pp. 63 and 235, which have served as a basis for my simplified maps.

4.1. The Dialects of Old English

4.2. The Dialects of Middle English

5. Nature of the Sources

The corpus contains in all 725 instances from texts written in the
Old English period (List OE 1). 78 of them are from vocabularies. Semantic classification of the material from vocabularies is not possible
as no context accompanies the words. The classified instances, 647 in
number (List OE 3), are from excerpted Old English texts, Bible texts and
non-Bible texts, containing ca. 730,000 and 754,000 running words respectively. The Bible texts have yielded 380, i.e. ca. 59%, of the classified instances, the non-Bible texts 267, i.e. only 41%, of these instances. Moreover, 31 of the instances from the non-Bible texts consist
of quotations from the Bible.

The excerpted texts from the Middle English period are Bible texts
containing ca. 2,779,000 running words and non-Bible texts containing ca.
1,030,000 running words. This disproportion, 71% for the Bible texts and
29% for the non-Bible texts, is due to the difficulty of finding Middle
English non-Bible texts suitable for this investigation, namely texts
that are at least to some extent literal translations. Of the total number of instances from the Middle English texts, 1,387 (List ME 1), ca.
1,170, i.e. 84%, are from the Bible texts.

5.1. Bible Texts

The predominance of instances from the Bible in my material is due to
the fact that the translations of the Bible texts show far greater fidelity to the originals than other translations generally do (cf. above).

Some of the Bible texts are also especially valuable for comparing vocabularies from different periods of a language, as they have been translated or copied over and over again in the course of the centuries (see
p. 37). None of the texts translated in the Old English period seem to
have attracted as much attention as the Psalter. There are in existence
thirteen Old English manuscripts containing this text. They are based
on two different Latin versions, the so-called "Roman" and "Gallican"
Psalters respectively (App. A, p. 122). The Old English versions form
two groups, those of the A-type and those of the D-type. Those of the
A-type are the Anglian Vespasian Psalter (dated 875-900) and the versions
dependent on it. Those of the D-type are the West Saxon versions independent of the Vespasian Psalter. Their oldest representative, the
Regius Psalter, is dated ca. 950. (See App. A, p. 119 f.) The Gospels

seem to have been next to the Psalter in popularity, if we are to judge from the number of extant manuscripts. In Skeat's edition (App. A, p. 122) four Old English manuscripts are printed in full together with variant readings of three other manuscripts. The oldest of these seven manuscripts is the Lindisfarne MS. (MS. CND4), an Anglian text from ca. 950 (p. 15). The oldest of the West Saxon manuscripts, the Corpus MS., has been dated ca. 1000.

My most important source from the Middle English period is the so-called Wyclif Bible. The earliest version (EV 1) is the text of MS. Bodley 959 from ca. 1385. It contains the Old Testament books Genesis - Baruch 3,20. Forshall & Madden's edition (henceforth FM) is based on six other manuscripts, the youngest dated "not later than 1420" (App. A, pp. 130-131). In relation to the texts of the Wyclif Bible the two Early Middle English Psalter versions, the Surtees Psalter and the Midland Prose Psalter (also called the West Midland Psalter), are of special interest in my material. The texts of the Wyclif Bible are mainly in the East Midland dialect of Late Middle English. The Surtees Psalter, a text of Northern or Midland origin from the late thirteenth century, probably depended directly or indirectly on an Old English glossed version, the Midland Prose Psalter (the London MS. from 1340-50; the Dublin MS., a revision of the text in the London MS., from 1375-1425) on a French glossed version (App. A, pp. 131-132). These two versions are useful for comparison, as they form a link between the Late Old English Psalter versions and the Late Middle English ones of the Wyclif Bible. A text which was not available to me is the Psalter and Psalms of David by Richard Rolle of Hampole, edited by H.R. Bramley, 1884 (Severs II, p. 539). The selections of this Psalter in H.E. Allen's edition, English Writings of Richard Rolle, Oxford, 1931, do not contain any of my words. Two editions containing parts of the New Testament have also been excerpted. They are A Fourteenth Century English Biblical Version (Paues, App. A, p. 132) and the Northern Pauline Epistles (NPE, App. A, p. 132).

Quotations from the Bible are frequent in religious non-Bible texts such as Cura Pastoralis, Regula S. Benedicti, Liber Scintillarum, De Vitiis et Peccatis, and De Virtutibus et Vitiis (App. A, pp. 124-127). My Old English material from non-Bible texts includes 31 such instances (see p. 19). Many of these quotations are from Bible texts of which no Old English versions exist, as for instance Sirach (Ecclesiasticus), Proverbs, Isaiah, Jeremiah, Ezekiel, and the New Testament Epistles. Such an in-

stance is Phillippians 3,19: <u>Quorum deus venter est, et gloria in con-</u>
<u>fusionem ipsorum</u>. The passage is quoted in <u>Cura Pastoralis</u>, and conse-
quently an Old English version of it occurs in King Alfred's <u>Pastoral</u>
<u>Care</u>. The word <u>confusio</u>, one of the words dealt with in this investiga-
tion, has been rendered by <u>bismer</u> (App. C, p. 185). The same passage
occurs in one of Aelfric's homilies, but there <u>confusio</u> is rendered by
<u>gescyndnys</u> (App. C, p. 185). The Middle English versions of the <u>Wyclif</u>
<u>Bible</u> (EV 2 and LV) and Paues (see above, p. 20) have in this instance
<u>confusioun/confusyoun</u> (App. C, pp. 208-209).

5.2. Non-Bible Texts

The proportion of instances from non-Bible texts is far greater in my
Old English material than it is in my Middle English material (see p. 19).
The great value of the Bible texts, being close translations, and the
difficulty of finding non-Bible texts that are literal translations, es-
pecially from the Middle English period, has already been emphasized.
Owing to this difficulty I have included a few poetic texts in my ma-
terial, even though such texts are generally free translations (see App.
A, pp. 132-133 and below, pp. 22-24).

King Alfred's <u>Pastoral Care</u>, which belongs to what has been called the
earlier period of Alfred's literary career (Baugh, 1967, p. 97), is a
close translation. So are the works ascribed to two of his assistants,
i.e. Waerferth's translation of Gregory's <u>Dialogues</u> and the translation
of Bede's <u>History</u> (see p. 13). The works of King Alfred's later period,
<u>Orosius</u> and <u>Boethius</u>, are, on the other hand, paraphrases rather than
translations, especially <u>Boethius</u> (App. A, p. 124). Although the Latin
text of <u>Boethius</u> abounds in instances of the relevant Latin words, I have
not been able to record more than ten instances from that work.

Important sources from the later, classical, Old English period are
the translations of <u>Regula S. Benedicti</u> and <u>Liber Scintillarum</u>. The
first translation of <u>Regula S. Benedicti</u> was made between 960 and 970 by
Aethelwold, Aelfric's teacher and one of the leaders of the Benedictine
Reform movement (p. 13). According to Schabram (p. 56) one of the extant
manuscripts, nine in number, dates from the tenth century. However, I
have not found any edition based on the text of this manuscript (MS. CCCO
197: Corpus Christi College, Oxford, No. 197). The earliest version of
Aethelwold's translation in my material is the text of a manuscript dated
ca. 1025 (MS. A). A version considered to be independent of the earlier

ones is the <u>Interlinear Version</u> in a manuscript from the middle of the
eleventh century. A late Old English version, the <u>Winteney Version</u>,
is contained in a manuscript written in the first quarter of the thirteenth century, i.e. in the Middle English period (see p. 14). MS.
<u>Cotton Tiberius A 3</u>,   which contains the <u>Interlinear Version</u>, also
contains a translation of Aethelwold's <u>De Consuetudine Monachorum</u>
(App. A, pp. 125 and 127-128).

Aelfric, the leading prose writer of the classical period (see p.13)
is represented in my material only by his translation of a few Old
Testament books (App.A,pp.122-123). His work consists mainly in homilies,
pastoral letters, lives of saints, and learned works of various kinds.
None of them are, as far as I have been able to discover, literal translations. "He treated his sources with great freedom, adapting his material to the needs of English pastor and flock." (Baugh, 1967, p. 101.)

Parts of the <u>Blickling Homilies</u>, a collection of Old English sermons
in a MS. from ca. 970, have been traced back to Latin texts in <u>Mignes</u>
<u>Patrologie</u> by Max Förster. He has published them in <u>Archiv für das</u>
<u>Studium der neueren Sprachen und Literaturen</u>, 116 (1906), pp. 301-305,
and 122 (1909), pp. 246-262, under the title of "Altenglische Predigtquellen I" and "Altenglische Predigtquellen II" respectively. Portions
of the <u>Blickling Homily</u> IV have been traced back to their Latin source,
<u>Patrologie Latina</u> XXXIX, 2266. They occur in Kirby and Woolf (1949),
pp. 65-78. None of my Latin words occur in these parts.

My most important non-Bible source from the Middle English period is
Higden's <u>Polychronicon</u>. Eight heavy volumes (App. A, p. 132) contain
the Latin text together with Trevisa's translation (henceforth Higd.
Trev.) finished in 1387 (Baugh, 1967, p. 268) and the translation of an
unknown writer from the fifteenth century in the <u>Harleian MS. 2261</u>
(henceforth Higd.Harl.). These translations have yielded ca. 105 instances, i.e. nearly half the number of Middle English instances from
non-Bible texts.

The <u>Destruction of Troy</u> (henceforth Destr. Troy) is a poetic text
which abounds in words for <u>shame/disgrace</u>. It is a free translation,
much more so than e.g. the <u>Life of St. Katherine</u>, which is also a poetic
work (App.A,pp. 132-133). Thus it is for the most part very hard to
make out which expression is to be considered as the translation of a
given Latin word. To demonstrate this and to show my manner of proceed-
ing, I quote two instances from this text:

Destr.Troiae, p. 165,22-24: Nunquam tanta dedecoris a te detergetur
infamia quanta es uiscose turpitudinis
ignominia denigratus

Destr. Troy, p. 264,8119-21: Of shame & shenship shent bes þou neuer:
Euery lede will þe lacke and þi lose file,
And þe fame of þi filth so fer will be
knowen

In most of my collected instances from this work one or more expressions
in the Middle English text are underlined with a broken line (see Notes,
App. C, p. 211). This is meant to indicate that though the expression or
expressions in question might possibly be regarded as a translation of a
particular Latin word, I have chosen to consider another expression,
namely the one which is underlined with a continuous line, to be the
better equivalent of the relevant Latin word.   In the instance quoted
above four expressions are underlined with a broken line and none with a
continuous line. I have interpreted the Latin sentence to mean something
like this: 'Never could so great blemish and dishonour be wiped away from
you, as you are viscously (stickily) besmeared with through the shame of
your filth'. As both shame and shenship occur in my material as translations of dedecus, not of infamia, I have listed them as translations of
that word (see App. C, p. 206). Cf. App. C, p. 205, where shame and shenship have been put in brackets after infamia indicating that they are
not listed as translations of that word (Lists ME 1-4). The other two
expressions underlined with a broken line, þe lacke and þi lose file, con-
sisting of an infinitive plus an object, are at any rate no literal translations. In my classification of meaning they would not be listed in the
same group as infamia. I refer to my classification "... activity intended to bring disgrace on ..." (Sense group A) - "... state of dishonour or shame, including that which qualifies for such a state ..." (Sense
group B). See pp. 41-43. For these reasons I have recorded none of the
four expressions as translations of Latin infamia.

Two additional instances from the passage quoted above have been recorded, viz. turpitudo:filth (... turpitudinis ignomina ...: ... þe fame
of þi filth ...) and ignominia:fame (of þi filth). (App. C, pp. 207 and
209.)

The second passage concerns translations of injuria:

Destr.Troiae, p. 32,28 f.: Inde est quod idem Iason et Hercules regi
Pelleo et aliis Grecie regibus a Troyano rege eis
iniuriam in mente illatam exponunt ...

Destr. Troy, p. 34,1005-6: Of dyshoner he did and his derfe wordes,
þat the grettyst of Grise gremyt þerat ...

In this case I have listed both <u>dyshoner</u> and <u>derfe wordes</u>[1] as translations of <u>injuria</u>.

---

[1] A French loan word or expression coupled with an older, native word
or expression (see pp. 85-86).

6. Arrangement of Collected Material: Lists OE 1, 2, and ME 1, 2

The arrangement in Lists OE 1 and ME 1 represents a first division of the material on the basis of the sixteen Latin words (see p. 11). The figures and letters which head the columns in the two Lists 1 refer to the figures and letters in the two Lists 2, where the individual forms (a:root words, b:derivatives, and c:compounds) of the Old and Middle English words recorded in my collection are presented.

The relevant sixteen Latin nouns are not exclusively rendered by nouns. Expressions with verbal and adjectival forms also occur. The heading 1 b:derivatives of bismer (List OE 1:1), for instance, includes the verb bismrian/bysmrian and the adjective bismerlecre (dǣd).

The order of the Latin words depends on their degree of correspondence with bismer-words. I define bismer-words so as to include bismer with orthographical variants, derivatives of bismer, and compounds with bismer as one part. The Latin word which has the largest number of corresponding bismer-words in relation to the whole number of Old English translations recorded for it (i.e. has the highest percentage of bismer-words) tops the lists. The second Latin word is the one which has the next highest percentage of bismer-words, etc. (see List OE 1:4). The first Latin word in List OE 1 is rendered, not only by bismer-words, but also by five non-bismer-words, i.e. swic, swicung, beswic, costnung, and hosp. As swic, swicung, and beswic are represented by four instances and the remaining two words only by one instance each, swic and its derivatives which form one group (a and b) have been given number 2. The remaining two words, costnung and hosp, which are in alphabetical order, have been given numbers 4 and 5 respectively. They are followed in numerical order by the new non-bismer-word which has the highest frequency among the new renderings for the second Latin word, etc. In this way the order in which the Old English words are ranged is an approximate measure of their synonymy with bismer. The same thing can be said about the order of the Latin words (see above). The Latin word inlusio, which has the highest percentage of bismer-words in the Old English translations, tops the Lists. It is rendered by a bismer-word in 31 instances out of 37, which means that in Old English the bismer-words dominate the translations of the word by 84%. The Latin word at the bottom of the Lists, confusio, is rendered by a bismer-word in only two instances out of 111, which is less than 2%. In the case of inlusio - confusio there is only one instance recorded for each of them where they have a non-bismer-word in common, and that is No. 4 (hosp). This seems to confirm the impression got by comparing their percentages of bismer-words, namely that the range of meaning covered by confusio belongs only to a very small extent in the same semantic field as that covered by inlusio. Furthermore, the two instances of bismer-words for confusio are translations of the same passage from two parallel manuscripts. The translation in the first manuscript might be a mistranslation, which has been copied by the writer of the second manuscript. However, if we look further at the translations of confusio in List 1 we find that confusio has many instances where the translations correspond to the translations of other Latin words which have a higher percentage of bismer-words. This shows that confusio does not fall completely outside the range of meaning of the Latin words collected on the basis of bismer-words.

7. Delimitation

My collection of instances from the Old English period contains nearly twice as many instances as those ca. 700 which are accounted for in my lists. This is an inevitable consequence of my method, as the principle for my collection of material has been to find Latin nouns rendered by bismer-words in Old English translations. I could not possibly know from the beginning which Latin words would turn out to have been rendered by bismer-words. As a starting point I recorded those Latin nouns whose meaning seemed to have something in common with the meaning of the bismer-words, i.e. words meaning 'blasphemy', 'contemptibleness', 'defilement', 'disgrace', 'disrepute', 'filthiness', 'insult', 'infamy', 'mockery', 'pollution', 'reproach', 'scandal', 'scorn', 'scurrilous song', 'shame', and 'shameful conduct'. These are the translations of the bismer-words in HM (1970) ranged in alphabetical order. Thus I have recorded instances of many Latin words which in the end proved never to have been rendered by any bismer-words. They are the following in alphabetical order: Abominatio, dedignatio, execratio, exprobratio, improbitas, indignatio, inproperium, obscenitas, probrum, pudor, scandalum, verecundia, and vituperatio.

A number of Latin nouns turned out to have been rendered by a bismer-word only once (see p. 11). These are the instances:

TEXT	LATIN WORD	ENGLISH WORD
WW VI, col. 201,38	cauillatio	bismrung
" " , " "	conuitium	bismrung
Bede I, 27,9:p. 95,2; (MS.B), p. 96,2143	inquinatio	bysmernes
Or. (MS.L), p. 216,15-16	macula	bismer
" (" "), p. 162,10	perjurium	bismerlicestan āde
I, Ps. 68,20	reverentia	gebysmerung
Dialogues I,5, p.41,6; (MS.C), p.46,18	rixa	bysmrun3
Aldhelm (MS.l),Napier,no.2933	rubor	bysmor
Or. (MS.L), p. 260,29	scelus	bismer

None of the Latin words above are included in my lists (App. B). However, most of them are to some extent dealt with later on (see Index, pp. 227-228). Only cauillatio, conuitium, execratio, obscenitas, perjurium, rixa, and rubor do not occur elsewhere in this study.

A word (expression) not included in my lists though it occurs rendered by a bismer-word more than once is nenias/naenias (vanitates)

(see p. 11). It has been recorded only from glossaries. <u>Nenias/</u>
<u>naenias vanitates</u> rendered by <u>bismerlēod/bismerlēos/bysmerlēoh/besmer-</u>
<u>lēoh</u> is to be found in Aldhelm (MS.H, Mone, nos. 6133, 6258, and MS.1,
Napier, nos. 5104, 5227). In WW XI and XII (MS. Cotton Cleopatra 3,
from the tenth century) <u>nenias</u> appears alone. It has been rendered by
<u>lēasspellunga</u> in WW XI, col. 452,6, and by <u>bismerlēod</u> in WW XI, col.
454,14 as well as in WW XII, col. 512,34. HM records <u>bismerlēod</u>
´scurrilous song´ followed by "Gl" (= Glossary), which indicates that
the word has been found only in Anglo-Saxon glossaries. <u>Lēasspellung</u>
´empty or false talk´ has a reference to "AO" (= Alfred´s <u>Orosius</u>) in
HM. The word is probably one of Alfred´s formations (cf. p. 9).

III. INTERPRETATION OF MEANING

The prominent position of Latin at the initial stage of Old English
prose writing and its great influence on the formation of the English
vocabulary through the work of translators provide good reason for
basing a study of this vocabulary on translations of Latin texts. As
also literary work of later periods to a large extent consists in translations of Latin texts, the Latin words could form a basis for selecting English items from different periods, and the sense of the Latin
words could serve as a point of departure in semantic analysis (see p.
9). Whether an English word which was used to render a certain Latin
word conveyed the meaning of this Latin word to a contemporary reader
is difficult to deduce. Especially in the early Old English period when
the usage of the words shows a high degree of instability (p. 88 f.) a
contemporary reader certainly often found a well-known word in a new
context. He certainly also very often found well-known words in new
compounds or derivatives coined for the purpose of rendering certain
Latin words (see pp. 9, 28, and 90-91). However, I have worked on the
assumption that a word used for a certain Latin word generally conveyed
the meaning of the Latin word. This implies that my work on the interpretation of the meaning is to a large extent taken up with the interpretation of the meaning of the Latin originals. I have, of course,
questioned this Latin - English equivalence when I have found special
reasons to do so, i.e. when the meaning of the English word as given in
current dictionaries seemed to contradict the meaning of the Latin word
that it rendered. See pp. 37-39 and 74-76. I have tried to interpret
the meaning of each word in each individual instance, which implies
that also morphological criteria have been taken into account for semantic classification (pp. 23, 42 and 44-48). Cf. also pp. 38-40.

1. Meaning of Latin Words According to Current Dictionaries

My main source for the meaning of the Latin words has been Lewis &
Short. Additional information has been taken from OLD, Georges, and
Forcellini. From these three dictionaries I have quoted what seemed to
be of importance as a complement to the information supplied by Lewis &
Short. Forcellini is a unilingual Latin dictionary, and for that reason
allowance must be made for omissions or, at worst, misinterpretations on
my part.

Here follows a list of the relevant Latin words with the meanings
assigned to them by those lexicographers:

(1) illusio (inlusio)

Lewis & Short: (i) A mocking, jeering; irony.
                  (ii) An illusion, deceit (eccl.Lat.), Vulg.
                       Ps. 37,7; Isa. 66,4.

Georges: (i) Die Verspottung, Ironie (Vulg. Sirach
                       27,31; Ps. 78,4; Isa. 66,4).
                  (ii) Die Täuschung, eitle Vorstellung (Vulg.
                       Ps. 37,7).

Forcellini about Ps. 37,7: Lumbi mei impleti sunt illusionibus
                       h.e. ignominia: ita vertit et Hieronym. Alii
                       cum Chaldaica versione: lumbi mei impleti sunt
                       combustione, de libidinis igne interpretantur.

(2) irrisio (inrisio)

Lewis & Short: A deriding, mocking, mockery.

(3) ludibrium

Lewis & Short: (i) A mockery, derision, wantonness.
                  (ii) Transf. A. A laughing-stock, butt, jest,
                             sport.
                         B. A scoff, jest, sport.
                         C. Abuse, violence done to a
                            woman.

(4) derisus

Lewis & Short: Mockery, scorn, derision.

(5) gannatura

Lewis & Short: A snarling, yelping: calumniae, Aldh.Laud.
               Virgin. 47; 56 al.

(6) infamia

Lewis & Short: Ill fame, ill report of a person or thing;
               bad repute, dishonor, disgrace, infamy.

OLD: (i) Bad reputation, ill-fame, notoriety, de-
                       famation, reproach.
                  (ii) Discredit, disgrace, official disgrace
                       (involving loss of certain rights).
                  (iii)A scandalous action, quality, circum-
                       stance; a term of abuse.

(7) blasphemia

    Lewis & Short: A reviling, slander, Vulg.Isa. 51,7;
                        towards God, blasphemy, Vulg. 2 Par. 32,17;
                        id. Matt. 26,65.

(8) dedecus

    Lewis & Short: (i)   Disgrace, dishonor, infamy, shame.
                              B. Concr. (as sometimes our word shame),
                              that which causes shame; a disgrace,
                              blot, blemish.
                    (ii) Moral dishonor, vice, turpitude, a vi-
                              cious action, shameful deed, unchastity.

    Georges: Die Unzierde, Unehre, Schande.
                        Meton. (i)   Eine verunehrende, entwürdigende
                                          Handlung oder Eigenschaft, ein
                                          entehrender Streich, eine
                                          Schändlichkeit, ein entehrendes
                                        Laster.
                          (ii) Der Schandfleck.
                        (iii) Als Schimpfwort: naturae dedecus
                                  ´Schandgeburt der Natur´.

(9) subsannatio

    Lewis & Short: Mockery by gestures, derision in pantomime
                        (Vulg. Ps. 34,16; 43,14).

(10) contumelia

    Lewis & Short: (Post-classic accessory from contumia)
                        abuse, insult, affront, reproach, invective,
                        contumely.
                        Transf., injury, assault, annoyance, vio-
                        lence, blows (cf. injuria).

    OLD   Insulting language or behaviour, or an in-
                        stance of it, indignity, affront.
                        Transf.,rough treatment.

(11) ignominia

    Lewis & Short: disgrace, dishonor, ignominy, esp. as the re-
                        sult of civil or military punishment.
                        (i) A legal and military term.
                        (ii) In general

    OLD: In later legal contexts not clearly distin-
                        guishable from infamia.

(12)   calumnia

Lewis & Short: Trickery, artifice, chicanery, cunning de-
                 vice.
                 (i) In a literal sense.
                 A. In general.
                 B. In particular.
                    1. A pretence, evasion, subterfuge.
                    2. A misrepresentation, false state-
                       ment, fallacy, cavil.
                    3. A false accusation, malicious
                       charge, esp. false or malicious in-
                       formation, or action at law, a per-
                       version of justice.
                    4. Hence, jurid. the bringing of an
                       action, whether civil or criminal,
                       in bad faith.
                 (ii) Trans., a conviction for malicious prose-
                      cution.

(13)   turpitudo

Lewis & Short: Ugliness, unsightliness, foulness, deformity
                 (syn. deformitas).
                 (i) In a literal sense very rare.
                 (ii) In a tropical or figurative sense: base-
                      ness shamefulness, disgrace, dishonor,
                      infamy, turpitude (syn. obsenitas, de-
                      decus).
Forcellini: Abstractum a turpis: deformitas.
                 2) Translate est probrum, dedecus, infamia,
                    labes macula, vitium.
                 3) Turpitudo sensu concreto sunt pudenda viri-
                    lia aut muliebria; quo sensu saepissime
                    usurpat Vulg. Interpr. Levit. 18,6 etc.

(14)   injuria

Lewis & Short: Any thing that is done contrary to justice
                 and equity, injury, wrong, violence.
                 (i) In a literal sense.
                 (ii) Transf., injurious, unlawful, or unjust
                      conduct.
                      A. Act, injustice, wrongdoing.
                      B. An injurious act, injury, outrage,
                         insult, affront.
                      C. Unjust severity, harshness, rigor.
                      D. Revenge or punishment for injury in-
                         flicted.
                      E. An unjust acquisition.
                      F. A damage, harm, injury of any kind,
                         even that which proceeds from inani-
                         mate things.

(15) opprobrium

Lewis & Short: A reproach, scandal,disgrace, dishonor, op-
                probrium (syn.: dedecus, probrum, infamia).
                Transf. A. A reproach, taunt, abuse, abusive
                            word or language.
                         B. Of persons, a reproach, disgrace.

Georges: (i) Der Vorwurf, Schimpf, die Beschimpfung.
                (ii) Meton.: A. Von Personen: der Schimpf,
                                die Schande.
                             B. Das Schimpfwort, die Schimpf-
                                rede, die Schmährede.

(16) confusio

Lewis & Short: (i) A Mingling.
                     A. In a proper sense: concrete, a mix-
                        ture, union.
                     B. In a tropical or figurative sense:
                        1. A mingling, mixing, uniting,com-
                           bining (rare).
                        2. A confounding, confusion, disorder.
                (ii) A reddening, blushing.

Forcellini: 4. Translate sumitur pro perturbatione animi.
                6. Hinc apud Vulg. Interpr. saepe sumitur pro
                   verecundia, pudore, Sir. eccl. 29,19; 4,25;
                   Abd. 10; Mich. 2,6.

It may be difficult to establish the exact meaning of an individual
word in its context, even if current dictionaries are available. The
difficulties are certainly the greater the less the reader knows about
the time at which or the circumstances in which the text was written.
Not only language but also social and political circumstances as well
as moral values change in the course of centuries. Reasons for reproach or dishonour are not the same at all times and in all places.
To-day, at least in our own society, a widow is not looked upon in the
same way as at the time of Isaiah, and when we think of Jesus' death on
the cross we often overlook the fact that such a death in the Roman
world was very shameful and originally reserved for slaves. The following quotations may serve as examples:

Isaiah 54,4: obprobrii viduitatis tuae non recordeberis:

             đaes bismeres đines wuduwanhādes đū ne gemansđ
             (Alfred, PC, p. 207,10 f.)

Hebr. 12,2: sustinuit crucem confusione contempta: ... despising the
            shame (AV).

Ancrene Riwle, p. 138,27-28, and p. 161,30-31:
'mortem autem crucis' significatur confusio:
to deade o rode: is schendlac betocned

Mediaeval Latin presents special problems. Lewis & Short as well
as the other dictionaries referred to above record instances from
ecclesiastical Latin. It is, however, not always possible to obtain
every shade of meaning of a word from these dictionaries. The word
illusio may serve as an example. Lewis & Short and Georges give the
following meanings:

1. Lewis & Short: A mocking, jeering, irony.
   Georges   : Die Verspottung, Ironie.

2. Lewis & Short: Illusion, deceit.
   Georges   : Die Täuschung, eitle Vorstellung.

Forcellini does not give any meaning beyond these interpretations
but takes up the instance of illusio in Ps. 37,8: lumbi mei impleti
sunt inlusionibus. In Lewis & Short and Georges this instance is recorded under the second heading, i.e. with the meaning 'illusion, deceit'. Forcellini states that the "Hebrew" Psalter in this instance
has the Latin word ignominia and adds: "Alii cum Chaldaice Versione:
lumbi mei impleti sunt combustione, de libidinis igne interpretantur."
None of the dictionaries referred to above seem to recognize the
meaning of 'libidinis ignis' for illusio. My instances from Bede's
History (App. C, p.176), however, are examples of illusio with this
meaning, or at least a meaning closely related to it. In this text as
well as in Gregory's Dialogues and Higden's Polychronicon (see pp. 35-
36) illusio implies the devil's influence on man, especially in man's
sleep. My interpretation of illusio in the History is that the word
has here a metaphorical meaning, i.e. illusio 'the devil's influence on
man in his sleep' stands for the result of this influence, which may be
'libidinis ignis' or 'pollution'. Note the instance from the History
quoted on p. 36 where inquinatio illa (in Old English usually rendered
by besmitenes/-nis) refers to illusio dormientis in the preceding
clause! Also Latin coinquinatio (rendered by Old English besmitenes)
has the same sense in this text, e.g. I 27,9, p. 86: MS. T,p. 80,15;
MS. O, 1.1915. In both these instances the Modern English translation
in Miller's edition (pp. 87,18 and 81,15) has the word pollution.

2. Information from the Context

2.1. Qualification in the Form of Adjunct Words, Prepositional Phrases or Relative Clauses

The immediate context of the head-word often contains some kind of
qualification which is a help in the interpretation of the head-word.
To illustrate this I quote a passage from Gregory's Dialogues:

IV,50 (p. 309,5 ff.):
..., aliquando vero inlusione/illusione, aliquando cogitatione
simul et inlusione/illusione ... (somnia etenim nisi plerumque ab
occulto hoste per inlusionem/illusionem fierent, ...):

... hwīlum ēac for bysmrunȝe þaes costiendan fēondes ... of þaes
fēondes bysmrunȝe ... of þaes fēondes bysmrunȝe ... (p. 339,4-9).

Latin vero inlusione stands for the devil's influence on man. Some
lines further down the devil is mentioned as the agent: ab occulto
hoste. The Old English translator includes the agent (the devil) in
the genitive.

In Higd.Harl. (II, 2,25, p. 430) the genitive has been added to
Middle English illusion as a translation of Latin illusio:

Ita ut sensibus humanis illusione sopitis res non videantur sicut
sunt ...: the wyttes oppressede with the illusion of the deuelle
...

The instances quoted above are classified in Sense group A I:Devil-
Men. See p. 55.

Finally, here is an example of translations of Latin turpitudo
which usually means 'unchastity' (Sense group B II). The example is
from Higden's Polychronicon VII, 7,7 (p. 358), and the translations
are from Higd.Trev. and Higd.Harl.:

Age ergo quod viri, quod militis est, ut proditio tua saltem turpi-
tudine careat.:
... þat þy tresoun be wiþ oute schame of cowardise (Higd.Trev.)
... it is a signe of a cowarde, and noo man (Higd.Harl.)

The underlined expressions are classified in B III:Misbehaviour.
See p. 55.

2.2. Contrast

A notion may be delimited by contrast. The following example is from Gregory's <u>Dialogues</u>:

IV,50 (p. 310,13-16):
Sancti autem viri inter <u>inlusiones</u> atque <u>revelationes</u> ipsas visionum voces aut imagines quodam intimo sapore discernunt, ut sciant vel quid <u>a bono spiritu</u> percipiant, vel quid <u>ab inlusione</u> patiantur.:
(p. 339,16-19): ... ac hāliʒe weras tosceadad mid sumum incundum wīsdōme þā swefn ʒe þā hēowunʒe þara swefna betux þām bysmrunʒum & aet þām sōdan onwriʒnessum, swa þaet hi witon, hwaet hwaet hī onfōd from þām ʒōdan ʒāste, ʒe eac hwaet hī þrowiad from þām fūlan bysmriendan.

Here the opposites <u>inlusiones:bysmrunʒum</u> - <u>revelationes:þām sōdan onwriʒnessum</u> 'true revelation' are given together with the agents, a bono spiritu:<u>from þām ʒōdan ʒāste</u> - ab inlusione: <u>from þām fūlan bysmriendan (ʒāste)</u>. Latin <u>ab inlusione</u> refers to <u>ab occulto hoste</u> on p. 310,12. See the preceding page.

2.3. Variation

A concept is repeated by another word as a further explanation. I quote an instance from Bede's <u>History</u>, I, 27,9 (p. 95,1-3):

Sin uero ex turpi cogitatione uigilantis oritur <u>inlusio</u> dormientis, patet animo reatus suus; uidet enim a qua radice <u>inquinatio illa</u> processerit, quia, quod cogitauit sciens, hoc pertullit nesciens.

<u>Inquinatio illa</u> refers to <u>inlusio</u>. <u>Inquinatio</u> is in Old English usually rendered by <u>besmitenis</u> 'defilement', 'dirtiness', 'pollution'. In one out of three parallel MSS. <u>inquinatio</u> has been rendered once by <u>bysmernes</u> (Schipper, I.2142). This instance has been discussed on p. 34.

2.4. Passages Outside the Immediate Context

Passages outside the immediate context as well as the general context of the piece of writing may explain the meaning of a word. The following is an example from Higden's <u>Polychronicon</u>, VI, 5,14 (p. 44):

... qui carnibus usi et aqua exemplo beati Job pepigerunt foedus cum occulis suis, ut nec quidem cogitarent de <u>turpitudo</u>, sed orationi jugiter incumbebant.:
... <u>foyle</u> ne <u>filþe</u> or <u>synne</u> (Higd.Trev.); ... <u>synne</u> (Higd.Harl.).

Further on in the text we find what kind of sin is meant here. On p. 46,3 ff.. it says:

Vinum, ergo sumentes monachi, ubi cum hilaritate vini surrepsit
oblivio, irruerunt in foeminas illas, ...:
þanne þe monkes drone wyn, and wex mery and glad, and forȝat þat
þey schulde have in mynde, and fil to and lay by þe wommen. (Higd.
Trev.);
The monkes drynkynge wine gladdely, and not remenbrenge theire holy
religion, falle on the women that ministrede to þeim, and followede
the pleasure of the flesche (Higd.Harl.).

The instances belong to Sense group B II:Unchastity in my classification
(see p. 55).

3. Parallel Versions

The usefulness of parallel manuscripts for comparing vocabularies
from different periods of a language has been pointed out (see p. 19 f.).
Also for the interpretation of otherwise obscure examples parallel
readings are a help. For an illustration see pp. 74-76.

4. Deviations from the Original

It cannot be taken for granted that a rendering in a glossed version
is the equivalent of the Latin word in question. A glossator may have
had more than one version of a Latin text before him or even one or
several already glossed versions, as the glossators of the Psalter most
certainly had. The Old English glosses are based on two different versions of Latin text, the "Roman" Psalter and the "Gallican" Psalter (see
App. A, p. 122). The eleventh century Old English glosses to the "Gallican" text depend more or less on earlier glosses to the "Roman" text.
As a consequence of this fact many Old English words in the glosses
based on the "Gallican" text interpret the corresponding Latin word of
the "Roman" text rather than that of the "Gallican" text. I give an
example from the Arundel Psalter:

Ps. 37,8: forðon sāwle mīn gefilled is besmyrnessum:
          Quoniam lumbi mei impleti sunt inlusionibus

The "Roman" text has here the Latin word anima instead of lumbi 'loins,
genital organs' (Lewis & Short).

An instance where an unexpected translation cannot be explained only
as a result of influence from the "Roman" text is the rendering of the

Latin word <u>reverentia</u> by <u>gebysmerung</u> ´disgrace´, ´insult´, or ´shame´ in
the <u>Lambeth Psalter</u>, Ps. 68,20. See p. 27. To find an explanation of
this phenomenon I resorted to a third Latin Psalter text, the so-called
"Hebrew" Psalter (App. A, p. 122). When I compared the three Latin
Psalter texts, I found that they usually had different Latin words in
those instances where <u>reverentia</u> appeared in one of them. In Psalm
68,20, the instance referred to above, where the <u>Lambeth Psalter</u> had the
translation <u>reverentia:gebysmerung</u>, the "Hebrew" Psalter had <u>ignominia</u>, a
word which certainly means ´shame´, ´disgrace´. I shall return to this on
pp. 74-76.

On pp. 23-24 I have quoted and discussed instances of free translations from my Middle English material. Also my Old English material has
instances of more or less free translations. Most of them are from the
two important works of King Alfred´s later period, <u>Orosius</u> and <u>Boethius</u>
(p. 21 and App. A, p. 124). Even in those passages which follow the
Latin text fairly closely minor deviations frequently occur. As examples
I quote below two instances from <u>Orosius</u>. The relevant Latin phrases
seem to express a state of shame or possibly the reason for it, which is
in both these instances unchastity. The Old English text has not only a
word for unchastity but also a word for an external activity intended to
put the person/persons in question to shame. In fact, the different
senses here referred to, that of state (often as a mental or physical
quality) and that of activity (i.e. an external activity intended to put
the object/objects of this activity to shame), form the basis for my division of the word material into two main Sense groups, A (Activity) and
B (State). See p. 55. In the first instance the external activity intended to put the object to shame consists of reproach, scorn, or derision, in the second instance it consists of a material punishment implying harm and shame for the object.

    1) Orosius, p.31,30-33: ... privatam <u>ignominiam</u> publico scelere ob-
                                  texit. (Praecepit,enim, ut inter parentes ac
                                    filios nulla deleta reverentia naturae, de
                                    conjugiis adpetendis ut cuique libitum esset,
                                    liberum fieret.)
               p.30,33-34: ... for đon þe hio hyre <u>firenluste</u> fulgān ne
                                 moste būtan manna <u>bysmrunge</u>, (hīo gesette ofer
                                 eall hyre rīce ...)

---

[1]The instance is from a MS. written in the early eleventh century,
<u>Cotton Tiberius B 1</u> (CTB1). It is the only example of a substantival
<u>bismer</u>-word other than <u>bismer</u> in my material from Alfred´s texts.

I have interpreted the Latin passage, ... privatam ignominiam publico
scelere obtexit, as 'she concealed her private ignomiy by public sins'.
Privatam ignominiam refers to the preceding clause: tandem filio inceste
cognito 'finally after having incestuously had sexual intercourse with
her son'. Publico scelere refers to the sentence that follows (Praecepit
enim, ... 'She ordained namely ...'). Here we are told that she (Semira-
mis, wife of King Ninus of Assyria and regent after his death) published
an edict permitting incest. The Old English clause quoted above seems to
mean 'as she could not indulge her sinful lusts without the reproach of
men (she ordained ...)'. Thus hyre firenluste (exposed to) manna bysmrunge corresponds to privatam ignominiam in the Latin text. Publico scelere (abl. instr.) has not been rendered. According to my classification
Latin ignominia must be listed under B (State of dishonour or shame), and
so must the Old English word firenlust, whereas Old English manna bysmrunge must be listed under A (An external activity intended to bring disgrace on or to show contempt for the object of the activity). See pp. 41
and 55.

   2) Orosius, p.65,4-5: Quoniam ibi in rege libidinum turpitudo punita,
                         ...:
           p.64,6-9: ... (for þon þe Babylonie mid monigfealdum un-
                     ryhtum & firenlustum mid heora cyninge būtan
                     aelcre hreowe libbende waeren, þaet hie hit nā
                     gebetan nolden,) aer þon hīe God mid þam
                     maestan bismere geeadmedde, ... (Lauderdale MS.,
                     early tenth century).

The Latin text means: 'As the shame(fulness) of sinful lusts in the king
had been punished (by God) ...'. Old Enlish aer þon hīe God mid þam
maestan bismere geeadmedde refers to the way they (i.e. the Babylonians)
are punished together with their king for their sinful life. As punishment they are deprived both of their king and of their power. God had
humbled them "mid bismere" . In my classification turpitudo, like
ignominia in the first instance above, must be listed under B:State.
Old English mid bismere, like manna bysmrunge in the first instance,
under A:Activity. Old English firenlust in the second instance, being
the equivalent of libidinum (gen.plur.) 'lusts', has not been recorded
in my lists.

   In both instances the Old English text has apart from a word for lust
(firenlust) also a word for an external activity intended to put the
object/objects to shame (bismer, bysmrung), whereas the Latin text has
only a word for such a state (ignominia, turpitudo). In the second in-

stance the word (turpitudo) has a qualification, libidinum (gen.plur.)
'lusts'.

IV. SEMANTIC CLASSIFICATION

1. The Two Main Sense Groups A: Activity and B: State

The bismer-words which have served as the primary basis for my
collection of material (see pp. 10-11) are rendered in HM by one or
several of the following nouns: blasphemy, contemptibleness, defilement, disgrace, dishonour, disrepute, filthiness, insult, infamy,
mockery, pollution, reproach, scandal, scorn, scurrilous song, shame,
and shamefull conduct. Some of these words clearly express an action
or an activity intended to show contempt for or to bring disgrace on
the object of the activity. Such words are blasphemy, mockery, insult,
reproach, and scorn. The first two are derived from transitive verbs,
the latter three are identical with the corresponding transitive verbs.
Among the other nouns which render the bismer-words, e.g. filthiness,
contemptibleness, disrepute, infamy, and shame, a sense of state or
condition seems to be prominent. The group also contains words which
stand for both aspects, that of activity and that of state. Such
words are disgrace and dishonour, which mean the condition or state of
one fallen from grace and honour, as well as the transitive activity
of bringing him into this position. Cf. Webster s.v. disgrace/dishonour.

The difference in meaning, transitive action or activity - state
or condition, has been settled upon for a first division of the material into two main Sense groups, A:Activity and B:State. The following
instances from the collection may serve to demonstrate the difference
in meaning referred to:

A. The Sense of Action or Activity

Matt. 26,65:
Ecce nunc audistis ᴜlasphemiam:
nū gīe hērdon efolsungas (CND4:Lindisfarne MS.)
nū ge gehȳrdon of hym gyltlice spraece (Corpus MS.)

Mark 14,64:
... audistis blasphemiam ...:
gehērdon gēe ðaet ebolsung ...(CND4:Lindisfarne MS.)
ge gehȳrdon his bysmer ... (Corpus MS.)

Cura Pastoralis (Hebr. 11,36):
Sancti ludibria et verbera experti ...:
Ða hālgan menn geðafedon on ðisse worlde monig bismer & monige
swyngean ... (Alfred's PC, p. 205,11 ff.)

Deut. 28,29:
Omnique tempore calumniam sustineas ...
... & dolie bysmor on aelcne timan ... (Heptateuch, p. 361);

Gregory's Dialogues:
... tam crudelem facere contumeliam praesumpsit (I.2, p. 24,7)
... swā waelhrēowne teonan ('insult') 3edyde ...(p.21,31-32; MS.H)
... swylce waelhrēownysse fraceþa ('insult') 3efremede...
(p. 21,33-34; MS. C);

Ps. 118,134:
Redime me a calumniis hominum ("Roman" text)
Āles mec from hearmum monna (Vespasian Psalter)
... hearmcwidum ... (Junius Psalter);

Ps. 88,51:
Memor esto obprobrii servorum tuorum ("Roman" text)
... edwīta dīowa dīnra (Vespasian Psalter)
... hospes þeowra þīnra (Regius Psalter)
... edwītspraece (Paris Psalter);

Boethius II, pr.7:
adorsus esset hominem contumeliis (p. 46,65)
... & hine bismrode (Alfred's translation, p. 45,5-6);

Leviticus 19,13:
Non facies calumniam proximo tuo ...
Ne bysmra ðū ðīnne maēg ... (Heptateuch, p. 296).

In the last two instances above the Old English translator uses the
verb bysmrian to render the Latin expression with the nouns contumelia
and calumnia. Note the form contumeliis (abl.instr.plur.).

B. The Sense of State or Condition

Sir.Eccl. 3,13:
Et dedecus filii pater sine honore est
& aepsenyss ('dishonour') suna faeder būtan wurþscype ys (Lib.
Scint., p. 174,9);

Sir.Eccl. 3,12:
Ne glorieris i. gratuleris in contumelia patris tui. non est tibi
gloria sed confusio
... nys þē wuldor ac sceand (Lib. Scint.,174,8);

Cura Pastoralis:
... ut unde adepta gloria creditur, inde utilis subsequatur confusio (32)
... daet hīe donne haebben mid ðy scame geholode (Alfred's PC, p.
209,19).

Cura Pastoralis (Philipp. 3,19):
Quorum deus venter est, et gloria in confusione ipsorum (43)
... & hīe dydon hiera bysmer him tō wyrðscype(Alfred's PC,p.316,23).

In my terminology the characteristics that distinguish the two
groups are as follows:

A: Words signifying an activity intended to bring disgrace on or to show contempt for the object of the activity. (Latin words: illusio, inrisio, ludibrium, derisus, blasphemia, subsannatio, contumelia, calumnia, injuria, and opprobrium.)

B: Words signifying the state or condition of shame and disgrace. (Latin words: ignominia, infamia, dedecus, turpitudo, and confusio.)

The Latin words under A:Activity can also be used to express a state, which is the state of the object exposed to the activity in question or the state incurred through the external activity. However, all the Latin words under A, except opprobrium, occur in this sense only sporadically. The instances are classified in a subgroup of A (Ab), not in B. My arguments for doing so are to be found on pp. 44-45 and 51-54.

The Latin words under B:State do not exclusively express a state or a condition, but also, to some extent, the behaviour or the quality through which the agent incurs the state in question. Arguments for classification of these instances in B:State are given on pp. 48-49.

2. Sense Group A: Activity and Its Division into Subgroups

The bismer-words cover 19% of the whole number of Old English words (tokens, not types) in A:Activity. Cf. Sense group B:State, where the bismer-words cover only 7% (see p. 48).

The Subgroups are also ranged according to their relative frequency of bismer-words within each group. Subgroup A I:Devil-Men has the highest frequency, viz. 83% (29 instances out of a total of 35), Subgroup A II:Men-God the next highest frequency, viz. 25% (12 out of 49), and Subgroup A III:Men-Men the lowest frequency, viz. 12% (47 out of 405). See List OE 3.

2.1. Subgroup A I: Devil-Men

The Devil's activity directed towards having an influence on men is in my instances represented by one Latin word, inlusio/illusio. Concerning the metaphorical meaning of the word in Ps. 37,8 and in Bede's History see pp.34-35 and 37-38. Cf.p.36, where an instance of the word used as a personification of the devil is quoted. The expression ab in-

lusione/illusione has in Gregory's Dialogues been rendered by from þam
fūlan bysmriendan ʒāste. Cf. Swedish den fule 'the devil' (Hellquist,
1957).

2.2. Subgroup A II: Men-God

This Subgroup contains words for men's activities intended to show
contempt or irreverence for God, the Holy Ghost, and things considered
sacred. Contempt or lack of reverence for God etc. can certainly be
shown in many different ways, by words as well as by actions. However,
these activities are, with very few exceptions, referred to by one word,
blasphemia, in the Latin texts.

2.3. Subgroup A III: Men-Men

Words for men's activities intended to disgrace or insult other men
are divided into three Minor groups, 1:Derision, 2:Calumny, and 3:In-
sult, indicating the nature of the activity (p. 55). The groups in question are ranged according to the same principle as the Subgroups. No.
1:Derision has the highest frequency of bismer-words, viz. 59%, No.
2:Calumny the next highest, viz. 20%, and No. 3:Insult the lowest frequency, viz. 6%. See List OE 3.

The two Minor groups A III 1:Men-Men-Derision and A III 3:Men-Men-
Insult present special problems. Some of the words, in Old English
particularly hosp and edwīt, in Middle English repref/reprof and shenship (Lat. opprobrium), seem to express not only the activity as directed towards an object, i.e. a transitive activity intended to put
somebody to shame, but also, if this activity is continuous, as something static. In the latter case they express the state of the object,
usually a person, being exposed to the activity in question (see p. 43).
To make a clear distinction between the two senses in individual instances is often difficult and may be a matter of judging whether the
sense of activity or the sense of state is stressed more. I have, however, tried to distinguish between the two senses and labelled the first
a and the second b. Sense a, the Original sense (a:O) is common for all
three of the Minor groups, A III 1:Men-Men-Derision, A III 2:Men-Men-
calumny, and A III 3:Men-Men-Insult, whereas sense b, the Transferred
sense = State (b:TS), only occurs in A III 1:Men-Men-Derision and A III
3:Men-Men-Insult. The words of a:O and b:TS are also used as a comple-

ment of the predicate. In this position they signify the object exposed
to the activity in question. The object is identified with this activity, i.e. the activity has been personified. This sense has been labelled c, the Transferred sense = Personification (c:TP), in my classification. See list on p. 55. To demonstrate these differences I give
a number of examples of the three senses, a:O, b:TS, and c:TP:

1) a:O (A III 3 a:Men-Men-Insult-O)

    Ps. 14,3: obprobrium non accepit adversus proximum meum:
           edwīt ne onfēng ... (Vespasian Psalter);
           hosp ne onfenʒ ... (Regius Psalter);
           nor taketh up a reproach ... (AV, Ps. 15,3).

    Ps. 68,10:obprobria exprobrantium tibi ceciderunt super me:
           edwīt edwītendra ... (Vespasian Psalter);
           hospas hyspendra ... (Regius Psalter);
           the reproaches of them that reproached ... (AV, Ps.
           69,9).

    Boethius II, pr. 7 (p.46,65): adorsus esset hominem contumeliis:
    Alfred's Bo. (p. 45,5-6): ... & hine bismrode.

2) b:TS (A III 1 b:Men-Men-Derision-TS)

    Jer. 48,26: erit in derisum:
           ... in to scornyng (Wyclif Bible,EV);
           ... in to scorn (Wyclif Bible,LV);
           Ye shall be in derision (AV).

    Lam. 3,14: factus sum in derisu:
           I am maad in to scorn (Wyclif Bible);
           I was a derision (AV).

    (A III 3 b:Men-Men-Insult-TS)

    Luke 1,25: ... respexit auferre opprobrium meum inter homines
           (Elisabeth being barren):
           ... hē geseah mīne hosp betux mannum (Corpus MS.);
           ... my schenschip ... (Wyclif Bible,EV);
           ... my repreef ... (Wyclif Bible,LV).

    Cant. 16,8: ... amputavi caput eius et abstuli opprobrium a
           filiis israel:
           ... & onweg āfirde edwīt of bearnum Israela
           (Vespasian Psalter).

    Ps. 118,39: amputa opprobrium meum:
           ācerf edwīt mīn (Vespasian Psalter);
           ofāceorf hosp mīnne (Regius Psalter).

3) c:TP (A III 1 c:Men-Men-Derision-TP)

    Ez. 22,4: dedi te opprobrium et inrisionem universis terris:
           ..., and scornynge to alle loondis (Wyclif Bible,EV)
           ..., and scornyng to alle londis (Wyclif Bible,LV).

... I made thee ... a mocking ... (AV)

Ps. 78,4: facti sumus obprobrium vicinis nostris subsannatio
           et inlusio ("Gallican" text)
           We are become a reproach to our neighbours, a scorn
           and a derision (AV, Ps. 79,4);

(A III 3 c:Men-Men-Insult-TP)

Ps. 78,4: facti sumus obprobrium vicinis nostris ("Gallican"
           text)
           We synd gewordene were cneorissum eallum
           edwitstaef ymbsittendum (Paris Psalter)

Ps. 21,7: ego autem sum vermis et non homo obprobrium
           hominum et abjectio plebis
           ic soðlice eam ... edwit monna ... (Vespasian
           Psalter);
           ic eom ... hosp manna ... (Regius Psalter);
           But I am a worm, and no man; a reproach of men ...
           (AV, Ps. 22,6);

Ps. 30,12: Super omnes inimicos meos factus sum obprobrium
           vicinis meis nimium ...
           ... geworden ic eam edwit ... (Vespasian Psalter);
           ... 3eworden ic eom hosp ... (Regius Psalter);
           I was a reproach ... (AV, Ps. 31,11).

In the instances under a:O (A III 3 a:Men-Men-Insult-O) the sense
of "activity" is obvious. Note Alfred's rendering by the verb bismrian
in the third instance. In the second instance (Ps. 68,10) the plural
form of the noun as well as the presence of the agent (exprobrantium:
edwitendra/hyspendra) stresses the sense of "activity". The meaning
in the first instance is clearly verbal: 'When somebody finds fault with
(blames) his neighbour, he never listens.' Compare also the instances
on pp. 41-42, where examples from A II:Devil-Men and also from A III:
Men-Men are given to demonstrate the sense of "activity" (Sense group
A) versus the sense of "state" (Sense group B). Note the Old English
translations blasphemiam:gyltlice spraece (Matt. 26,65), opprobrium:
edwitspraece (Ps. 88,51), and calumniis:hearmcwidum (Ps. 118,134).

In the expressions under b:TS (A III 1 b:Men-Men-Derision-TS and
A III 3 b:Men-Men-Insult-TS) the state or the situation of the object
exposed to the activity in question seems to be stressed more than the
activity itself. The activity rests upon the object like a load (A III
3 b:Men-Men-Insult-TS). It was taken away (carried away) from Elisa-
beth (Luke 1,25) and from the people of Israel (Cant. 16,8). In Ps.
118,39 it adheres to the object and has to be "cut away". The adverbial phrases with the preposition in (in derisum/in derisu) under b:TS

(A III 1 b:Men-Men-Derision-TS) imply a condition or situation.   In
the second instance (factus sum in derisu: I was a derision) the
translator of AV has replaced the adverbial phrase (in with ablative,
sense b:TS) by a complement of the predicate, which is sense c:TP in
terms of my classification .

An instance of contumelia: tēona (App. C, p.181) which shows
ambiguity of meaning caused by the genitive (subjective or objective?) is the following from Lib. Scint., p. 174,7 (Sir.Eccl.
3,12-13):

> Ne glorieris i. gratuleris in contumelia patris tui. non est tibi
> gloria sed confusio: ne wuldra þu on teonan faeder þīnes nys þe
> wuldor ac sceand.

Given the meaning of contumelia in my terminology as ´an activity of
disgracing somebody by means of insulting reproaches or actions´
(A III 3:Men-Men-Insult), two interpretations are possible, namely
´Don´t exult at your father´s disgrace, i.e. your father´s situation
of being (your father being) exposed to disgracing activities from
outside´(A III 3 b:Men-Men-Insult-TS) and ´Don´t exult at your father´s
activities of disgracing other persons´(A III 3 a:Men-Men-Insult-O).
I have chosen the first interpretation.

The instances under c:TP (A III 1 c:Men-Men-Derision-TP and A III 3
c:Men-Men-Insult-TP) are examples of inrisio (Ez. 22,4), subsannatio
(Ps. 78,4), inlusio (Ps. 78,4), and opprobrium (Ps. 78,4, 21,7, and
30,12) used as a complement of the predicate to qualify a person. The
activity has been personified, and it refers to the object of the
activity (p. 45). Note the translations in AV: a derision, a scorn,
and a reproach!   Note also the coordination of obprobrium: a reproach and vermis et non homo: a worm and no man (Ps. 21,7)¡ `In AV
the coordinate expressions are divided by a semicolon to mark the
difference in kind between individuals (worm, man) and a concept (reproach).

Sometimes the word for the activity, used as a complement of the
predicate, seems to signify the person not only as an object of disgracing activities but, as a consequence of this, also as a cause of
disgrace to another person or a group of persons. By insulting or
disgracing a certain person or certain persons, others are also dis-
graced, in the following instance (I Kings, Sam¿, 11,2) a whole nation:

> ... ut eruam omnium vestrum oculos dextros ponamque vos
> obprobrium in universo Israel: ... and y put ʒou reproue in al

Yrael (Wyclif Bible EV);
... and y sette ʒou schenschip in al Israel (Wyclif Bible LV).
Nahash the Ammonite besieges Jabesh in Gilead. The men of Jabesh offer
to make a covenant with Nahash. He accepts, but his condition is that
he may thrust out all their right eyes and make them a reproach in
Israel, obviously a reproach to Israel for their not having brought
them relief. In the following, however, we read that they were relieved
by Saul and the people of Israel, who slew the Ammonites (I Kings, Sam.,
11,11).

3. Sense Group B: State and Its Division into Subgroups

The bismer-words cover only 7% of the whole number of Old English
words (tokens) in this Sense group. It has been divided into three subgroups, I:Misfortunes, II:Unchastity, and III:Misbehaviour, implying
three groups of reasons for the state of shame or disgrace in question
(see p. 43). Subgroup I:Misfortunes has the highest frequency of
bismer-words, viz. 15%, subgroup II:Unchastity the next highest frequency, viz. 6%, and subgroup III:Misbehaviour the lowest frequency,
viz. 3%.

The words assigned to B:State render the Latin words ignominia, infamia, dedecus, turpitudo, and confusio. According to current dictionaries (see pp. 30-33) these Latin words have in common the meaning
of dishonour or shame, in my terminology "the state of dishonour or
shame". Infamia, dedecus, and turpitudo signify not only the state of
dishonour or shame but also that which qualifies for such a state, i.e.
the act (activity) through which the agent brings shame upon himself or
reveals his bad character. Dedecus and turpitudo also stand for mental
or physical qualities which cause the possessor disgrace or shame.

Thus both Lewis & Short and OLD record for dedecus, besides the
meaning of dishonour or shame as a state, also the meaning of 'shameful conduct, misbehaviour' as well as 'blemish' and 'repulsive appearance'. A repulsive appearance has often been interpreted as a sign of
bad character. According to Leisi (1973) the Old English language does
not distinguish between beauty and goodness nor between repulsive
appearance and bad character. He says on p. 223: "Es gibt weder eine
edle Hässlichkeit noch eine böse Schönheit." My material includes

17 instances   of dedecus translated into Old English.   In seven of them
words which refer to outward appearance occur, namely unwlite (5 times)
and the verb unwlitegan (twice).   The five instances unwlite are from
vocabularies (see p. 19 and App. C, p. 186).   HM renders unwlite by
'dishonour' only.   Its opposite wlite, however, means according to HM
'brightness:appearance, form, aspect, look, countenance', 'beauty,
splendour' and 'adornment'.   The remaining two instances, i.e. those
in which the verb unwlitegan has been used, are from two parallel MSS.
of the Pastoral Care (App. C, p. 183). The passage tells us that vice is
heavy as it causes the member to swell and become disfigured (Vitium
quippe est ponderis, cum humor viscerum ad virilia labitur, quae pro-
fecto cum molestia dedecoris intumescunt: ... đonne asuild hit &
ahefegad & unwlitegad).   None of my Middle English renderings of dedecus
(29 in mumber) are words which refer to outward appearance.

The original meaning of turpitudo seems to have been physical deformity or ugliness.   Lewis & Short says that this literal meaning is
"very rare".   The word occurs mostly in the figurative sense of 'base-
ness', 'shamefulness', 'disgrace', and 'dishonour'.   Forcellini also
records the meaning of 'pudenda virilia aut muliebria' for Leviticus
18,6 etc.   In AV the instances of turpitudo from Leviticus are rendered by nakedness.   Compare the German word die Scham 'die äusseren
Geschlechtsorgane, besonders die weiblichen' (Brockhaus, 1972), the
Swedish word blygd 'shame', 'feeling of shame', 'genitals' (Hellquist,
1957), as well as the Latin word pudenda 'genitals', a derivation of
pudere 'feel ashamed'.   Not only turpitudo but also ignominia has this
meaning in Leviticus 18,15, 18,17, 20,17, 20,19, and 20,20.   AV has in
all these instances nakedness.   This meaning is not recorded in the
current dictionaries for ignominia.   In other instances, e.g. in Ezekiel
16,36, 16,37, 23,10, 23,18, and Jeremia 47,3, ignominia:nakedness (AV)
has a figurative sense.   Mostly apostasy, symbolized by whoredom, is referred to.   In Ezekiel Jerusalem and Samaria are harlots.   In instances
from my material ignominia is also rendered by words which refer to
other sins, e.g. cowardice: Fabius Maximus, ignominia filii deprecatus:
þaet þā senātum forgeaf þaēm suna þōne gylt (Alfred's Orosius, see App.
C, p. 184).   Fabius Maximus's son had behaved like a coward by running
away in a battle.

In fact, it is often difficult to distinguish between the meaning

of 'dishonour' as a state and the meaning of the 'misbehaviour' or
the 'quality' through which it is incurred. Very often parallel
translations interpret the original differently in this respect. Take
for instance Naum 3,5: ignominiam tuam, in the Wyclif Bible, EV and
LV, rendered by yuel fame, in the Ancrene Riwle, p. 145,12-13,
where the passage is quoted, by bine scheomfule sunnen. Another example is Rom. 1,26: passiones ignominiae, in the Wyclif Bible, EV, yuel
fame, in the Wyclif Bible, LV, schenschip, and in AV vile affections.

As was pointed out above, the Latin words for "state of dishonour
or shame" also, at least to some extent, signify the reason for this
dishonour. The dictionaries (see pp. 30-33) include such meanings
for dedecus, turpitudo, and infamia, but not for ignominia. In my
material renderings which refer to the reason for a state of shame
occur for all four of them. This fact may justify a classification
of the words according to the reason for the dishonour (see p.48).
The reasons in question can be divided into two main groups: misfortunes or afflictions in one group and misbehaviour, shameful conduct,
or sins in the other. The first-mentioned group has been kept undi-
vided, the second on the other hand has been subdivided into two
groups, one for unchastity, which predominates among the different
kinds of misbehaviour,etc., and one for other kinds of misbehaviour,
etc. The result of this division is three groups, B I:Misfortunes,
B II:Unchastity, and B III:Misbehaviour. See p. 55.

3.1. Subgroup B I: Misfortunes

Out of the whole number of Old English instances classified in B:
State, viz. 158, misfortunes or afflictions were involved as reasons
for dishonour in 46 instances, i.e. 30%. Out of the corresponding
Middle English instances, 514 in number, misfortunes or afflictions
were involved as reasons for dishonour in 70 instances, i.e. 14%.

3.2. Subgroup B II: Unchastity

The instances of this group express dishonour on account of unchastity, the action of unchastity, and also the naked body (see p. 49).
The words of this sense are often used in similes for other sins,
especially apostasy.

In the Old English instances unchastity was involved in 33 cases
out of 112 , which is the total number of instances of dishonour in

connection with sins or offences. This makes 29%. The corresponding
figures for the Middle English instances are 185 out of 444, i.e.
42%.

3.3. Subgroup B III: Misbehaviour

I did not consider it to be of any special value to try to distinguish between all the different kinds of misbehaviour or shameful
conduct that were the cause of dishonour in my material. This would
have given a great number of subgroups with few instances in each.
Therefore I brought all instances, in which misbehaviour or shameful
conduct other than unchastity were involved, together in this group.
It holds half the number of instances in B:State, i.e. 79 (out of a
total of 158) Old English instances and 259 (out of a total of 514)
Middle English instances.

4. Expressions from A III b: Men-Men-TS Compared with Expressions from B: State

On pp. 44-45 I have pointed out that some of the activity words
classified in A III:Men-Men, especially Old English edwīt and hosp,
Middle English repref/reprof and shenship (Lat. opprobrium), seem to
express not only the activity of putting somebody to shame, i.e. a
transitive activity, but also, if this activity is continuous, something static. The stress is on the situation of the object being exposed to the activity rather than on the activity itself. Expressions
in which the words have this meaning show in many cases the same
formal syntactic pattern as those in which the words of B:State occur.
Certainly, this fact could be put forward as a reason for classifying
them in B:State ("Words signifying the state of dishonour or shame").

The following two instances from Isaiah exhibit a characteristic
feature of Hebrew biblical poetry and prose, the so-called parallelism (parallelismus membrorum). The above-mentioned words of A III b:
Men-Men-TS and words of B:State (here Lat. confusio and ignominia)
occur in coordinated clauses:

	Sense group	
Isaiah 47,3:		
revelabitur ignominia tua	B	... thi shenshipe/schame
et videbitur opprobrium	A III b	... thi repref/schenschipe
tuum		(Wyclif Bible)

Sense group

Isaiah 54,4:

quia <u>confusionis</u> adulescentiae tuae oblivesceris	B	... the <u>confusioun</u> of ʒouthe ...
et <u>obprobrii</u> viduitatis tuae non <u>recordaberis</u>	A III b	the <u>repref</u> of ... (Wyclif Bible)
quia <u>confusionis</u> adulescentiae tuae oblivesceris	B	... đaere <u>scame</u> & đaere scande ...
et <u>obprobrii</u> viduitatis tuae non <u>recordaberis</u>	A III b	& đaes <u>bismeres</u> đines wuduwanhādes ...(Alfred's PC, p. 207,11 ff.)

In the Psalter, Ps. 68,20, the words occur coordinated in the same
clause:

Tu enim scis <u>inproperium/opprobrium</u> meum	A III b	... <u>edwīt mīn</u> ...
et <u>confusionem</u> ... meam	B	<u>gedrōefnisse mīne</u> (Vespasian Psalter)

<u>Opprobrium</u> is present in all three instances. It occurs in the first
instance together with <u>ignominia</u>, in the second and third instances together with <u>confusio</u>, two words which have a rather high degree of synonymy. Both of them have the meaning of ´shame as a state´ or ´a feeling of shame´(see pp. 71-73).

An instance which shows <u>opprobrium</u> in clear opposition to <u>confusio</u>
with regard to the senses settled upon for the division of the material
into the two main Sense groups, A:Activity and B:State, is the Psalter,
Ps. 68,8:

quoniam propter te sustinui <u>opprobrium/inproperium</u> operuit <u>con-
fusio</u> faciem meam: for þē forþī þe ic forbaer <u>hosp</u> oferwrēah <u>ge-
scyndnes</u> mīne ansȳne (Lambeth Psalter).

<u>Opprobrium/inproperium</u> here stands for the external treatment which the
object has to endure, <u>confusio</u> for ´a feeling of shame, a blushing´. In
this instance <u>hosp</u> has been classified in A III a:Men-Men-O (i.e. activity in a literal sense, see p. 44 f.)

The senses of <u>opprobrium</u> seem always to include the meaning of external activity. In support of this statement one can observe its frequent use as a complement of the predicate to signify an identification
of the object with the activity (A III c:Men-Men-TP). I quote an instance from the Psalter, Ps. 21,7:

Ego autem sum vermis et non homo, <u>opprobrium</u> hominum et abiectio
plebis: ic sōđlice eam ... <u>edwīt</u> monna & āworpenes folces (Vespasian Psalter).

The instances discussed make it seem reasonable to interpret the
parallelism in the instances from Isaiah (above) as synthetic rather

than synonymous parallelism (see Engnell, 1962-1963, or Svensk Uppslagsbok, s.v. parallellism). If this interpretation is acceptable, the two members of each sentence express different aspects of the state of shame, one of which implies an external activity intended to put the object to shame (A:Activity; Lat. opprobrium) and another which implies the inherent character or the feeling of the person in question (B:State; Lat. confusio and ignominia).

It is quite obvious that the words of both Sense groups, those of A III b:Men-Men-TS and those of B:State imply a state, but there is a fundamental difference between them. The words of A III b:Men-Men-TS express the state or the situation of a person who has to endure disgracing treatment. The words of B:State express dishonour or disgrace as a state, but 'disgracing treatment' is not included. The meaning of the words in B:State usually implies a mental or a physical quality of a person. It may also be a feeling, i.e. a feeling of shame. In those instances where they express an act or an activity it is the question of a shameful act or conduct by which a person brings disgrace upon himself or betrays his bad character. Consequently B:State does not include any instances where the relevant words occur as a complement of the predicate signifying a person as the object of an external activity intended to disgrace him. Cf. p. 46 about the instances of A III c:Men-Men-TP.

The two Latin versions of the Psalter, the "Roman" and the "Gallican", (pp. 37-38) often show mutual differences in regard to the instances classified as a:O, b:TS, and c:TP in A III:Men-Men. I quote two instances:

Ps. 43,14 (AV: Ps. 44,14):

"Roman" text: Posuisti nos in obprobrium (A III b) vicinis nostris
                 derisu et contemptu (A III a) his qui in circuitu
                 nostro sunt

Vespasian Ps.:   ðu settes usic in edwit (A III b) nehgehusum urum
                 mid bismerunge and forhogadnisse (A III a) ...

"Gallican" text:Posuisti nos obprobrium (A III c) uicinis nostris
                 subsanationem et derisum (A III c) his qui ...

Lambeth Ps.:   þu gesettest us to hospe nehgeburum urum tale l.
                 bysmur l. on hlacerungum & hleahter ... (I have
                 placed all these expressions in A III b).

AV: Thou makest us a byword (A III c) among the heathen,
                 a shaking of the head (A III c) among ...

The same differences between the "Roman" and the "Gallican" texts as in Ps. 43,14 also appear in Ps. 78,4 (AV: Ps. 79,4):

Roman text: Facti sumus <u>in obprobrium</u> (A III b) vicinis nostris <u>derisu</u> et contemptu (A III a) his qui ...

Gallican text: Facti sumus <u>obprobrium</u> (A III c) uicinis nostris <u>subsannatio</u> et <u>inlusio</u> (A III c) his qui ...

AV: We are become <u>a reproach</u> (A III c) ... <u>a scorn</u> and <u>a derision</u> (A III c) ...

The easiest way of handling these instances would have been to keep them together in one group with reference to the fact that the actual differences in meaning are rather small. However, I found the instances of b:TS and c:TP interesting in as much as they could be said to form a kind of intermediate stage between the sense of 'activity' (Sense group A) and that of 'state' (Sense group B).

5. List of Division into Sense Groups

A:Activity   (Words signifying an activity intended to bring disgrace on
             or to show contempt for the object of the activity; Lat.
             illusio/inlusio, inrisio, ludibrium, derisus, blasphemia,
             subsannatio, contumelia, calumnia, injuria, and opprobrium
             /obprobrium)

   I:Devil-Men   (Illusion, the devil's deceitful influence on man; Lat.
             illusio/inlusio)

   II:Men-God   (Men's activities intended to show contempt or irrever-
             ence for God, the Holy Ghost, or things considered sa-
             cred; Lat. blasphemia, subsannatio, contumelia, and
             injuria)

   III:Men-Men   (Men's activities intended to disgrace or insult other
             men; Lat. illusio/inlusio, inrisio, ludibrium, blasphe-
             mia, subsannatio, contumelia, calumnia, injuria, and
             opprobrium/obprobrium)

     1:Derision   (Derision, mockery; Lat. illusio/inlusio, inrisio,
             ludibrium, derisus, and subsannatio)

       a:O   (Original sense)

       b:TS   (Transferred sense = State, i.e. words for the activity
             used to express the state of being exposed to the
             activity in question)

       c:TP   (Transferred sense = Personification, i.e. personifica-
             tion of the activity, used as a complement of the pre-
             dicate to express the object of the activity)

     2:Calumny   (Malicious charge, calumny, claim; Lat. calumnia)

     3:Insult   (Insulting reproaches or actions; Lat. blasphemia,
             contumelia, injuria, and opprobrium/obprobrium)

       a:O   (See above under 1:Derision!)

       b:TS   (- " -   )

       c:TP   (- " -   )

B:State   (Words signifying the state of dishonour or shame; Lat. in-
          famia, dedecus, ignominia, turpitudo, and confusio)

   I:Misfortunes   (Dishonour on account of misfortunes and afflic-
          tions; Lat. dedecus, ignominia, and confusio)

   II:Unchastity   (Dishonour on account of unchastity; unchastity and
          the naked body; often in similes for other sins,
          e.g. apostasy; Lat. dedecus, ignominia, turpitudo,
          and confusio)

   III:Misbehaviour (Dishonour on account of misbehaviour or shameful
          conduct other than unchastity; misbehaviour, shame-
          ful conduct, sins; Lat. infamia, dedecus, igno-
          minia, turpitudo, and confusio)

V. VOCABULARY OF DIFFERENT SENSE GROUPS

1. Lists OE 3-5 and ME 3-4

Lists OE 3 and ME 3 give the number of instances of each word recorded for each Sense group, OE 4 and ME 4 the total number of instances
recorded for each Sense group century for century as well as the number
of instances of each word recorded for each Sense group century for
century. List OE 5 shows the distribution of the collected Old English
word material over dialects century for century.

Lists OE 4 and OE 5 include the twelfth and thirteenth centuries, centuries which belong to the Middle English period. This is due to the
fact that certain manuscripts dating from those centuries are copies of
Old English originals; they are hence best treated as Old English. Cf.
p. 14 and Baugh (1967), p. 117.

2. The Words Discussed Individually and in Relation to Each Other within the Sense Groups

2.1. Sense Group A: Activity

2.1.1. Subgroup A I: Devil-Men and the Minor Group A III 1: Men-Men-Derision

The Sense groups have been ranged according to their relative frequency of bismer-words (see p. 43). A I:Devil-Men has the highest frequency (83%), A II:Men-God the next highest (24%), and A III:Men-Men
the lowest frequency among the Subgroups of A:Activity (12%).

However, if the Minor groups of Subgroup A III:Men-Men are counted
separately, one of them, A III 1:Men-Men-Derision, surpasses A II:Men-
God and comes next to A I:Devil-Men in frequency of bismer-words. It
has bismer-words in 20 instances out of a total of 35 (see List OE 3).
This circumstance has caused me to deal with a Subgroup and a Minor
group of another Subgroup under the same heading.

2.1.1.1. The Old English Bismer-Words

In OED two different etymological interpretations are mentioned for
Old English bismer, which is identical with Old High German bismer ´ri-
dicule´. Schmeller´s interpretation is looked upon as the more probable. Schmeller connects Old High German bismer (bí + smer) with Middle
High German smier ´a smile, laughing´, smieren ´to smile´. This interpretation is well in line with the meaning of bismer in Sense group
A III 1:Men-Men-Derision. The other interpretation in the OED reads as
follows: "Others have compared OHG smero, OE smeoru, OTeut.^{x}smerwo- ´fat,
grease, butter´, which seems, on phonetic as well as other grounds, less
probable." This etymology, however, corresponds to the meaning of
bismer in Sense group A I:Devil-Men (Lat. inlusio/illusio). Cf. Lat. inlusio repeated by inquinatio, a word usually rendered by Old English besmitenis, once by bysmernes (p. 36). Old English besmitenis means ´de-
filement, dirtiness, pollution´(HM). Cf. also p. 34 concerning the metaphorical meaning of Lat. inlusio/illusio. Let us assume with OED that
Schmeller´s etymology is the right one, and that -smer[1] is the Old English form of Middle High German smier ´a smile´. Then it seems at any
rate very probable that Old English bismer acquired the meaning of A I:
Devil-Men on account of popular association with Old English smeoru/
smeru ´fat, grease, ointment´.

My earliest instance of bismer-words from Anglian texts are those
from the Vespasian Psalter (dated 875-900). They are inlusio:bismer-
niss (A I:Devil-Men) in Ps. 37,8, and derisus:bismerung (A III 1:Men-Men-
Derision) in Ps. 34,16, 43,14, and 78,4. The extant manuscripts of King
Alfred´s Pastoral Care (PC) are perhaps as old as, or possibly a little
younger than, the manuscripts of the Vespasian Psalter. See App. A, p.
124. An instance from PC classified in A I:Devil-Men is ludibrium:
bismer. Concerning Alfred´s extensive use of bismer see p. 10. The
bismer-words hold a larger proportion of the total number of classified
instances in the ninth century than in the following centuries (List OE
4). If we look at List OE 5 we find that the decrease in use of the
bismer-words concerns only the West Saxon texts, not the Anglian ones.
There the proportion held by the bismer-words is even larger in the
eleventh century than in the earlier centuries. However, the instances

---

[1]Long vowel reduced to -e- owing to reduction of stress in the second
element of a compound. See OEG, par. 372.

from "Anglian" texts of the eleventh century represent the vocabulary of
earlier centuries. See pp. 15 and 94. All instances of the root word
bismer have been recorded from West Saxon manuscripts. See List OE 5.

2.1.1.2. The Old English Non-Bismer-Words

Words other than bismer-words in A I:Devil-Men are swic, swicung, and
big swic/bi3-swic (Lat. inlusio/illusio). See App. C, p. 176.

Big swic and bi3-swic are probably variants of Old English biswic/
beswic/geswic 'treachery, deceit, snare'(HM). Concerning the inter-
change of forms with ī and ig see OEG, par. 271. In A III 1:Men-Men-De-
rision hleahter/hlehter/leahter (Lat. derisus and subsannatio) is next to
the bismer-words in frequency. Other words used for Lat. subsannatio
are tāl, golfetung (gaffetung) 'scoffing, mocking', and hlacerung 'unseemly behaviour or words'(HM). See App. C, pp. 177-178.

All these forms of non-bismer-words, except hlehter and leahter,
occur only in late West Saxon texts.

2.1.1.3. The Middle English Words

The most important Middle English words of A I:Devil-Men and A III 1:
Men-Men-Derision are scornyng, scorn, illusion, and /vnder-/mouwing, all
four adopted or derived from French words. The French words referred to
are Old French escorne 'scorn' and escorner 'himiliate, mock at'(deriva-
tions of Lat. ˣexcornare 'deprive of horns'), French illusion (an adaptation of Lat. illusionem), and Old French moe/moue 'mouth, lip, pout'
(OED, Onions, 1966, and Skeat, 1910).

Of these words scorn/scarn is the first to appear in English. My
earliest instances are from the Ancrene Riwle (1225-49). There schorn/
schornung render Lat. derisus. Skeat (1910) records schorn/scharn from
the Ancrene Riwle and from Early English Homilies of the Twelfth Century
(EETS Orig.Ser. 53, 1873, II 169, 1.1). The instance from the Homilies
reads as follows: ac mest manne him gremede mit scorne 'scornfully re-
viled him'. The OED has skarn from Ormin, dated "c 1200".

My earliest instance of illusioun (Lat. illusio) is from the Midland
Prose Psalter (London MS. dated 1340-1350), where the word has the sense
of A I:Devil-Men. The earliest instance quoted in the OED also has this
sense. It is from English Prose Treatises by Richard Rolle of Hampole
(MS. ca. 1340) and reads as follows: "Wha-so þan will here aungells
sange, and noghte be dyssayuede by feynynge ... ne by illusyone of þe

enemy." My instances from the Wyclif Bible (MSS. dated 1385-1420, see
App. A, p.130) give an idea of the competition between the older words,
scorn and scornyng, and the later illusioun/illusion in the sense of
A III 1:Men-Men-Derision. In the earlier versions, EV 1 and EV 2, Lat.
illusio (Sir.Eccl. 27,31 and Isaiah 66,4) has been rendered by illusioun, in the later version, LV, by scornyng. In EV 1 and EV 2 scorne/
scoorne has been added to illusioun (Sir.Eccl. 27,31) by another hand.
It is quite clear that adaptations of Latin words, such as illusioun/
illusion, confusioun/confusion, etc., came into existence and were originally used as translations of the Latin words from which they had been
adapted. In my instances the adaptations of Latin words are exclusively
used to render the corresponding Latin words. They were literary words,
only understood to a small extent by the common people. The ambition to
make the Bible texts understood by the common people may have induced a
revisor (in this case probably John Purvey, see App. A, pp. 130-131) to
substitute the older and better known word scornyng for the learned word
illusioun, which had been used by the original translator (probably
Nicholas of Hereford).

My earliest instance of **mouwing/undermouwyng** is from the Wyclif
Bible, EV 1 (ca. 1385). The earliest instance in the OED is also from
the Wyclif Bible, though from EV 2. It is the one in Hosea 7,16, where
Lat. subsannatio (A III 1:Men-Men-Derision) has been rendered by mowyng
or scornyng. The later version, LV, has in this instance scornyng. Cf.
the translations of Lat. illusio in Sir.Eccl. 27,31 and Isaiah 66,4
discussed above.

Words appearing only two or three times are desceit/deseit (Old French
deceite), bygile (derived from Old French guile), hethyng (from Old Norse
haeða 'to mock, scoff'), and bismer.

2.1.2. Subgroup A II: Men-God

The activity of Subgroup A II:Men-God (see p. 44) is expressed in
125 instances out of a total of 140 by blasphemia in the Latin sources.
In ecclesiastical Latin blasphemia also occurs for 'men's activities
directed towards other men: slandering, reviling'(see p. 31). I have
some instances of this meaning in my Middle English material from the
Bible. They are classified in A III 3:Men-Men-Insult. In both senses,
Men-God and Men-Men, the Middle English translators use **blasphemye/blas-
femye**, an adaptation of the Latin word. **blasphemye/blasfemye** renders

only blasphemia, never any other Latin word.

The translations of blasphemia show a clear difference in the two
Old English dialects, Anglian and West Saxon. All the instances from
Anglian texts in my material have ebolsung/etc. for blasphemia. In the
West Saxon texts the bismer-words (bismer, bismer-spraec, and bismerung)
cover 46% of the translations (12 instances out of 26). As large a
proportion, i.e. 12 instances, consists of expressions or words which
occur only for blasphemia. They are tallice word, gyltlice spraec,
woffung, hyrwincg[1], wiþersacung, and yfelsacung. The remaining two instances are from Alfred's Pastoral Care, where blasphemia has been rendered by tael (App. C, pp. 176-177).

My material includes two instances of yfelsacung:blasphemia, one
classified as Anglian and one as West Saxon (List OE 5:3, p. 150). The
one classified as Anglian is from the Dialogues, MS. C, a West Saxon
copy of an Anglian original (see p. 15). The one classified as West
Saxon (see above) is from a prayer in MS. Lambeth 427 (see App. A, p.
127). A slightly younger version of this prayer in MS. Arundel 155 has
in this instance hyrwincʒ[1]. Max Förster (Anglia 66, 1942, pp. 52-55)
comments on these two parallel instances in the following way: "Dass
die Ausdrücke von L [i.e. MS. Lambeth 427] die ursprünglicheren sind,
wird auch dadurch bestätigt, dass sie mehrfach den Sinn der lateinischen
Vorlage genauer wiedergeben als die Ersatzwörter von A [i.e. MS. Arundel
155], so z.B. yfelsacunʒ 'blasphemia' gegenüber hyrwincʒ."

Both West Saxon bismer-spraec and Anglian ebolsung/eofulsung/etc.
were obviously formed for the purpose of rendering Latin blasphemia.
West Saxon -spraec is a literal translation of -phemia which derives
from -phemos '-speaking' (OED). Anglian ebol-/eoful-/etc. seems to be
a literal translation of blas- which derives from blapsis 'evil'
(Collins). In HM ebol- is marked "(N)=yfel-" 'Northumbrian form corresponding to yfel-' and eoful- "(A)=yfel-" 'Anglian form corresponding
to yfel-'. Ebolsung/eofulsung/etc. could be derived from the corresponding verb ebolsian/eofulsian/etc. (ebol-/eoful- + -sian). Cf. for
instance Old English maere 'famous', maersian 'to make or become famous', and maersung 'fame, report, renown'. Other forms in my material

---

[1]In HM hierwing/hyrwing is provided with a reference to a particular
passage, Lib. Scint., 137,12. Such references are added only in the
case of rare words, - more especially hapax legomena (HM, p. vi).

(App. C, pp. 176-177), e.g. ebolsong, efolsong, eofolsong, and efalsong, could be interpreted as compounds whose latter part derives from singan 'chant, intone, recite, etc.'. An example of the noun yfelsang in a West Saxon text from the tenth century (Confessionale Ecgberhte) is the following, which is interesting as it gives an interpretation of the word: " ... daet daet yfelsang waere on God, sede for yfelne man maessan sunge ...". I have quoted the instance from Jordan (1906), p. 17. Cf. the compound yfelsacung (p. 60), whose latter part is a derivative of sacan 'dispute, disgrace, fight'. However, Jordan (1906), p. 18, and Holthausen (1963), s.v. eofulsian, relate the verb efolsian/eofulsian/ etc. to a form ^{x}ef-halsian and ^{x}eb-halsian (^{x}eb-hal 'Lästerung' + -sian) respectively. Cf. the Old English verb halsian 'take oath, swear'. The forms efalsung/hefalsung in my material support this interpretation.

To sum up, three different etymological interpretations could be justified with regard to the following forms which occur in my material: Ebolsung/eofulsung/efolsung (from ebolsian/etc. = ebol/etc. + -sian), ebolsong/efolsong/eofolsong (a compound = ebol-/etc. + -song from singan), and efalsung/hefalsung (from ^{x}ef-halsian/^{x}eb-halsian = ^{x}eb-hal + -sian). These forms could be regarded as separate formations or as variants of one formation, the original one. Variants of this kind often develop on account of popular association with semantically and phonetically re-lated words (cf. bismer, p. 57). I have preferred to treat them as orthographical variants of one word, a compound with ebol-/eoful-/efol-/ etc. 'evil-' as one part (see List OE 2, No. 14).

Anglian words appear not only in such West Saxon texts as are copies of Anglian originals (p. 15). Saxon authors, for instance Wulfstan and Aelfric, also used Anglian words. Menner (1948) says (p. 8) that An-glian words in Wulfstan's sermons are easily explained by the preacher's search for fine phrases or by his imitation of earlier homilists. These Anglian words were easily grasped by educated listeners in Saxon terri-tory, he adds. The large Anglian element in Aelfric's vocabulary has been emphasized by Meissner (1934/35). Schabram (1965), p. 92, mentions an instance of the older Anglian type oferhyd- in Aelfric's vocabulary (App. A, p. 127). Though Schabram's expectations of the reader's reac-tion to this discovery may be a bit surprising I quote his comment: "Wir brauchen zwar keinen Anstoss daran zu nehmen, dass ihm [Aelfric] die anglische Wortsippe überhaupt bekannt war ...".

2.1.3. The Minor Group A III 2: Men-Men-Calumny

All the instances in this group are translations of calumnia, the
12th Latin word in List 1. In List OE 1, which includes unclassified instances (p. 19), only 13% of the translations of calumnia are bismer-
words (List OE 1:4). In the Sense group (List OE 3), however, the percentage of bismer-words amounts to 20%.

Many of the words which render calumnia render also words of A III 3:
Men-Men-Insult, e.g. Old English hosp, teona, tāl, and telnis. Words
occuring only for calumnia are hearm, hearmcwide, hearmcwidolnes, hearm-
sprǣc, līcettung, lēas, hōltihte, and yrmðu. The instances of telnis
and hearm/-cwide/-cwidolnes derive from Anglian texts or texts dependent
on Anglian originals. The Paris Psalter, too, has hearmcwide (cf. p. 64).

The Middle English translations have chalenge/chaleng/chalengyng (Old
French chalenge derived from Latin calumnia) for calumnia in 77 instances
out of a total of 82 (i.e. 94%). My earliest instance is from the Midland
Prose Psalter, London MS., dated 1340-50. There calumnia has been rendered by chalang/-e. In the OED two instances, one of chalange and one of
chaleng, are quoted from texts dated "before 1300". The form chalengyng
is represented by only two instances in my material. They are from the
Wyclif Bible, EV 1 and EV 2. In LV they have been replaced by chalenge
which is the normal form in all three versions of the Wyclif Bible. In
the great majority of instances from this source the word is preceded by
wrong or fals. EV 1 and EV 2 up to Baruch 3,20 have wrong chalenge, EV 2
after Baruch 3,20 to the end of the Old Testament as well as LV throughout have fals chalenge. See App. A, p. 131.

The MED records the following senses for chaleng/-e/-yng:

1. (The act of making) false or malicious accusations; slandering
   calumny, scolding.

2. The act of claiming or demanding (either rightly or wrongly).

In my material the first of the recorded senses for calumnia is by far the
most common. All Old English words which render calumnia seem to have
this sense. However, among my five Middle English instances of words
other than chalenge/etc.(see above) there is one which has craving (Old
English crafing 'claim, demand'). It is from the Surtees Psalter, a text
dated "late thirteenth century". The remaining four have blame, chalenge
and blame, blamenge, and eny thynge to be discussed afterwarde (App. C,
p. 193).

2.1.4. The Minor Group A III 3: Men-Men-Insult

The words of A III 3:Men-Men-Insult render Latin contumelia, injuria, and opprobrium. In my Middle English material there are also a few instances which are translations of blasphemia in this sense. They are from the Wyclif Bible. Blasphemia normally has the sense of A II:Men-God.

2.1.4.1. The Old English Bismer-Words

Contumelia being the 10th, injuria the 14th, and opprobrium the 15th Latin word in List 1, the proportion of bismer-words in this group is small. Only 21 out of a total of 339 Old English instances, i.e. 6%, are bismer-words (see List OE 3). The majority of them, more exactly 17, are from King Alfred's translations.

2.1.4.2. Old English Edwīt and Hosp

The most frequent words in A III 3:Men-Men-Insult are edwīt and hosp. They represent between them 56% (100 instances of edwīt and 91 instances of hosp) of the total number of instances in this group. Except for eight instances all of them render opprobrium. The exceptions are three instances of edwīt and three of hosp for injuria, as well as two of edwīt for contumelia.

In the three Latin versions of the Psalter (App. A, p. 122)   inproperium alternates with opprobrium. There is no instance of inproperium occurring in all three versions. In 36 instances out of a total of 37, inproperium has been rendered by edwīt or hosp. The translations of Latin inproperium are not included in my lists. (See p. 27.)

Edwīt is the word for opprobrium/inproperium in the Anglian Vespasian Psalter (dated 875-900), where it occurs 16 times for opprobrium and five times for inproperium. The Regius Psalter (dated ca. 950), which is regarded as the oldest representative of the independent West Saxon Psalter versions, has in all these instances the word hosp. The Old English Psalter versions dependent on the Vespasian Psalter, called the Psalters of A-type, i.e. the Junius Psalter and the Cambridger Psalter, follow with few exceptions their original in the use of edwīt. The exceptions are one instance of hosp in the Junius Psalter and two instances of hosp in the Cambridger Psalter. The Salisbury Psalter, which is a Psalter of D-type, i.e. dependent on the Regius Psalter, follows its original in the use of hosp without exceptions. Also the Lambeth Psalter, a late West Saxon compilation, has hosp throughout, though in some instances together with other words, e.g. bysmerung.

In the so-called Paris Psalter, an eleventh-century MS. containing a metrical version of Psalms 51-150, edwīt is the only word for opprobrium and inproperium. Cf. hearmcwide for calumnia on p. 62. Concerning Anglian elements in the Paris Psalter I quote a few lines from Krapp's edition, Introduction, p. 17: "The language of the text as it now stands in the manuscript is prevailingly West Saxon, but certain forms in it were assumed by Sievers (Beiträge X, 474,483) to be of Anglian origin and to indicate that the translation was originally made in the Anglian dialect." The consistent use of edwīt for Latin opprobrium/inproperium can be seen as a support for Sievers' assumption.

In Alfred's Pastoral Care edwīt occurs for contumelia, once in each of the two parallel MSS. (MS. C and MS. H 20) from the ninth century (App. C, pp. 178-179). In the same MSS. two Latin words from my un-classified material (p. 27), exprobratio (PC, MS. C, p. 294,11; MS. H 20, p. 295,10) and probrum (PC, MS. C, p. 260,5; MS. H 20, p. 261,5) are rendered by edwīt. In Alfred's Orosius (MS.L, dated early tenth cen-tury) edwīt renders infamia once (App. C, p. 183).

A few instances from the Rule of St.Benedict (Aethelwold's transla-tion and the Winteney Version) have hosp, edwīt, or a combination of both, for opprobrium (App. C, p. 181) and injuria (App. C, p. 180).

2.1.4.3. Old English Teona

Teona is next to edwīt and hosp in frequency within the group. To-gether with a few instances of tēan-/tēon- in compounds (tēancuide, tēon-rēden, tēonraēden, and tēonfull þing) it renders 22% of the total number of instances in A III 3:Men-Men-Insult. All instances of tēan-/tēon- in compounds and all instances of tēona except one occur in sense a, i.e. they express the activity in a literal sense (see pp. 41-42, 44-45, and 47).

Tēona as well as tēan-/tēon- in compounds render only contumelia and injuria, never opprobrium. They represent 42% of the instances of con-tumelia and 57% of the instances of injuria. My earliest instances of tēona render Latin injuria in Anglian texts from the ninth century (List OE 5:2). From the tenth century onwards tēona dominates the translations of injuria and contumelia not only in Anglian but also in West Saxon texts. Tēona also dominates in Gregory's Dialogues and in Bede's Histo-ry (works ascribed to two of King Alfred's assistants), whereas in King

Alfred's translations neither t$\bar{e}$ona nor t$\bar{e}$an-/t$\bar{e}$on- in compounds occur.

2.1.4.4. Old English Words Other than T$\bar{e}$ona and T$\bar{e}$an-/T$\bar{e}$on- in Compounds Used to Render Latin Contumelia and Injuria

Scand, grama, and edw$\bar{\imath}$t/hosp cover between them 19% of the translations of contumelia, 11% of the translations of injuria. See List OE 1. These percentages in combination with the percentages representing the translations of contumelia and injuria by t$\bar{e}$ona/etc. (see above under 2.1.4.3.) seem to indicate a fairly high degree of synonymy for contumelia and injuria, at least if judged on the basis of the Old English translations. There are also instances in my material in which contumelia is substituted for injuria and vice versa. An example is Cura Pastoralis, 33, col. 62 (App. A, p.124). Here contumelia jaculatione is repeated some lines further down by injuriarum jacula.

There are, it is true, among the translations of injuria a great number of words which have been used only for injuria, thus marking the distinction between injuria and contumelia or between injuria and other Latin words in the field. They are anweardnys[1] (24), w$\bar{\imath}$te, unriht w$\bar{\imath}$tnung, w$\bar{\imath}$tnan/w$\bar{\imath}$tnian (42), laeðo (43), demm (44), t$\bar{y}$nan (45), abylgð (47), baeligniso (48), earfoðe (49), trega (50), un$\bar{a}$r (51), uneðnys (52), wraecs$\bar{\imath}$ð (53), wraeððo (54). The numbers in brackets refer to the numbers in List OE 2. Eight of these fifteen words are recorded from King Alfred's translations, and so they primarily testify to the peculiarity of his vocabulary. The eight words I refer to are those numbered 42, 44, 47, 49, 51, and 53. Alfred's translations make up only 16% (ca. 241,000 running words) of all the excerpted Old English texts (ca. 1,482,600 running words), and only 12% (80 instances) of all the classified Old English instances (647) are from his translations. Alfred uses 14 different Old English words, one of which is bismer, for Latin injuria. Only one of these 14 words appears elsewhere as translation of injuria. The word is laeðdo, which, as well as in Alfred's translations, appears once in an Anglian text, the Lindisfarne MS. (CND4). Cf. Alfred's use of edw$\bar{\imath}$t dealt with on p. 64. Alfred has a peculiar vocabulary for contumelia as well. Only in his translations do we find contumelia rendered by bismer, woroldbismer, scand, edw$\bar{\imath}$t, and hisping.

---

[1]The translation anweardnys:injuria is from Alcuin (App. A, p. 127). Cf. Alfred's translation unweordnes:dedignatio (p. 90).

2.1.4.5. Middle English Wrong

The most frequent Middle English word in A III 3:Men-Men-Insult is wrong. It has been used in 140 cases out of a total of 585 in this group, i.e. 24%. See List ME 3. Only contumelia and injuria have been rendered by wrong, which occurs in 18% of the instances of contumelia, and in 66% of the instances of injuria. See List ME 1. Cf. the corresponding percentages for teona, p. 64.

Wrong is a Scandinavian loan word which appears in late Old English (Onions and Skeat). The earliest instance quoted in the OED is the following from Wulfstan's Homilies (xlii 203) dated "a 1100": þā unriht-dēman, ðe ... wendaþ wrang tō rihte and riht tō wrange. The period during which the Scandinavian element was making its way into the English vocabulary is the tenth and eleventh centuries. The loan words, however, generally appear somewhat later in written records, many of them not until the beginning of the thirteenth century. See Baugh (1959), p. 124. In my material the earliest instance of wrong is from the London MS. of the Midland Prose Psalter (dated 1340-50).

2.1.4.6. Middle English Repref/Reproof/etc.

The word next to wrong in frequency within A III 3:Men-Men-Insult, repref/reproof/etc., renders almost exclusively Latin opprobrium (List ME 1) and inproperium (pp. 63-64). With 135 instances (List ME 3) it covers 23% of the translations in the group. My earliest instances are those from the Wyclif Bible, EV 1 (ca. 1385). The OED, however, records one instance of reproue (Old French reprove) from a text dated "a 1300".

2.1.4.7. Middle English Shenship/Schenschipe/etc.

Shenship is the third word in frequency (next to wrong and reprof/repref/etc.) within the group. With 115 instances, all of them rendering Latin opprobrium, it covers 20% of the translations in A III 3:Men-Men-Insult.

However, the majority of the instances of shenship in my material, viz. 153 out of a total of 268, are classified in Sense group B:State, where shenship renders Latin ignominia, confusio, and in a few cases dedecus. Thus shenship is a word which transgresses the borderline between the two Main Sense groups, A:Activity and B:State (see p. 80 and pp. 84-85), and in fact the only Middle English word that does so to any appreciable extent. Other words which occur in both A:Activity and B:State are represented in one of the two groups by only one or two instances. See List ME 3.

List ME 4 shows that the earliest instances of opprobrium:shenship (A:Activity) are recorded from manuscripts written in the fifteenth century. In fact, the rendering of opprobrium and inproperium (A:Activity) as well as confusio and ignominia (B:State) by the same word, shenship, is a phenomenon that occurs only in the Wyclif Bible. It starts in EV 2 at Baruch 3,20 and continues in LV. The translation of opprobrium and inproperium by shenship is never to be found in EV 1 (MS. ca. 1385). Nor is it to be found in EV 2 before Baruch 3,20. Concerning the break at Baruch 3,20 see App. A, p.131. The two versions of the New Testament, EV and LV, show by comparison a decrease in the use of shenship for opprobrium and inproperium. In EV reproue/repreue (repref/etc. in EV 1 and EV 2 before Baruch 3,20) alternates with shenship. In LV, however, only one instance out of a total of six has shenship. The remaining five have repreef. Confusio is in both versions of the New Testament rendered by confusion. Ignominia is in EV rendered by yuel fame, in LV by shenship.

I have collated my instances with the corresponding ones in the Authorized Version (AV), which is a revision of translations made by Tyndale and Coverdale during the first half of the sixteenth century. Tyndale translated the New Testament from the Greek as well as parts of the Old Testament, to which Coverdale added his translation of the remainder of the Old Testament. See pp. 367-370 in Baugh (1967) and p. 114 in Legouis (1950). In AV the distinction between the senses in terms of my classification into the two Main Sense groups, A:Activity and B:State, is entirely reestablished. There the word corresponding to opprobrium/inproperium is with very few exceptions reproach[1]; the words corresponding to confusio are shame or confusion.

---

[1]Modern English reproach is descended from Middle English reproche (French reproche, 12th c., = Provençal repropche, Spanish reproche, Italian rimproccio). The earliest instance of Middle English reproche recorded in the OED is from a text written "c 1420". The word is not represented in my material.

2.1.4.8. Middle English Words Other than Wrong, Repref/etc., and
Shenship/etc.

Latin contumelia and injuria show a considerably lower degree of
synonymy if judged on the basis of the Middle English translations
than if judged on the basis of the Old English translations. Compare
the percentages of translations by Old English tēona/etc. (p. 64),
scand, grama, edwīt/hosp (pp. 63 and 65), and by Middle English
wrong (p. 66), which is the only Middle English word used for both
contumelia and injuria.

The Middle English translations of contumelia show a far greater
variety than those of any other Latin word dealt with in this investigation. None of the words used to render it cover more than 20%
of the translations. The most frequent words are dispit (20%),
wrong (17%), dispisyng (17%), strif/strijf (13%), blamyng (8%), re-
pref/etc. (6%), and the verb turmenten (4%). The remaining 15% are
shared by 14 different words or expressions. Of these 14 words or
expressions 8 occur only once each in the whole collection. See
Lists ME 1-2, Nos. 1, 8-11, and 29-44, in App. B, p. 155 f.

The most frequent word for injuria, next to wrong (p. 66), is the
adaptation of the Latin word, i.e. injury/etc. It occurs in 18 instances out of a total of 189, which makes 10%. The earliest instance
recorded in the MED and in the OED is from the Wyclif Bible, EV, Col.
3,25 (in the MED dated ca. 1384, in the OED 1382): Qui enim injuriam
fecit: He that doth iniurie or wrong. In Forshall and Madden's
edition (henceforth FM) wrong is marked as being omitted in two MSS.
(called O and X). The Wyclif Bible, LV, has iniurie but FM has a
note stating that wrong is added in the margin of the MS. in question. This addition of wrong to iniurie indicates that the scribe
or a later revisor felt that the word iniurie required an explanation
in order to be commonly understood. Cf. pp. 58-59 about scorn/scorn-
yng and illusion.

Neither wrong nor injury/etc. occur in the three Middle English
texts from the thirteenth century, the Ancrene Riwle, the Life of St.
Katherine (two South-West Midland texts from the first half of the
thirteenth century), and the Surtees Psalter (a Northern or Midland
text from the late thirteenth century). The two South-West Midland
texts have wouh/woh (OE wōh), the Surtees Psalter has unright and
unrightwisness (OE unriht and unrihtwīsnes). The instances of wouh/

woh here referred to are the only ones in my Middle English material.
Old English wo̅h is not represented in my material. The OED (s.v. wough),
however, has a number of instances from Alfred´s texts and also from
other Old English texts. The word is to be found in Beowulf as well.
The meaning ´crooked´ and ´perverse´ is given in the glossary of
Klaeber (1950).

   The two Middle English words repref/etc. and shenship/etc. (see p. 66)
cover together 85% (243 instances out of a total of 285) of the translations of Latin opprobrium. Among the words which cover the remaining
15% (42 instances) upbraidyng and reproce/repruce/repruse/reproceing/etc.
are the most frequent ones. Upbraidyng, derived from the verb upbraid
(Old English upbre̅dan), **is a new formation in Middle English.** The
earliest instance quoted in the OED is from a text dated "c 1205". In
my material the word is represented by 18 instances. The majority, 16
instances, are from the Surtees Psalter ("late thirteenth century").
The remaining two are from the Midland Prose Psalter, the London MS.
(ca. 1340-50). My 15 instances of reproce/etc. are also from the London
MS. of the Midland Prose Psalter. **Reproce, repruce,** and **repruse** are
Old French (Norman ?) or Anglo-French variants of French reproche (see
p. 67, footnote 1, and p. 101). The OED records instances of the word
from this text. In the Dublin MS., which is a revision of the text in
the London MS. (App. A, p. 131), reproce/etc. is replaced by reprofc/
reproue/reprouyng. Cf. above, p. 67, about the Wyclif Bible, where
repref/etc. is used in EV 1 and in EV 2 before Baruch 3,20.

2.1.5. Summary of Sense Group A: Activity

The bismer-words are the most frequent Old English words in A I:
Devil-Men and A III 1:Men-Men-Derision. Next to the bismer-words in
frequency in A III 1:Men-Men-Derision is hleahter/leahter/hlehter,
which occurs only in texts from the **second** or so-called classical Old
English period. The Middle English words ranked in order of frequency
within each group are in A I:Devil-Men desceit/deseit, illusion, scornyng, bismer and in A III 1:Men-Men-Derision scornyng, scorn, illusion,
and under-/mouwing.

In A II:Men-God the bismer-words are the most frequent West Saxon
words. The Anglian texts have ebolsung/etc. In the Middle English
translations blasfemye/blasphemie, an adaptation of the Latin word blasphemia, dominates almost completely.

A III 2:Men-Men-Calumny has different Old English words in Anglian
and in West Saxon texts. The Anglian texts have hearm, hearmcwide/
-cwidolnes, telnis, and scomu/sceomu. The West Saxon texts have hosp,
tal, teona, and bismer-words. Over 90% of the instances from Middle
English texts have chalenge/etc.(Old French chalenge derived from Lat.
calumnia).

In A III 3:Men-Men-Insult Old English hosp, edwit, and teona dominate.
Edwit is the Anglian word for Latin opprobrium. Hosp dominates the
translation of opprobrium in the West Saxon texts. My earliest instance
of hosp is the one from the Junius Psalter (ca. 925) mentioned on p. 63.
Teona occurs both in Anglian and West Saxon texts for Latin contumelia
and **injuria**, though its frequency in West Saxon texts is more than
double its frequency in Anglian texts. See List OE 5:1-2. The most important Middle English words are wrong, **repref**/etc., and shenship, which
are represented by more than 100 instances each in my material. Words
represented by less than 20, but not less than 9 instances, are the
following: dispit, despisyng, upbraidyng, iniury, reproce/-ing, strif,
blasfemye, harm, wouh, and blamyng. They are ranked in order of frequency within the group.

Of the Middle English words enumerated above three are Old English
words that have survived in Middle English. They are bismer, harm (OE
hearm), and wouh (OE woh).

2.2. Sense Group B: State

Sense group B:State holds one third of the whole number of classified instances, viz. 672 out of a total of 2022 (see Lists 3).

The meaning of B:State is less important in the Old English bismer-
words (see p. 48). The collected 672 instances (158 Old English and
514 Middle English ones) render the Latin words infamia, dedecus, ignominia, turpitudo, and confusio, i.e. the 6th, the 8th, the 11th, the
14th, and the 16th word in Lists 1. Nearly half of these 672 instances,
more exactly 324, consist of translations of confusio, the last word
in Lists 1, and consequently the one which has the lowest percentage of
bismer-words in the Old English translations, which is 2%. Infamia,
the word which has the highest frequency of bismer-words among the five
Latin words of B:State, is represented by only five Old English and
nine Middle English instances of translation (Lists 3). Six of the
eleven instances in List OE 1 are from vocabularies (App.C, pp.186-187)
and consequently unclassified.

2.2.1 Special Features of Latin Words in B: State

The meanings of Latin confusio and ignominia (B:State) will be discussed and compared to the meanings of Latin pudor, verecundia, and
reverentia (three words of my unclassified material, see p. 27) mainly
on the basis of instances from the three Latin Psalter versions, the
Roman, the Gallican, and the Hebrew Psalters, where not only confusio,
pudor, and verecundia seem to be interchangeable, but also confusio,
pudor, verecundia, reverentia, and ignominia. Compare the following instances from the three versions:

```
Ps. 34,26
Roman text    : ... induantur pudore     et reverentia
Gallican text: ... induantur confusione et reuerentia
Hebrew text   : ... induantur confusione et verecundia

Ps. 43,16
Roman text    : ... uerecundia mea ... et confusio vultus mei
Gallican text: ... uerecundia mea ... et confusio faciei meae
Hebrew text   : ... confusio mea    ... et ignominia faciei meae

Ps. 68,8
Roman text    : ... operuit reverentia faciem meam
Gallican text: ... operuit confusio faciem meam
Hebrew text   : ... operuit confusio faciem meam

Ps. 68,20
Roman text    : ... confusionem et verecundiam meam
Gallican text: ... confusionem meam et reuerentiam meam
Hebrew text   : ... confusionem meam et ignominiam meam
```

Ps. 70,13
Roman text   : ... operiantur confusione et pudore
Gallican text: ... operiantur confusione et pudore
Hebrew text   : ... operiantur obprobrio et confusione

Ps. 88,46
Roman text   : ... perfudisti eum confusione
Gallican text: ... perfudisti eum confusione
Hebrew text   : ... operuisti eum ignominia

Ps. 108,29
Roman text   : ... reverentia et ... confusione
Gallican text: ... pudore   et ... confusione
Hebrew text   : ... confusione et ... confusione (sic)

2.2.1.1. Confusio

According to Lewis & Short, my main source for the meanings of the
Latin words (see p. 29), confusio means:

1) a mingling, a mixture, a confounding, confusion, disorder;
2) a reddening, a blushing.

In the great majority of my instances confusio seems to have a meaning
closely related to that of ´a reddening, a blushing´, i.e.´a feeling of
shame´.[1] Concerning this meaning, the second one in Lewis & Short, the
following information is to be found in Forcellini: "Translate sumitur
pro perturbatione animi; Hinc apud Vulg. Interpr. saepe sumitur pro
verecundia, pudore." ´Metaphorically used for perturbation of the mind
(the soul); hence in the Vulgate often used for verecundia and pudor.´

Confusio with the meaning of ´a mingling, a mixture´ is only represented by a few instances in my material. In the Epinal, Erfurt, and
Corpus MSS. (the Oldest Glossaries, 1885) from the eighth and ninth centuries, and in the Cleopatra MS. (WW, XI) from the tenth century confusio is rendered by gemaengiung, gemengiung, gemengung, and besides in
the Corpus MS. the translation chaos:duolma is explained by "prima confusio omnium rerum". These instances, being from Glossaries, are not included in my classification. From Hymnus Athanasii (36), which occurs
in seven of the Old English Psalter MSS., I have the following instance:
"Vnus omnino non confusione substantie: sed unitate persone". In four of
the versions gemang, gemeng, gemengnes, and gemengednys are used; the
remaining three have wilnun3, gescindnes, and gedrēfydnys, respectively,
for confusio. With some hesitation I placed these instances in B II:

---

[1]Cf. the translation in the Paris Psalter, Ps. 68,8: confusio:hlēor-
sceamu ´confusion of face´(HM).

Unchastity. In HM s.v. gemengednes 'sexual intercourse' is recorded
from Alfred's Pastoral Care, and wilnung/wilning 'desire, longing (good
or bad)' both from the Pastoral Care and from Orosius.

Confusio in Boethius (p. 106,16) has been rendered by gewrixle 'turn,
change' in Alfred's Boethius (MS. C; p. 125,12).

In the following instances from my Middle English material the meaning of 'disorder, mixture' is obvious:

Higden, Vol. I, p. 94: post confusionem linguarum
        Higd.Trev. : ... spredinge ...
        Higd.Harl. : ... confusion ...

        Vol. I,p. 208: post turrim confusionis constructam
        Higd.Trev. : ... tour Babel ...
        Higd.Harl. : ... toure of confusion ...

        Vol. I, p.344: post linguarum confusionem
        Higd.Trev. : men speked many langages
        Higd.Harl. : confusion of langages

        Vol. II,p.250: Vocatus est autem locus ille Babel, quod
                      sonat confusio ... et ideo immunis a
                      linguas confusione
        Higd. Trev. : ... schedynge ... schedynge ...
        Higd. Harl. : ... confusion ... confusion ...

  The Ancrene Riwle,
      p. 100,32-34: Ysboseeth interpretatur 'vir confusionis'; et
                nonne talis est qui in medio inimicorum ad
                dormiendum se prosternit?
      p. 121,18-20: ... bimased mon ...

      p. 101,13:   occidunt Ysboseeth: id est virum confusionis
      p. 121,35:   ... þene bimasede gost

  Acts, 19,29:   et impleta est civitas confusione
  Wyclif Bible,EV 2:... confusioun
    "   " ,LV :... confusioun

The instances quoted above are not included in my classification.

2.2.1.2. Verecundia and Pudor

As the words verecundia and pudor have the sense of 'a feeling of
shame' in common with confusio (and ignominia ?), I collected the instances of them during my work (see p. 27). However, unlike confusio
and ignominia, they are never rendered by bismer-words in the Old English translations and are, because of this, not included in my tables
and lists.

The principal Old English words for verecundia and pudor is scomu/etc.

It has been used for verecundia in 24 cases out of a total of 30 and for pudor in 20 cases out of a total of 33. Cf. confusio, which has been rendered by scomu/etc. in 26 cases out of a total of 112 (List OE 1).

Verecundia and pudor do not exclusively express 'a feeling of shame' but also qualities which could be said to imply the ability of a person to feel shame. Pudor has been rendered by clēnnes/claēnnes[1] 'cleanness, purity, chastity', hygdignis[2] 'chastity, modesty', gehealdsumnys[3] 'devotion, chastity', sīd(efulnys)[4] 'virtue, modesty', and pudor ac verecundia by claēnlice sȳdefulnys[5].

2.2.1.3. Reverentia

In the Old English Psalter versions reverentia occurs 22 times altogether. It has been rendered by scomu/etc. (Ps. 68,8, 68,20, and 108,29), aewiscnes[6] 'shameless conduct, reverence', ārweorþung, ārwurþnes 'reverence, honour', andracung 'fear, awe' (Ps. 34,26), forwandung 'shame'(Ps. 68,8, 68,20, and 108,29), and gebysmerung (see below). A mistranslation is reverentia:cirrendrae in Eadwine's Canterbury Psalter, Ps. 108,29. A present participle of the verb cierran 'turn, return' has been used for reverentia probably misread as being a participle or a gerundive of the Latin verb reverti 'return'. The principle words for reverentia in other Old English translations seem to be ārweorþung and ārweorþnes. According to Lewis & Short reverentia means not only 'reverence, respect, veneration, awe', but also 'shyness, shame' and 'timidity arising from high respect or fear'. This implies that reverentia has the sense of 'a feeling of shame' in common with verecundia, pudor, confusio, and ignominia (?).

Finally I shall return to the translation reverentia:gebysmerung in the Lambeth Psalter, Ps. 68,20 (see p. 38):

Gallican text :Tu scis inproperium meum et confusionem et
       reuerentiam meam:
Lambeth Psalter :þu canst mīne hosp 1. mīn onhrōp & gescaendnysse 1.
        sceamunge mīne & mīne gebysmerunge;

---

[1] Clēnnes (Hymn 11,12, added to the Vespasian Psalter); claēnnes (Boethius II, pr. 4, p. 32,18: Alfred's Boethius, p. 22,14; Aldhelm, MS. H, Mone, nos. 4178, 4489, and Aldhelm, MS. 1, Napier, nos. 4176, 4479, 5176).

[2] Hygdignis (Dur.Ri., p. 110,2-3).

[3] Gehealdsumnys (De Vitiis, p. 234,8).

[4] Sīd(efulnys) (Aldhelm, MS. 7, Napier, no. 347).

[5] Claēnlice sȳdefulnys (Rule C, p. 76,12-13:p. 77,2-3).

[6] In HM aewiscnes 'reverence' is recorded from CP (= the Pastoral Care), 34,26. This is a misprint for Ps. 34,26 (see p. 11, footnote 1).

Arundel Psalter : ... scame ...;
Salisbury Psalter: ... forwandunȝa ...

The editor of the Arundel Psalter observes (p. 17) that the word scame
might have been adopted from a glossed Roman text, which served as an
original for the translator. In this instance the Roman text has verecundia, a word mostly rendered by scomu/etc. in the Old English translations (see p. 74). However, it does not seem necessary to explain the
translation reverentia:scamu in this instance as an adoption from the
corresponding instance, verecundia:scamu, in a glossed Roman text. The
instance reverentia:scamu discussed here is only one out of nine instances in the Old English Psalter versions. The remaining eight instances are glosses to the Roman Psalter text.

The translation reverentia:gebysmerung, on the other hand, is a single
instance. It cannot be explained as an adoption from other glosses, nor
as a result of influence from the Latin word verecundia of the Roman
Psalter text. The sense which reverentia has in common with verecundia,
pudor, and confusio, viz. 'a feeling of shame'(see p. 73), seems to fall
outside the range of meaning embraced by the bismer-words. As far as I
have been able to find out, neither verecundia nor pudor have ever been
rendered by a bismer-word, and confusio only in two instances out of a
total of 112.[1] A possible explanation for the translation reverentia:
gebysmerung, however, may be found in the influence from the Hebrew
Psalter text, which has in this instance the word ignominia (see pp. 71
and 76). The Lambeth Psalter, the source of the instance reverentia:
gebysmerung, shows characteristics which distinguish it from the other
Old English Psalter glosses. It is a compilation made by a learned man.
It is rich in vocabulary. Many Latin words have been rendered by two or
three Old English words. It must be reasonable to assume that the
man in question collated the Gallican Psalter, which was the current Latin text at his time, with other available Latin Psalter texts (App. A,
p. 122). The difference in vocabulary between the Latin texts (see p.
71) may have been his reason, or at any rate one of his reasons, for
giving more than one Old English word for a Latin word in the Gallican
Psalter text.

---

[1]The two instances are from the two parallel manuscripts of Alfred's
Pastoral Care. It is a quotation from the Bible, Philippians 3,19:
quorum deus venter est, et gloria in confusionem ipsorum, where confusio
has been rendered by bismer.

2.2.1.4. Ignominia

The meaning of ignominia has been discussed in connection with the meaning of the other Latin words of B:State on pp. 48-51. Here its relation to the bismer-words will be taken up with reference to the instance of reverentia:gebysmerung from the Psalter, Ps. 68,20 (see above, pp. 71 and 74-75).

In my material there are three instances where ignominia and bismer-words are involved. All three have been recorded from Alfred's Orosius. One of them, ignominia related to bysmrung, has already been dealt with and explained as being a free translation (see pp. 38-39). The remaining two, which concern ignominia and bismer, follow here:

1) Orosius, p. 146,33-34: Ac hē heora eft āegþer ge mid bismere onfeng, ge hīe eac on þone ... eard gesette, ...
   p. 147,22 : et mox cum foedissima ignominia in exercitu Antigoni dispersi sunt.

The Old English clause, which has the active voice, refers to how somebody received captives. Consequently, mid bismere signifies in terms of my classification (see p. 55) 'men's activities intended to disgrace or insult other men'(A III:Men-Men). The Latin clause, which has the passive voice, could be interpreted as referring to the shame incurred or felt by the captives on account of the humiliations they are exposed to. This interpretation would justify the classification of ignominia in B:State, where it normally belongs.

In the second instance, however, no obvious incongruity between ignominia and bismer with regard to the two aspects, Activity (Sense group A) - State (Sense group B), seems to exist, even if the Old English clause is no literal translation:

2) Orosius, p.122,7-8: ...& him beforan drīfen swā swā nīedlingas
   þaet heora bismer þy māre wāere
   p.123,4 : ... oneratos ignominia consules remiserunt

Both ignominia and bismer have been classified in B I:Misfortunes.

Though ignominia as well as verecundia, pudor, and confusio (see pp. 71-74) seem to fall mainly outside the range of meaning embraced by the bismer-words, gebysmerung as an occasional translation of ignominia is more readily explained than gebysmerung as an occasional translation of reverentia.

2.2.2. Subgroup B I: Misfortunes

2.2.2.1. Old English Words

The most frequent of the Old English words in B I:Misfortunes is gedroefnis/gedroefednis/-nes/gedrēfnes/gedrēfednis/-nes/-nys. It occurs in 14 instances, which make up 30% of the whole number of instances in the group. The Anglian Vespasian Psalter (dated ca. 875-900) has only forms with the stem vowel -oe-, gedroefnis and gedroefednis. Gedroefnis, the original form without -ed- as the connecting link between stem and suffix, appears in one instance, gedroefednis in three instances. The Junius Psalter, which is the oldest of the Psalter versions dependent on the Vespasian Psalter, has two instances of gedroefednes/gedrōfednes and two instances of the form with stem vowel -ē-, one of gedrēfnes,and one of gedrēfednes. All later texts have only forms with -ē- in the stem and -ed- as the connecting link between stem and suffix.

The word next in frequency within the group is gescindnes/gescyndnis/gescaendnys, which covers 24% of the translations in the group. See List OE 3, No. 22, which also includes two instances of scand and one instance of the verb scyndan. About two instances of the original form without suffix, gescendd/ȝescentd, one in the Vespasian and one in the Junius Psalters, see p. 79 under B III:Misbehaviour.

The bismer-words have a higher percentage here than in the other two subgroups of B:State, viz. 15%.

Other words of importance in the group are sceomu/scamu/sceamu (see p. 83) and scamunȝ/sceamung/scaemunȝ (see p. 79), which cover together 17% of the translations (List OE 3, No.6).

The remaining ca. 14% are shared by a number of words occurring only once or twice each.

2.2.2.2. Middle English Words

In B I:Misfortunes shenship covers 42%, confusion 29%, schame 15%, and deshonour 4% of the translations. The remaining 10% are shared by words occurring only once or twice each. (See List ME 3.)

The earliest instances of shenship in my material are from the Surtees Psalter (dated "late thirteenth century"). These instances, however, are classified in B III:Misbehaviour (see p. 79). List ME 4(1) shows that shenship has extended its range of meaning in the fifteenth

century. My instances from the thirteenth and fourteenth centuries
show the word only in the sense of B:State, those from the fifteenth
century also in the sense of A III 3:Men-Men-Insult. See pp. 66-67.

B I:Misfortunes has 15% of the recorded instances of confusion/con-
fusioun, B II:Unchastity 6%, and B III:Misbehaviour 79%. The Midland
Prose Psalter, London MS. (dated 1340-50), is my earliest source for
this word. The earliest instance in the OED is recorded from a text
dated "c 1290".

The two Lists, OE 4(2) and ME 4(3), show that Old English scomu/etc.
is more comprehensively used than Middle English shame/schame. All instances, except one, of Middle English shame/schame are classified in
B:State, whereas 20% of the instances of Old English scomu/etc. appear
in A:Activity, 80% in B:State (see p. 83).

Deshonour has been recorded from a text written ca. 1400 (Castle-
ford) and from a text written ca. 1450 (Destr.Troy). See App. A, p.
117.

My instances of yuel fame (in B I:Misfortunes only two) are from the
Wyclif Bible, EV 2 (after Baruch 3,20) and LV, i.e. from MSS. dated ca.
1400 or later (see App. A, p. 117). Cf. p. 102.

2.2.3. Subgroup B II: Unchastity

2.2.3.1. Old English Words

The Words ranged in order of frequency within the group are: scond-
licnes/sceand-/scand- covering 45% of the instances, gemang/gemeng/ge-
mengnes/gemengednys 12%, and fȳlþ 9%. The remaining 34% are shared by
words occurring only once or twice each, among them bismer-words.

Scondlicnes/etc. renders only turpitudo and it occurs only in B II:
Unchastity. The instances recorded are from Alfred's PC (one from each
of the two parallel MSS.) and from Bede's History (four from each of
three parallel MSS.).

Old English fȳlþ has been found solely in late West Saxon texts
(Menner, pp. 6-7). The three instances, making up 9%, render turpitudo
in a West Saxon text from the middle of the eleventh century (Lib.Scint.).
See App. A, p. 126.

2.2.3.2. Middle English Words

The two most frequent words in B II:Unchastity, filth and filthhed,

cover together 56% of the translations. See List ME 3. Only one instance of the simple form has been recorded for the thirteenth century
(List ME 4:2). The form is fulde and the text is the Ancrene Riwle
(dated 1225-49). List ME 4:2 shows that the use of filth in B II:Un-
chastity increases during the Middle English period. In the fifteenth
century it dominates the translations to a degree of 40%. The derivative, filthhed, appears considerably later. The earliest instances in
List ME 4:2 are from MSS. written towards the end of the fourteenth
century, EV 1 and EV 2 of the Wyclif Bible. In LV of the Wyclif Bible
the word has been replaced by filth in all instances except four.

The other words of the group are shenship covering 24%, yuel fame 7%,
confusion/confusioun 5%, and schame 3%, of the instances. The remaining
5% are shared by a few occasional translations. (See List ME 3.)

2.2.4. Subgroup B III: Misbehaviour

2.2.4.1. Old English Words

B III:Misbehaviour shows a great variety in the Old English translations. The words ranked in order of frequency within the group are:
scomu/sceomu/scamu/sceamu covering 34% (three instances of scamung/etc.
included), gescende/ gescindnes/gescyndnis/gesciendnys/gescendnes/etc.
30% (two instances of scand/sceand, two of forescending, and one instance of āscyndnes included), gedrōfednes/gedroefednis/gedrēfednys/ge-
drefydnys 8%, tēona 4%, unƷewiss 4%, and orwyrd 4%. The remaining 16%
are shared by a number of words occurring only once or twice each, among
them two instances of bismer-words.

List OE 3 shows that 59% of all instances recorded of scomu/etc. are
classified in B III:Misbehaviour. Being a word represented in both
Main Sense groups, A:Activity and B:State, it is dealt with on p. 83
under the heading "Words Occurring in both Main Sense Groups, A and B".

Gescende/-nes/etc. and gedrōfednes/etc. have been discussed on p. 77.

2.2.4.2. Middle English Words

The words in order of frequency within B III:Misbehaviour are: confusion covering 44%, shenship 30% (two instances of schendnes/-ful- and
two of schendlac included), schame 8%, yuel fame 7%, vilenye 2%,
sclaundre 2%, and sunne 1%. The remaining 5% are shared by a number of

words occurring only once or twice each.

2.2.5. Summary of Sense Group B: State

The most important words of B I:Misfortunes are: Old English ge-
droefnis/gedroefednis/etc., gescendnes/etc., bismer, and scomu/etc.
Middle English shenship, confusion, and schame. In B II:Unchastity
the words are: Old English scondlicnes/etc., gemang/gemengnes/etc. (see
pp. 72-73), and fylþ; Middle English filthhed, filth, shenship, and
yuel fame. B III:Misbehaviour has: Old English scomu/etc., gescendd/
gescendnes/etc., and gedrofednes/etc.; Middle English confusion, shenship, schame, and yuel fame. All the words are ranked in order of frequency within each subgroup. None of the words cover less than 7% of
the translations within the relevant subgroup.

Only B II:Unchastity has words that do not occur elsewhere in my
Sense groups, viz. Old English scondlicnes/etc., gemang/gemengnes/etc.
(pp. 72-73), fylþ,   as well as Middle English filthhed. Middle English
filth appears, besides in B II:Unchastity, also in B III:Misbehaviour,
though there only in two instances.

Old English forms appearing solely in Anglian texts and texts dependent on Anglian originals are gedroefnis/gedroefednis/gedrofednes and
scomu/sceomu, i.e. forms with the stem vowel -ō-/-oe- and -o-/-eo- respectively (see pp. 77 and 83).   Also the forms without the connecting
link -ed-, gedroefnis and gedrefnes, appear exclusively in those texts.
Gescendd, i.e. the form without the suffix -nes/-nis/-nys, has been recorded only from the Anglian Vespasian Psalter and a version dependent
on it, the Junius Psalter.

Two of the Middle English words above are of French origin, namely
confusion and fame. The remaining ones are of native origin. Filthhed
and shenship are new formations in Middle English. They are derived
from native forms by means of native suffixes. See p. 100.

3. Words Occurring in Both Main Sense Groups, A and B

3.1. Old English Words

The Old English words which occur in both A and B are the bismer-words, tēona, scomu/etc., orwyrd/orwurd, scand/scond, and yfel. There are a few more in my material, but as they are represented by only one instance each in one of the two groups, they are unimportant in this connection.

3.1.1. The *Bismer*-Words

Out of a total of 99 classified instances of bismer-words only 11 appear in B:State (List OE 3). They are from Alfred's texts, where they render infamia (four times), ignominia (once), dedecus, turpitudo, and confusio (twice each). List OE 1 includes the three instances of free translation which concern Latin ignominia and turpitudo in relation to bismer and bysmrung (see pp. 38-39 and 76).

Alfred renders also Latin macula, a word with the sense of 'state' (B:State), by bismer. Macula is not included in my lists (see p. 27).

In List OE 1 unclassified instances of bismer-words, 11 in number, from vocabularies are included. Only two of them render a Latin word of B:State. The two instances are dedecus:bismer from two parallel MSS. containing glosses to Aldhelm's "De Laude Virginitatis" (App.C, p. 186).

3.1.2. *Tēona*

Old English tēona, the most frequent word to render contumelia and injuria (A III 3:Men-Men-Insult), occurs in three instances for ignominia (B:State). The three instances are from two late West Saxon texts, the Lambeth Psalter and Liber Scintillarum (Lib.Scint.).

One of the three instances is from Ps. 82,17 which exists in nine different Psalter versions. Only one of them, the Lambeth Psalter, has tēona. Three of the other West Saxon versions have ungewiss, one has unwitende, and one has the verb sceamian (þaet hiora ansȳn ... sceamige). The Anglian versions have orwyrd.

The remaining two instances, which are from Lib.Scint., read as follows:

1) Aegestas et ignominia ei qui deserit disciplinam:Waedl & tēona
    þam sē forlaet lāre (p. 113,16)

The instance is a quotation from the Bible, Proverbs 13,18, where AV has the word shame for ignominia.

2) Ignominia omnium sacerdotum propriis studere diutiis: tēona ealra sacerda āgenum hicgean (p. 158,11-12)

The same word for ignominia and contumelia, viz. bismer, has been used in King Alfred's Orosius (MS. from the tenth century). Compare also the Anglian word orwyrð/orwurð dealt with below. In the Middle English translations the two words, ignominia and contumelia, have been rendered differently throughout. See List ME 1.

3.1.3. *Orwyrð/Orwurð*

List OE 3:1 contains five instances of orwyrð/orwurð, three in B: State and two in A:Activity. The instances are from Anglian texts and texts considered to be descended from Anglian originals.

The three instances in B:State have been recorded from three parallel MSS., the Anglian Vespasian Psalter and the two versions dependent on it, the Junius and the Cambridger Psalter. The word renders ignominia in Ps. 82,17, which is the instance referred to in HM under orwyrð/ orwurð. The West Saxon Psalters have other words in this instance (see App. C, p. 184).

The two instances in A:Activity are from Gregory's Dialogues:

1) quantasque pateretur verborum contumilias (II,23, p.114,20-21):
hū maniȝe tēonan & orwyrdu þāra nunnena fracoðwyrda hē ȝe-prowode (MS. C; p. 152,6-7);
hū fela tēonena hē ȝeþolode hyra yfelra worda (MS.H; p. 152,4-6).

In MS. C, which is considered to be descended from an Anglian original, orwyrd together with an adjunct, fracoðwyrda, have been added to tēona, the ordinary word for contumelia. In MS. H, which is a West Saxon re-modelling of the older translation (App. A, p.126), orwyrd is omitted and tēona (tēonena) is provided with the adjunct yfelra worda instead of fracoðwyrda. This seems to indicate that both orwyrd/orwurð and fracoðwyrda are Anglian words preserved from a supposed Anglian original. This instance is the one referred to in HM under fracoðword 'insulting word', and according to Hecht (the editor of the text) 2, p. 142, footnote 2, the only instance of this compound that has been found.[1]

The second instance of orwyrd:contumelia is the following:

... maioribus hunc verborum contumeliis (III,37; p. 218,19):
& on3unnon hine onscunian mid maran orwyrdum fracodlicra worda
(Dialogues, MS. C; pp. 250,28-251,1).

This instance does not exist in the second manuscript, MS. H, which was quoted in the first instance (p. 82).

3.1.4. *Scomu/Sceomu - Scamu/Sceamu*

Old English scomu/sceomu[2] is to be found only in Anglian texts, scamu/sceamu[2] only in West Saxon texts. It is the second word in frequency for the Latin confusio (B:State). See List OE 1. As I have mentioned on p. 73 it is also the most frequent word for verecundia and pudor, words which would have been assigned to B:State if classified in this investigation.

The Anglian forms, scomu and sceomu, appear not only in B:State but also in A:Activity. I have eight instances in all classified in A:Activity. They are from the three Northumbrian texts, the Lindisfarne (CND4) MS., the Rushworth (Ru[2]) MS. (Mark 12,4; Luke 3,14 and 11,45), and the Durham Ritual (App. A, pp. 122 and 127). The parallel West Saxon texts have tēona (Latin contumelia in Mark 12,4 and Luke 11,45) and tāl (Latin calumnia in Luke 3,14).

The instances of scamu/sceamu from the West Saxon texts are classified in B:State. The sole exception is one instance from Alfred's Soliloquies (MS. from the twelfth century), where ludibrium (A III 1 c: Men-Men-Derision-TP) has been rendered by on þam bysmore and on þaere sceame (A III 1 b:Men-Men-Derision-TS).

Out of a total of 37 classified Middle English instances of schame[3] 36 have been classified in B:State and one in A:Activity (List ME 3).

---

[1]Fracod, the first part of the compound, is an Anglian word (Menner, 1948, p. 1). It occurs in my material for contumelia once in the Dialogues, MS. C, and once in the Lindisfarne (CND4) MS., which is also an Anglian (Northumbrian) text. In both these instances the parallel West Saxon versions have tēona. See App. C, pp. 178-179.

[2]A glide -e- developed between sc and a back vowel (OEG, p. 68).

[3]The Ancrene Riwle, a West Midland text from 1225-49, is the only text in my material which has the forms schome and scheome.

3.1.5. *Scand/Scond*

Ten out of a total of twelve classified instances of scand/sceand/ scond are from the two parallel MSS. of Alfred's Pastoral Care, which implies that they represent only five instances of translation. In three of them the word renders contumelia and in one injuria (A III 3: Men-Men-Insult); in the fifth instance ðaere scame & ðaere scande renders confusionis (B:State). The remaining two classified instances are from two late West Saxon texts, the Paris Psalter and Lib.Scint., in which confusio is rendered by scand and sceand respectively. (See App. C, p. 185.) In addition my material contains two instances from vocabularies where scand/scond renders two Latin words of B:State, scond:dedecus in WW XI from the tenth century and scand:ignominia in WW IV from the first half of the eleventh century (App. C, p. 186).

The instances above indicate that Alfred is alone in using scand/scond in A:Activity. He also seems to be alone in using scand/scond for abo-minatio (p. 27). The Pastoral Care has three instances in each of the two MSS., H20 (PC, pp. 153,21, 155,9 f.) and C (PC, pp. 152,21, 154,9 f.). The translations are from a passage where Ez. 8,9 is quoted and commented upon (Cura Pastoralis XXI, 45).

3.1.6. *Yfel*

Yfel as a noun has been recorded only from Alfred's texts. There it renders injuria (A III 3:Men-Men-Insult) and turpitudo (B:State), twice each. Three of the instances are from Boethius (ca. 960) and one from the Soliloquies (MS. from the twelfth century).

Alfred alone uses yfel also for scandalum (PC, MS. H20, p. 453,5), scelus, and improbitas (see pp. 88-89: King Alfred's Vocabulary). These translations belong to my unclassified collection (p. 27).

Yfel as an adjective, on the other hand, is common in Old English, and yuel/evel occurs only as an adjective in my Middle English material.

3.2. Middle English Words

Shenship, the word that tops List ME 3, is the only word of importance used for both senses, that of A:Activity and that of B:State, in the Middle English translations. It belongs to the most frequent words in all three subgroups of B:State, where it renders ignominia, confusio,

and dedecus. Shenship is also one of the most important words in A III
3:Men-Men-Insult, where it renders opprobrium. Its use in this sense,
however, seems to have been temporary, in fact limited to Bible texts
written in the early fifteenth century (p. 67). That opprobrium shares
a translation with the words of B:State is significant. Among the
words of A:Activity it is by far the most important one in the two
senses b:TS (Transferred sense = State) and c:TP (Transferred sense =
Personification). See p. 44 f. As regards semantic coverage shenship
is second only to Old English bismer, though it is represented only in
those senses where bismer had its weakest representation, i.e. in A III
3:Men-Men-Insult (opprobrium) and in B:State (see p. 93 and the two
Lists, OE 4:1 and ME 4:1).

Words normally belonging to one of the two Main Sense groups appear
occasionally in the opposite group. In such cases the word is usually
joined to another word in a coordinate expression which renders one
Latin word. On p. 83 the instance of ludibrium rendered by Old English
on þām bysmore and on þære sceame was mentioned as the only one in
which Old English sceamu/etc. renders a Latin word of A:Activity.

In the following instance from Higd.Trev. unworschippe and blamynge
are joined to render dedecus, a Latin word of B:State:

... de praesulis dedecore ... (p. 162): ... of þe unworschippe and
blamynge of þe bisshop ... (p. 163).

The native word unworschippe was used earlier for dedecus[1], whereas the
French word blamynge in other texts renders only contumelia or calumnia
(A:Activity). In Appendix C (p. 206) blamynge has been put in brackets
indicating that it is not listed as translation of dedecus in Lists
ME 1-4 (see p. 23).

The only instance of dyshoner occurring for a Latin word of A:Activ-
ity is the following:

dyshoner ... and derfe wordes (Destr.Troy, p. 32:1005-1006).

In this instance the native derfe wordes has been added to the French
word dyshoner to render one Latin word, viz. injuria.

---

[1] Boethius III, p. 4: Videsne quantum malis dedecus adiciant dignita-
tis? in Alfred's translation, MS. from ca. 1110, rendered by: hū
micelne unweorðscipe ... In the OED the instance is recorded as being
the oldest one of this word, but there the MS. has been dated "c 888",
which seems to be too early (see App. A, p. 124: Boethius, MS. B).

In instances like these it seems hard to decide whether the two coordinate words/expressions ought to be interpreted as having the same
meaning, i.e. the same meaning with regard to the two senses A:Activity
and B:State in terms of my classification, or whether two words/ex-
pressions of different meaning were put together on purpose by the
translator in order to achieve a certain effect. Cf. pp. 51-53, where
coordinate expressions **used** for rhetorical effect, originally in
Hebrew biblical poetry, are discussed.

VI. VOCABULARY OF DIFFERENT PERIODS

1. The Early Old English Period (Late Ninth and Early Tenth Centuries)

1.1. The Vocabulary of the Different Sense Groups

1.1.1. The *Bismer*-Words

Bismer has been recorded only from West Saxon texts, bismerung/bismr-un3[1] and bismernis/-nes only from Anglian texts and texts dependent on Anglian originals (see App. B, p. 148).

The instances of bismer, 27 in number, are from King Alfred's texts, the Pastoral Care (two MSS. from the late ninth century) and Orosius (MS. L from the early tenth century[1]), which are the only West Saxon texts in my material from this period. These instances are distributed among the Sense groups in the following way: two in A III 1:Men-Men-Derision, 15 in A III 3:Men-Men-Insult, and 10 in B:State. In B:State there is also an instance of bismerlecre dæd rendering Latin infamia from Orosius. See pp. 48-50 about the meaning of 'the misbehaviour' or 'the quality' through which a state of shame/disgrace is incurred.

In Orosius also scelus and macula have been rendered by bismer, but these instances are not included in my lists (see p. 27).

The Anglian Vespasian Psalter (from ca. 875-900) and the Psalter text dependent on it, the Junius Psalter (from ca. 925), have one instance each of bismernis/-nes for Latin inlusio (A I:Devil-Men) and three instances each of bismerung/bismrun3 for Latin derisus (A III 1:Men-Men-Derision).

The two groups A II:Men-God and A III 2:Men-Men-Calumny have no instances of bismer-words from the Early Old English period.

---

[1]In Sweet's edition of Orosius a MS. from the early eleventh century (Cotton Tiberius B 1:CTB1) has been used to supplement a gap in the Lauderdale MS. (MS. L). See App.A, p.124. This piece contains one instance of bysmrung, the only one of this word from Alfred's texts (see p. 38, footnote 1). Alfred's Boethius (MS.C from ca. 960) and Soliloquies (MS. from the twelfth century) have one instance each of a bismer-word. Boethius has contumelia:bismrian (App. B, p.179) and Soliloquies has ludibrium:bysmor (App. B, p. 178).

1.1.2. The Non-*Bismer*-Words

1.1.2.1. King Alfred's Vocabulary

King Alfred's translations are represented by in all 48 instances (tokens) of non-bismer-words. For convenience the instances from his Boethius (12 from MS.C, dated 960; one from MS.B, ca. 1110) as well as those from his   Soliloquies (three from a MS. written in the twelfth century) are included here. Sense group A II:Men-God holds four of these instances, A III 1:Men-Men-Derision one, A III 3:Men-Men-Insult 25, and B:State 18.

The peculiarity of Alfred's vocabulary has been pointed out repeatedly. Alfred alone uses bismer-words in B:State (pp. 81 and 93). In my material the non-bismer-words usually do not render the same Latin words in Alfred's texts as they do in other Old English texts. Such words are for instance scand/scond (p. 84), tael (p. 60), edwit (p. 64 and below, p. 90), gylt (pp. 49 and 89), teona (p. 89), and hosp (p. 90). A word recorded solely from Alfred's translations as a noun is yfel (p. 84). Many of Alfred's words for Latin contumelia and injuria appear exclusively in his texts (p. 65). Compare also footnotes on p. 89. In fact, only three of Alfred's non-bismer-words, scamu/sceamu, scondlicnes/sceondlicnes/scandlicnes, and gedrefednes, have been used by other translators in the same way as they were used by him. However, the second word, scondlicnes/etc., occurs, apart from in Alfred's Pastoral Care, only in one text, viz. in Bede's History, a translation ascribed to one of Alfred's Mercian assistants (pp. 21 and 78). The third word, gedrefednes, is represented in my material from Alfred's texts by solely one instance, which is from Boethius (MS. C, dated 960).

A feature even more conspicuous than his exceptional use of words is the great variety in his renderings of a Latin word. Both Anglian and later West Saxon texts show greater consistency. This is especially evident in the vocabulary of A III 3:Men-Men-Insult, the group that holds more than half of the whole number of classified Old English instances (List OE 3) and also more than half of the instances recorded from Alfred's texts (see above). Alfred uses 13 different words or expressions for injuria, which is represented by 21 instances, and 6 different words for contumelia, represented by 18 instances in his texts. However, 22 of these 39 (21 + 18) instances are from two parallel MSS.

namely those of the Pastoral Care, which have the same translations in
my instances. Thus 22 instances represent in reality only 11 instances
of translation, which means that Alfred uses a new word nearly every
time he has to render injuria or contumelia. Only three words have been
used more than once, namely bismer in six, scand/scond in four, and
wītnan/wītnian in two instances of translation. In other texts, Anglian
as well as West Saxon, injuria and contumelia have been rendered by
tēona (in a few instances by tēan- in compounds) to a degree of 67%,
i.e. in 72 instances out of a total of 108. Neither tēona nor compounds
with tēan- are to be found among Alfred's renderings of injuria and contumelia. That tēona, however, was not a word unknown to him is shown by
his translations of another Latin word, not included in my lists, scelus,
which has been rendered by tēona in Or. (p. 53,18, MS.L, p. 52,22)[1]. The
other West Saxon texts render scelus by scyld or gylt[2] (the word that
dominates in the Middle English translations). Other translations showing the uniqueness of Alfred's vocabulary are the instances of improbitas
and indignatio (see p. 27). Seven instances of improbitas are rendered
by seven different words or expressions. They are dysige (PC, MS. H20, p.
405,21), unryhte & dysige (PC, MS. H20, p. 407,18), yflena yfel (Bo. IV,
p. 96,16; p. 113,4), yfelnes (Bo., IV, p. 98,52; p. 114,20), yfel (Bo. IV,
p. 102,78; p. 120,28), unđeaw (Bo. IV,p. 105,145; p. 123,32), and yfelena
weorđe (Bo.,IV, p. 112,140; p. 133,21). All instances from other West
Saxon texts have onhrōp. Three instances of indignatio are rendered by
three different words, ierre[3], unweardscipe[4] (PC, MS. C, p. 222,8:Ephes.
4,31), and unweordung[5] (PC, MS. C, p. 222,13).   Among 53 renderings of

---

[1]Cf. scelus:bismer (p. 27), scelus:yfel (Or., MS.L, p. 236,16), scelus:
unþeaw (Or., MS.L, p. 260,28), and scelus:synne (PC,MS. H20, p. 399,17).

[2]Gylt occurs only once in my Old English material. The instance is
from Alfred's Or. (MS.L), where it renders ignominia (see p. 49).

[3]Ierre/yrre (Latin ira, Old French yre, Middle English ire) is the
only Old English word in my material which is of Latin origin (p. 10). In
Jer. 4,4: Alfred's PC, p. 435,9 (MS. H20) it renders Latin indignatio, and
in Ephes. 4,31: Alfred's PC, p. 222,8 (MS. C) Latin ira. See OED s.v. ire.

[4]In Alfred's Boethius (MS. B from ca. 1110) unweordscipe renders dedecus once (see p. 85, footnote 1).

[5]Unweordung does not occur elsewhere in my material.

indignatio in other Old English translations yrre occurs only twice,
once in each of two parallel MSS. from the eleventh century (the Heptateuch, Lev. 10), whereas unweordscipe and unweordung do not occur.

The third Latin word of A III 3:Men-Men-Insult, opprobrium, occurs
rendered by bismer twice. The instances are from the two parallel MSS.
of the Pastoral Care (App. C, p. 182). Latin opprobrium, in my Old
English material represented by 199 instances (List OE 1), is with few
exceptions rendered by edwīt in the Anglian (see p. 15), by hosp in the
West Saxon texts. None of these two words were unknown to Alfred. He
used edwīt for contumelia, infamia, exprobratio, and probrum (see p.
64), but not for opprobrium.[1] Hosp is also to be found in Alfred's
translations, but not for opprobrium. In his Boethius (I,met.5.1.36;
p. 156) hosp renders crimen.

Sense group B:State has 18 instances of non-bismer-words from
Alfred's texts. Two third of these instances, i.e. 12, are from the two
parallel MSS. of the Pastoral Care, which implies that they represent
six instances of translation. Consequently the 18 instances represent
only 12 instances of translation. They have been rendered by 10 different words. This means that the instances in B:State also testify to
Alfred's habit of varying his renderings.

Compounds and derivatives appearing only in Alfred's texts are
woruldbismer (for contumelia, App. C, pp. 178-179), unār (for injuria,
App. C, p. 181), unweordscipe (for dedecus and indignatio, p. 89), and
unweordnes (for dedignatio; PC; MS. C, p. 264,19; MS. H20, p. 265,19).
Undeaw, which according to Käsman (1951, p. 39 f.) was coined by Alfred,
renders in his material vitium 'vice', in my unclassified material
improbitas (p. 89), probrum (Boethius, IV, p. 96,1-2; p. 112,15), and
scelus (p. 89, footnote 1). Also unweordung (for indignatio, p. 89)
seems to have been coined by Alfred.[2] Compare also p. 9, where instances of compounds in Alfred's texts have been quoted from Fetzlaff
(1954), and p. 28 about the word lēasspellung.

---

[1] Also Waerferth, one of Alfred's Mercian assistants (p. 12), seems
to have used edwīt for opprobrium. At any rate this translation is to
be found in Waerferth's Dialogues, MS. C, which is from the eleventh
century but considered to be descended from an Anglian original (p. 15).

[2] HM records the instance referred to and a second one from a late
West Saxon text (Rule C, App. A, p. 128).

It was suggested that Alfred had to find expressions for new concepts (p. 9). The rich Latin vocabulary of the theological and
philosophical works translated by Alfred and his assistants must have
brought new shades of meaning difficult to render into English. Chris-
tian ideology had brought with it new moral values which implied for
instance new reasons for shame (A I:Devil-Men and B II:Unchastity),
and also new targets for disgrace (A II:Men-God), but none of the Bible
texts seems to have been translated into English before the time of
King Alfred's reign. The earliest extant MS. of an English Bible text,
the Anglian Vespasian Psalter, has been dated 875-900. The earliest
extant MS. of a West Saxon Bible text independent of an Anglian original
is the Regius Psalter, which is considered to have been written ca.
950, i.e. 50 years after Alfred's death. The passage quoted on p. 12
from the preface to the Pastoral Care gives us an idea of the situation
when Alfred starts his translative work. He tells us that he could not
find anybody south of the Thames who could translate a letter from Latin into English, obviously his reason for choosing Mercian assistants
(p. 12).

Characteristics of Alfred's vocabulary, such as an exceptional use of
the Old English words (p. 88) and a great variety in the renderings of
each Latin word (pp. 88-90), seem to give evidence of endeavours to
adapt the old native word material to new use. Compounds and derivatives formed to render certain Latin words (p. 90) are the results of
such endeavours. Alfred's vocabulary can be said to reflect the problems he faced in his work and at the same time his creative ability,
perhaps also stylistic ingenuity, in dealing with them.

1.1.2.2. The Anglian Vocabulary of the Early Old English Period

My Anglian word material of the Early period derives from two Psalter
texts, the Anglian Vespasian Psalter (dated 875-900) and the West Saxon
version dependent on it, the Junius Psalter (dated ca. 925).

The Anglian non-bismer-words of A III 3:Men-Men-Insult have been discussed in connection with King Alfred's vocabulary (pp. 88-91). It was
stated that teona dominates the translations of injuria and contumelia
in Anglian as well as in West Saxon texts other than King Alfred's and
that edwit is the Anglian, hosp the West Saxon word for opprobrium, a
word rendered by bismer in Alfred's texts. Injuria appears twice in the
Psalter. The Vespasian Psalter has tiona/teona:injuria, the Junius
Psalter, which includes only one of the two instances, has teona:inju-
ria. Contumelia is not represented in the Psalter. The Vespasian and
the Junius Psalters have together 34 instances of edwit:opprobrium. Besides the Junius Psalter has one instance of hosp:opprobrium.

Calumnia (A III 2:Men-Men-Calumny), which is not represented in Alfred's translations, appears once in the Psalter. It has been rendered
by hearm in the Vespasian Psalter, by hearmcwide in the Junius Psalter.
The later versions dependent on the Vespasian Psalter have hearmcwide/-
cwidolnes.

Confusio (B:State) has been rendered seven times in each of the two
texts. The words of the Vespasian Psalter are gedroefnis/gedroefednis
(B I:Misfortunes), scomu, gedroefednis, and gescende (B III:Misbehav-
iour), those of the Junius Psalter are ȝedroefednes/ȝedrefednes/ȝedref-
nes (B I:Misfortunes), scomu/scamu, ȝedrofednes, and ȝescente (B III:Mis-
behaviour). The translations of confusio give evidence of a gradual introduction of the West Saxon forms. The Vespasian Psalter has solely
forms with the stem vowel -oe-, i.e. gedroefnis/-ed-. The Junius Psalter
has two instances of ȝedroefednes and two of the forms with the stem
vowel -e-, ȝedrefnes/-ed-. The form with the stem vowel -e- and the
connecting link -ed- is the sole one of this word in the texts of the later period. The Vespasian Psalter has scomu, the Junius Psalter one instance of scomu and one of the West Saxon form scamu. Both texts have
gescende/gescente, whereas all later texts have only forms with the suffix -nes/-nis.

Ignominia has been rendered once in each of the two texts by orwyrd
(B III:Misbehaviour), an Anglian word (see p. 82).

2. The Classical Old English Period (Ca. 950 – 1100)

In the early ninth century Wessex began to extend its influence over the neighbouring kingdoms. All England and Wales acknowledged the overlordship of a Wessex king in 830. Under Alfred and his son Edward West Saxon dominance over Mercia was warranted. Mercia had sought the aid of Wessex against the Danes (p. 12) and had in consequence gradually lost her independence. In 918 Edward, king of Wessex after Alfred, took over the rule of Mercia after the death of his sister, who had been married to the alderman of Mercia and had ruled alone after his death a few years earlier. See Robinson (1923), p. 16, and Baugh (1959), p. 56.

A consequence of the growing political influence of Wessex was that the West Saxon dialect became the literary language in the later, so-called classical, Old English period. However, though Alfred's dialect prevailed, very few of the words he used, at least in the semantic field we are here concerned with, continued to be used in the same way by other translators (see pp. 88-91).

2.1. The Vocabulary of the Different Sense Groups

2.1.1. The *Bismer*-Words

Bismer, which was used by Alfred in the senses of A III 1:Men-Men-Derision, A III 3:Men-Men-Insult, and B:State (p. 87), continued to be used to a small extent in A III 1:Men-Men-Derision, but neither in A III 3:Men-Men-Insult, nor in B:State. The two Sense groups A II:Men-God and A III 2:Men-Men-Calumny, which have no instances of bismer-words from the Early period, have a few instances each of bismer from West Saxon texts written in the eleventh and twelfth centuries.

Bismerung/bismrung, which does not appear in Alfred's texts, i.e. those based on MSS. from the early period,[1] is the most frequent of the bismer-words in the classical period. The word dominates in Sense group A I: Devil-Men and in those instances of A III 1:Men-Men-Derision that have been recorded from texts dependent on Anglian originals. A III 3:Men-Men-Insult has three instances from the Lambeth Psalter, a West Saxon text dated ca. 1025. There bysmerung 1. hosp renders opprobrium three times. This group also has the instance of bysmrung from Alfred's Orosius re-

---

[1]Cf. pp. 38 and 87, footnote 1, about one instance of bysmrung from Alfred's Orosius (MS. dated "early eleventh century").

ferred to above (see p. 93, footnote 1).

Bismernis/-nes/etc. renders inlusio (A I:Devil-Men) in the Anglian
Vespasian Psalter and in three texts dependent on it (App. A, p. 120).

New formations in the eleventh century are bismer-spraec/etc., which
renders blasphemia (A II:Men-God), and gebismerung, which renders inlusio
(A I:Devil-Men and A III 1:Men-Men-Derision).

B:State has no instances of bismer-words from texts based on MSS. from
the classical Old English period.

The SUM columns in List OE 4:1 show that 27% of all collected instances
from texts based on MSS. written in the ninth century (21 instances out of
a total of 78), 14% of those from the tenth (22 out of a total of 162),
and 16% of those from the eleventh century (47 out of a total of 296)   are
bismer-words. These figures indicate a sharp decline in the use of
bismer-words in the tenth century, then from this level a slight rise in
the eleventh century. If we look at the Anglian and West Saxon dialects
separately (List OE 5:1, which includes unclassified instances from the
vocabularies) we find that only the Anglian dialect shows a rise in the
eleventh century (the ninth has 4:37 = 11%, the tenth 9:99 = 9%, and the
eleventh 14:98 = 14%), while the West Saxon dialect shows a continuous decline (for the ninth 17:45 = 38%, for the tenth 15:80 = 19%, and for the
eleventh 42:251 = 17%). However, all instances recorded from the eleventh
century in the "Anglian" column are from texts based on copies of Anglian
originals written in the ninth century, which means that they represent
the vocabulary of that century rather than that of the eleventh century.
See p. 15. So the eleventh-century "rise" is a bogus one.

2.1.2. The Non-*Bismer*-Words

Sense group A III 3:Men-Men-Insult, which holds more than half the number of classified instances (339 out of a total of 647), gives evidence of
a differentiation or stabilization of the West Saxon vocabulary after the
time of King Alfred. See pp. 88-91, where also unclassified translations
of a number of Latin words indicating such a development have been discussed. Teona/etc. dominates the translations of contumelia and injuria
in all West Saxon texts; edwīt and hosp those of opprobrium, edwīt in
West Saxon texts dependent on Anglian originals and hosp in other West
Saxon texts. The genuinely Anglian texts, MS. CND4, MS. Ru[2], and the Durham Ritual, have other words for contumelia, injuria, and opprobrium (see
(App. C, pp. 178-182). Teancuide appears in MS. CND4, but only once.

The remaining subgroups of A:Activity, i.e. A I:Devil-Men, A II:Men-God, A III 1:Men-Men-Derision, and A III 2:Men-Men-Calumny, are small groups, holding in all 150 Old English instances. Alfred's translations are very weakly represented in them, only by four instances in each of the two groups, A II:Men-God and A III 1:Men-Men-Derision, by none at all in A I:Devil-Men and A III 2:Men-Men-Calumny. Consequently very little, if anything at all, can be said for certain about a development from the **early** to the **later Old English period** as far as the West Saxon vocabulary of the four groups in question is concerned.

In A I:Devil-Men there are a few instances of words other than the bismer-words (see p. 58). They are from West Saxon texts of the eleventh century, where inlusio has been rendered by swic, bi3-swic (beswic?), big swic (beswic?), swicung 'deceit, deception, illusion', and costnun3 'temptation, trial' (HM).

The instances of A II:Men-God show a clear division between the two dialects, Anglian and West Saxon. Anglian texts or texts dependent on Anglian originals have for Latin blasphemia: ebolsung/efolsung/etc. (ebol/efol = yfel, see p. 61), West Saxon texts from the eleventh and twelfth centuries bismer-words (see p. 60), in a few instances dysines, woffung, talliche word, gyltlice spraec, hyrwincg, and wiþersacung.

In A III 1:Men-Men-Derision the instances from West Saxon texts of the late tenth and the eleventh centuries have, apart from bismer-words (see p. 93), (h)leahter/hlehter, taelhlehter 'laughter, derision'(Lat. derisus), 3ecanc 'jeering, scorn, derision'(Lat. ludibrium), tal, hlacerung 'unseemly behaviour', golfetung (gaffetung) 'scoffing, mocking' (Lat. subsannatio).

The instances of A III 2:Men-Men-Calumny (Latin calumnia), as those of A II:Men-God (Latin blasphemia), have different words in Anglian **texts** (or texts dependent on Anglian originals) and in West Saxon ones. The Anglian texts have hearmcwide/-cwidolnes[1], telnes, and scomu/sceomu; the West Saxon texts have bismer-words (see p. 93), hosp, teona, and tal.

Sense group B:State, which is next to A III 3:Men-Men-Insult in terms of size, holds in all 158 Old English instances. In West Saxon texts from the Later period, other than those that are copies of Alfred's texts (see p. 88), gescendnes/-nys/etc. is the most frequent word in B I:**Misfortunes** and B III:Misbehaviour. In B I:Misfortunes the second and third most fre-

---

[1]The simplex hearm occurs only in one instance, which is from the Anglian Vespasian Psalter (see p. 99).

quent West Saxon words are gedrēfednes/-nys and scamung, in B III:Misbe-
haviour scamu/sceamu, scamung, and gedrēfednes/-nys. In the Summary of
Sense group B:State (p. 80) scamung, being represented only by three instances in each of the two groups, has been left out. In texts dependent
on Anglian originals gedrēfednes/-nys is the most frequent word in B I:
Misfortunes, scomu/sceomu in B III:Misbehaviour.

   The early Anglian forms gedrōefnis, gedrōefednis/gedrōfednis, gedrēfnes, and gescendd/gescentd have been replaced by gedrēfednes/-nys and
gescendnes/etc. respectively in texts from the later period. (See p. 77.)

   Latin turpitudo (B II:Unchastity) has been rendered by scondlicnes/
sceond-/scand- in Bede's History (see p. 78), by fylþ, sceamu, and hāeman
(a verb!) in West Saxon texts of the later period. Sceamu and hāeman
occur only twice each. Gemang/gemeng and gemengnes/-ednys render Latin
confusio (B II:Unchastity) in West Saxon texts (see App. B, p. 152).

3. The Late Middle English Period (Ca. 1350 – 1500)

Seven[1] of the words in my Old English material are to be found in my Middle English material. They are bismer, fȳlþ, grama, hearm, tēona, scamu, and yfel.

Three of these seven words, viz. bismer, gram/grem (Old English grama), and tene (Old English tēona), did not survive in Modern English. In my Middle English material they are represented by only seven instances in all. Two of these instances are from the Surtees Psalter (bismer:inlusio and gram:opprobrium), two from Higd.Trev. (bismer:ludibrium),and the remaining three (grem:injuria, grem:dedecus, and tene:injuria) from the Destr.Troy, a poetical text written ca. 1450.

Old English yfel (see p. 84), Modern English evil, appears in my Middle English material only as an adjective, i.e. in yuel fame. Compare Modern English ill fame (ill from Old Norse illr).

The remaining three Old English words, scamu, hearm, and fȳlþ, are beside two new short-lived formations, shenship and filthhed, the only words of native origin among the 21 most important words which cover the relevant semantic field in the Late Middle English period, here delimited to embrace the second half of the fourteenth and the first half of the fifteenth century. One of these 21 Middle English words, viz. wrong, is a Scandinavian word. The remaining 15 are French loan words.

Three of the words in my Old English material, which have survived in Modern English, do not appear in my material from the Middle English period. They are hleahter/leahter/hlehter (List OE 2, No. 7), dysines/desynys[2] (List OE 2, No. 15), and wraeddo[3] (List OE 2, No. 49), Modern

---

[1]Old English unweorðscipe has not been included here. It is represented in my Old English material by two instances from Alfred's texts, one from the Pastoral Care (unweorðscipe:indignatio) and one from Boethius, MS. from ca. 1110 (unweorðscipe:dedecus), in my Middle English material by one instance from Higd.Trev. unworschippe:dedecus (see pp. 85 and 89.

[2]Old English dysines/desynys has been recorded only from two parallel West Saxon MSS. containing the Gospels. It renders blasphemia in Mark 7,22.

[3]Old English wraeddo appears only once in my material, viz. for injuria in the Durham Ritual. Middle English wrathe is not recorded in my Lists, though it appears in the Destr.Troy. See App. C, p. 197, where it is to be found in brackets after wrange (injuria). None of the words in brackets have been recorded in the Lists (see pp. 23-24).

English laughter, dizziness, and wrath.

3.1. The Vocabulary of the Different Sense Groups

Sense group A I:Devil-Men has illusion, desceit/deseit, and scornyng; A II:Men-God blasfemye/blasphemye/etc.; A III 1:Men-Men-Derision
scornyng, scorn, and /under-/mouwing, and A III 2:Men-Men-Calumny
chalenge/etc. often preceded by wrong or fals.

A III 3:Men-Men-Insult holds 585 Middle English instances, i.e. nearly half of the whole number of classified instances from Middle English
texts, which is 1375. The Old English words hosp, teona, and edwīt
have been replaced mainly by wrong, repref/etc., and shenship. Compared
with these Middle English words, which are represented by 391 instances,
the following are of low frequency, being represented by less than 20
but not less than 9 instances each: dispit, dispisyng, iniury, strif,
blasfemye/blasphemye/etc., harm, and blamyng. Three additional words,
upbraidyng, reproce/-ing, and wouh, represented by 17, 15, and 9 instances respectively, occur in texts from the thirteenth and early fourteenth centuries but have been replaced by other words in the texts
from the late fourteenth century. Upbraidyng and reproce/-ing have been
replaced by repref/etc. (see p. 69) and wouh by wrong (see p. 100).

Sense group B:State holds in all 514 instances from Middle English
texts[1]. The words ranked in order of frequency within each subgroup
are: shenship, confusion, and shame (B I:Misfortunes); filthhed, filth,
shenship, yuel fame, and confusion (B II:Unchastity); confusion, shenship, shame, and yuel fame (B III:Misbehaviour). These words make up
472 instances altogether (92%). In the remaining 42 instances a great
number of different words occur, many of them only in one or two instances each. See List ME 3.

---

[1]These 514 instances include 23 from two texts written in the thirteenth century, the Surtees Psalter and the Ancrene Riwle. Eight instances from the Surtees Psalter have schenschip (four in B I:Misfor-
tunes and four in B III:Misbehaviour) and five from the Ancrene Riwle
schome/scheome (one in B I:Misfortunes and four in B III:Misbehaviour).
The remaining 10 instances are included in those "42 instances" in which
"a great number of different words occur".

3.2. Native Words

3.2.1. *Shame*

In Old English the West Saxon forms scamu and sceamu were used only in sense B:State. It is the only word that has kept its position in the semantic field nearly unchanged from the Old English to the Middle English period (see p. 83 and App. B, Lists OE 3 and ME 3). List OE 3 includes the Anglian forms scomu and sceomu. In the Scandinavian languages we find the same word, namely Old Norse skǫmm, Danish and Swedish skam. Shame cannot be regarded as a Scandinavian loan word,[1] but the Scandinavian word may have backed up the Old English word and thus contributed to its survival.[2]

3.2.2. *Harm*

Old English hearm, Middle English harm, is a common-Teutonic word and well established in the Scandinavian languages. Cf. Icelandic harmr, Danish harme, Swedish harm.

In my material hearm appears only in one instance, which is from the Anglian Vespasian Psalter (dated 875-900). There it renders Latin calumnia. Later Psalter versions dependent on the Vespasian Psalter have in this instance the compounds hearmcwide and hearmcwidolnes (see p. 61 and List OE 5:5). Also the compound hearmspraec renders calumnia but as far as my material is concerned solely in a vocabulary (WW VI, App. C, p. 186). In the Middle English translations harm renders injuria (App. C, pp. 195-197).

---

[1] The Old English sound written sc was early palatalized to sh (written sc), whereas Scandinavian loan words retained their hard sk-sound (Baugh, 1959, p. 113). Cf. skirt (Old Norse skyrta) and shirt, both from primitive Germanic *skurtion (Hellquist s.v. skjorta).

[2] Scandinavian influence must have been especially strong in the East Midland dialect, from which standard English descends (see Bennett & Smithers, 1966, pp. 12-13, and Quirk & Wrenn, 1969, p. 2). It is the dialect of the area where the Danes settled when Alfred had defeated them and forced them to withdraw from Wessex in the late 870's. Cf. p. 12. It became known as the Danelaw (Dane-lage/Dane-lagh), i.e. the district in which Danish law prevailed (OED and Baugh, 1959, pp. 111-112). During the following centuries the Danish settlers gradually adopted the English language but enriched it with many Scandinavian loan words.

3.2.3. *Filth*

Fȳlþ (Middle English filth) is a late word in Old English. My material includes only three instances of Old English fȳlþ. They are from a West Saxon text written in the middle of the eleventh century (p. 78). The oldest instance quoted in the OED is from the Corpus MS., dated ca. 1000 (App. A, p. 122), Matt. 23,27, where it renders Latin spurcitia 'filth, dirt, dung' (OLD). In my instances it renders Latin turpitudo (B II:Unchastity). In the Middle English translations filth and filthhed (see below) dominate the translations of turpitudo (B II:Unchastity) to a degree of 97% (103 instances out of a total of 106).

Filth (Old Saxon fulitha) is one of **many** derivatives of adjectives with the suffix -th (primitive Germanic ^{x}-iþa/-iþo) that have survived in Modern English. It derives from foul, Old English fūl, Icelandic fúll, Danish ful, Old Swedish ful 'infamous, nauseous' (Hellquist s.v. ful).

3.2.4. *Shenship* and *Filthhed*

Both shenship and filthhed are new formations in Middle English. Together with a great number of formations with the abstract suffixes -ship (Old English -scipe) and -hed/-hede (Modern English -head), a variant of -hod (Old English -hād, Modern English -hood), these two words had a short life (pp. 67 and 80).

Shenship (**schenschippe, schenschip, shendship**,etc.) **derives from** the same root as **shame** and **scand** (primitive Germanic ^{x}skam-ðō). The meaning of shenship has been dealt with on pp. 66-67.

3.3. Scandinavian Words

3.3.1. *Wrong*

Wrong, the most frequent of the Middle English words in Sense group A III 3:Men-Men-Insult, is a Scandinavian word. It appears in late Old English, though in my material only in texts from the middle of the four- **teenth** century onwards (pp. 66 and 68). As the translation of injuria it ousted Old English tēona/Middle English tene as well as Old English wōh/Middle English woh/wouh (p. 68). Wrong (derived from primitive Germanic ^{x}wringan 'bend') and woh/wouh seem to have exactly the same meanings, namely originally 'crooked, bent', in extended use as nouns 'evil, injury, harm'. See the OED s.v. wrong and Hellquist s.v. vrång!

3.3.2. *Ill*

Middle English ill/ille/ylle (Old Norse illr) has replaced Middle English yuel (Old English yfel) in Modern English ill fame. My material includes only one instance of this expression, i.e. ylle fame:infamia (B III:Misbehaviour), which is from the NPE (App. A, p. 132), a text dated "late fourteenth century". The earliest instance in the OED is an ille fame:infamia from a text dated 1483. Cf. yuel fame/iuel fame, p. 102. However, the earliest instance in the OED of ille as an adjective is from a text dated "a 1200" ʿbefore 1200ʿ, as a noun from a text dated "a 1300" (Cursor Mundi).

3.4. French Words

French words appear in two of my three sources from the thirteenth century (p. 14), viz. in the Ancrene Riwle, which has schorn/-ung:derisus/derisio (A III 1:Men-Men-Derision), blasphemie:blasphemia (A II:Men-God), scandle/schandle/schaundle[1]:scandalum[2] (Latin text, pp. 8,21, 32,7, and 149,3-4; English text, pp. 5,25, 47,11, and 172,36-37), and in the Surtees Psalter, which has sclaundre/sclaunder[1]:scandalum[2] (Ps. 49,20 and 105,36).

The earliest of my sources from the fourteenth century, the Midland Prose Psalter, London MS. (dated 1340-50), has scorne:derisus, scornynge: subsannatio (A III 1c:Men-Men-Derision-TP), and sclaundre/sclaunder[1]: scandalum[2] (Ps. 48,14/48,13; 49,20/49,21; 68,23/68,27; 105,36/105,33; 118,165; 139,6, and 140,9/140,10). Cf. above. It is also my earliest source for seven French words, viz. illusioun:inlusio (A I:Devil-Men), desceit:inlusio (A III· 1c:Men-Men-Derision-TP), chalange:calumnia (A III 2:Men-Men-Calumny), confusioun/confusion:confusio (B:State), blamyng[3]: uituperatio[2] (Ps. 30,14/30,16), abominacioun:abominatio[2] (Hymn 6,24), and indignacioun:indignatio[2] (Ps. 29,6/29,5; 77,49/77,54; 84,4/84,3; and 101,11). A word which appears only in this text is reproce/repruce/repruse/-ing:opprobrium (see p. 69).

---

[1] Both words, scandle/etc. (Old Northern French escandle, Modern English scandal) and sclaundre/etc. (Old French esclaundre, Modern English slander), derive ultimately from Latin scandalum, Greek skandalon ʿsnare, stumblingstockʿ (OED s.v. slander). Only sclaundre/etc. appears in my sources from the fourteenth and fifteenth centuries, where it renders, besides scandalum, also ignominia and infamia (List ME 1).

[2] Scandalum, uituperatio, abominatio, and indignatio are words from my unclassified material (see p. 27).

[3] Wrong(ful) blamyng renders contumelia (A III 3:Men-Men-Insult), whereas blameng and blame render calumnia (A III 2:Men-Men-Calumny).

The Wyclif Bible, EV 1 (ca. 1385), is my earliest source for re-
pref/etc., despit, and strijf/strif. My earliest instance of iniurie
is the one from the Wyclif Bible, EV, Col. 3,25, quoted in the MED and
in the OED (see p. 68). The MED dates the text ca. 1384, the OED 1382.
Despisyng appears for the first time in Higd.Trev. (dated "late fourteenth century"), and yuel fame in the Wyclif Bible, EV 2, after
Baruch 3,20, i.e. ca. 1400 or later (see p. 78 and App. A, pp. 117 and
130-131).

I have compared the earliest instances quoted in the OED with the
earliest instances in my material for the relevant French words and
found that the OED gives earlier instances than I do for eight of
them. Ranged in chronological order in accordance with the dating of
their sources in the OED they are: strijf (the Ancrene Riwle, "a 1225";
cf. App. A, pp. 117 and 133, where the text has been dated 1225-49),
deceyte ("1275"), confusion ("c 1290"), chalange, despite, and iuel
fame (Cursor Mundi, "a 1300"), abominacion ("c 1325), and reprofe/
reproue/reprove (Richard Rolle of Hampole's Psalter, App. A, p. 131,
"a 1340").

The instances given above seem to indicate that many of the French
words did not attain their dominant position in the English vocabulary
until the middle of the fourteenth century, some of them even later.
French had been the language of the ruling class and together with
Latin the language of learning and culture since the Norman Conquest
(1066), but it was not until the English language began to prevail
over French that a gradual mixture of the two vocabularies took place.
Cf. Baugh (1967), pp. 111-112, and Kjellmer (1973), p. 156. After
1250 the spread of English among the upper class begins (Baugh, 1959,
p. 185). However, the process of reestablishment certainly extended
over centuries. The years 1349, 1362, and 1385 were mentioned on p.
14 as important dates in the course of this reestablishment. In Baugh
(1959), p. 184, the year 1425 is suggested as an approximate date for
a general adoption of English in writing.

VII. REASONS FOR CHANGES IN SEMANTIC FIELD

The last of the questions which were formulated in order to outline
the aims of my study (p. 7) reads: "How could words from a foreign vocabulary oust whole groups of old well-established words?" I have considered
linguistic factors, such as polysemy, homonomy, and semantic inappropri-
ateness, which normally contribute to the disappearance of old words
(Kjellmer, 1973, p. 141 f.), but I have not been able to connect any of
these factors with the disappearance of any of the Old English words in
the semantic field of shame/disgrace. However, the reshaping of the
Middle English vocabulary went beyond what can be called normal, and was
brought about to a great extent by non-linguistic events (p. 13). The
circumstance that the English language in the centuries after the Norman
Conquest (1066) represented the culture of a socially and politically inferior group in relation to French culture implies that "loan word prestige" must have been an important factor at work in the introduction of
the Romance vocabulary of the English language.

The majority of the French words which ousted the old vocabulary of the
relevant semantic field have doubtless been introduced into the Middle
English vocabulary by way of the literary language. In this period as
well as in the Early Old English period translators have contributed to
the reshaping of the literary vocabulary. Cf. p. 9. My investigation,
which is based on translations of Latin texts, shows primarily the influence of the Latin sources.

1. Loan Word Prestige

Being the language of the ruling class in England after the Norman Conquest, French became, together with Latin, the language of learning and
culture. When English was recognized as the official language after nearly two centuries of French predominance (p. 102) large parts of the old
Germanic vocabulary had disappeared and been replaced by French words. In
the semantic field of shame/disgrace all words except three had disappeared or lost their importance (p. 97). It is easy to imagine that the
native words in many cases had a rustic or blunt ring in the chivalrous
society of the thirteenth and fourteenth centuries. Many of the words in
the relevant semantic field may have been especially liable to sound indecorous. The bismer-words express disagreeable matters, perhaps in particular those of the two Sense groups A I:Devil-Men and B II:Unchastity.

The tendency to avoid the use of a common native word for an unpleasant
concept is well known. However, if we look at the vocabulary of the
opposite semantic field, that of honour/glory, for instance, we shall
find that it has an even lower rate of survival for the old words. Not
one of the many words for honour and glory in Beowulf has survived in
Modern English. The words I refer to are the following: ār 'honour,
kindness, benefit, help'; blǣd 'power, glory, renown, vigor of life';
duguð 'power, excellence, manhood, glory'; gilp 'boast' (HM: 'fame,
glory, glorious deed'); lof 'praise, glory'; maerðo 'fame, glory, glorious deed'; tīr 'glory'; þrym(m) 'might, force, greatness, glory';
weorðmynd/wordmynd 'honour, glory'; wuldor 'glory, heaven'. The Modern
English translations are those given in Klaeber (1950). The words rendered by honour or glory in HM are, beside those recorded from Beowulf,
the following: ārung, ārweorðnes, ārweorðung, dōm, dōmweorðung, gielping, gleng, hlīsa, maernes, maeð, rīceter, risne, þrymdōm, þryð, weorðfulnes, weorðlicnes, weorðnes, weorðscipe, weorðung, wlenc, wuldor-
blǣd, wuldorfaestlicnes, and wuldorþrymm. Only one of these words,
viz. weorðscipe, Modern English worship, has survived.

   It seems clear, therefore, that the "agreeable" or "disagreeable"
nature of the semantic field is of minor importance when it comes to pin-
pointing reasons for the disappearance of our Old English words. Even
if special reasons in many cases may have contributed to facilitate the
influx of the French vocabulary in the Middle English period one of the
most important factors must have been the prestige emanating from
French culture. Most of the words in the two semantic fields, that of
shame/disgrace and that of honour/glory, cover senses which are highly
abstract. They were therefore more at home in literature and among the
upper classes than in ordinary conversation among the common people.

2. Influence of Latin Originals

   A vital question when we are concerned with the introduction of
French loan words into the English literary vocabulary in an investigation based on translations of Latin texts must be: To what extent have
the Latin sources influenced the translators in their choice of a new
word instead of an old one?

The influence of the original is conspicuous when the translator uses a derivative of a Latin word to render the Latin word in question. In my material illusion/illusioun, blasphemy/blasphemie, iniury/iniurie, confusion/confusioun, and chalang/chaleng always render Latin inlusio, blasphemia, injuria, confusio, and calumnia respectively.

In 88 out of a total of 90 Middle English instances Latin blasphemia is rendered by blasphemy/blasphemie. The two exceptions are hokor[1] from the Life of St. Katherine (ca. 1225), and despisyng from Higd. Trev. (MS.dated "late fourteenth century"). The great majority (78 instances) are classified in A II:Men-God. The remaining ten instances of blasphemy/blasphemie:blasphemia have the sense of A III 3:Men-Men-Insult. The Middle English translators do not distinguish between the two senses of Latin blasphemia. Neither do they render contumelia nor subsannatio, which occasionally appear in the sense of A II:Men-God, by blasphemy/blasphemie. Their dependence upon the Latin original is complete.

Latin calumnia has been rendered by chalang/chaleng/chalengyng (mostly preceded by fals or wrong) in 77 instances out of a total of 82. The exceptions are craving[2] from the Surtees Psalter (MS. dated "late thirteenth century"), the three instances of blame/blameng:calumnia from Higd.Trev. and Higd.Harl., and one instance of eny thynge to be discussed afterwarde:calumnia from Higd.Harl. (App. C, p. 193).

Examples from my unclassified material are the translations of Latin scandalum and abominatio (see p. 27). Scandalum, rendered in Old English translations by twelve different words, has been rendered in the Middle English translations by scandle/schandle/schaundle and sclaundre/sclaunder/sclaundir (p.101, note 1) except in five instances from the Surtees Psalter where schame has been used. However, unlike the derivatives of Latin words dealt with above, sclaundre/etc. does not exclusively render the Latin word from which it derives. In my material it also renders ignominia and infamia (see p. 101). Latin

---

[1] Hokor (Old English hocor 'insult, derision') appears only twice in my material, the instance above and one instance in the Ancrene Riwle, where it renders Latin inrisio. See App. C., pp. 189-190.

[2] This instance of craving (Old English crafing 'insult, derision') from the Surtees Psalter, Ps. 118,134, is the only one of this word in my material.

abominatio has been rendered by nine different words in the Old English translations. The Middle English translations have abhominacion/
abhominacioun except in three instances. Two of these instances are
from two texts written in the thirteenth century, viz. the Ancrene
Riwle, which has schendfulness, and the Surtees Psalter, which has
wlating (Old English wlatung/wlaetung 'nausea, disfigurement'). The
third instance is from the Midland Prose Psalter, the London MS.
(dated 1340-50), which has one instance of wlateing and one of abhominacioun for Latin abominatio. The Midland Prose Psalter, the Dublin
MS. (dated 1375-1425), on the other hand, has abhominacion in both
these instances (Ps. 87,9/87,8 and Hymn 6,24/6,16).

Most of the instances mentioned above as exceptions, i.e. the instances in which the Latin words have been rendered by words other
than their French derivatives, are from one of the three texts written
in the thirteenth century (see p. 14). Neither illusion/illusioun,
iniury/iniurie, chalang/chaleng, confusion/confusioun, nor abhomina-
cion/abhominacioun appear in my instances from these texts.

Exceptions were also quoted from Higd.Trev. and Higd.Harl., the two
translations of Higden's Polychronicon (App. A, p. 132). If we compare
these two texts, however, we find that Higd.Harl., the younger of the
two translations, shows far greater dependence on the Latin original
than the older translation, Higd.Trev.   In the instance where Higd.
Trev. has despisyng for Latin blasphemia (see above), Higd.Harl. has
the French derivative blasphemy.   Other examples are the translations of Latin inlusio, injuria, opprobrium, and confusio. In Higd.
Harl. we find inlusio, opprobrium, confusio rendered by the corresponding French adaptations, illusion, opprobry/obprobry, confusion/
confusioun without exception, and injuria rendered by iniury/iniurie
in 11 instances out of a total of 12. None of the four French words
in question occur in Higd.Trev. (App. C, pp. 188, 196, 199, and 209).
Compare also unclassified instances with confusio in the sense of 'disorder, mixture' on p. 73.

The fact that French derivatives of Latin words were increasingly
used to render those words,   reflects the part played by the translators in the transformation of the Middle English literary vocabulary.
Two of the derivatives dealt with above, namely blasphemie (Latin blasphemia) and scandle/schandle/schaundle (Latin scandalum), appear as

early as the beginning of the thirteenth century, whereas others, for
instance <u>iniury/iniurie</u> (Latin <u>injuria</u>), do not appear until the end
of the fourteenth century. See pp. 101-102. Borrowing the French
derivatives gradually became a habit in the prevailing atmosphere of
French supremacy.

VIII. SUMMARY

This investigation deals with semantically equivalent sets of words
in the Old and Middle English vocabularies. The words, which can be
said to have the concept of ´shame, disgrace´ as a common denominator,
derive from translations where they render a set of 16 Latin words, viz.
those Latin words that have been translated by Old English bismer-words
at least twice (p. 11). Seven centuries, the ninth - fifteenth centuries, are represented in my material. Great changes in a language
during such a long time are quite natural, but as a consequence of the
Norman Conquest (1066) the changes in the English language were particularly far-reaching. In some lexical spheres the Germanic vocabulary
of the English language was to a great extent ousted by the Romance vocabulary of the French language. The Old English words for ´honour,
glory´, for instance, seem to have disappeared almost completely (p.
104). Only seven of all the Old English words recorded for the opposite
concept, that of ´shame, disgrace´, appear among the Middle English
words recorded for the same concept (Lists OE 2 and ME 2). The seven
words are: bismer, fӯlþ, grama, hearm, tēona, scamu, and yfel. Three
of them, viz. bismer, grama/Middle English gram/grem, and tēona/Middle
English tene, are very weakly represented in my Middle English material
(p. 97). They did not survive in Modern English.

In order to study the changes taking place in the semantic field of
´shame, disgrace´, I compared the vocabularies of that field from mainly
three periods of the English language, the early Old English period
(late ninth - early tenth centuries), the later, so-called classical,
period (ca. 950 - 1100), and the late Middle English period (ca. 1350 -
1500). My material derives only from translations of Latin texts.

The meanings of the Old English bismer-words form my semantic field
(p. 8). It embraces chiefly two aspects of ´shame, disgrace´, one of
activity (Sense group A) and one of state (Sense group B).

The use of the bismer-words in both these senses seems to be one of
the characteristics of King Alfred´s vocabulary, where the bismer-words,
as far as my material is concerned, are represented by one word, bismer,
except in three instances (p. 87 and its footnote). In contemporary
Anglian texts as well as in texts from the later Old English period the
bismer-words signify only Sense A:Activity.

Both main Sense groups, A:Activity and B:State, have been divided in-

to three subgroups, I, II, and III. The names of the subgroups in A:
Activity, A I:Devil-Men, A II:Men-God, and A III:Men-Men, refer to
agent and object of the activity, whereas those of the subgroups in B:
State, B I:Misfortunes, B II:Unchastity, and B III:Misbehaviour, refer
to reasons for the state in question. A III:Men-Men, in terms of size
the most important of the subgroups, has been subdivided into three
minor groups covering three different kinds of activity, A III 1:Men-
Men-Derision, A III 2:Men-Men-Calumny, and A III 3:Men-Men-Insult (see
p. 55).

The early Old English period is represented by a few Anglian texts
(p. 15) and by King Alfred's West Saxon versions of Cura Pastoralis
and Orosius. Alfred's vocabulary differs greatly from the vocabulary
of the Anglian translators and also from that of the later West Saxon
ones. The words of the relevant semantic field do not usually render
the same Latin words in Alfred's texts as they do in other Old English
texts. Another conspicuous feature in Alfred's vocabulary is the re-
markable variety in his renderings of certain Latin words. Other translators show greater consistency. This is especially evident in the instances of A III 3:Men-Men-Insult, which alone holds more than half of
the whole number of classified Old English instances (p. 88). In fact,
Alfred seldom uses the same word or expression twice for a Latin word
of the relevant semantic field. These phenomena seem to reflect the
problems Alfred faced in his work, though they may also reflect ambi-
tions on his part to translate the exact meanings of each Latin word in
its different contexts. Compounds and derivatives formed for the purpose of rendering certain Latin words give evidence of Alfred's endeavours to adapt the old native word material to new use. The expedient
of borrowing derivatives of the Latin words in question from another
language was not at hand as it was in the Middle English period. Nobody
seems to have translated any of the essential religious texts into West
Saxon before Alfred's reign. Alfred's assistants were Mercian (Anglian).
In the preface to his Pastoral Care Alfred tells us that he could not
find anybody south of the Thames who could translate a letter from Latin
into English (p.12), a statement that gives us an idea of the situation
at the time when he started his translative work.

Though Alfred's dialect prevailed (p. 93), his use of the individual
words was not accepted by his followers. As regards the relevant semantic field only two words, scamu/sceamu (p.88) and to some extent bismer

(p. 93), were later used in the same way as they were used by him.

The most important words of the later, so-called classical, Old English period are, in A I:Devil-Men bismer-words from Anglian and West Saxon texts, swic, big swic/biȝ-swic (beswic), and swicung only from West Saxon texts; in A II:Men-God ebolsung/etc. from Anglian texts, bismer-words from West Saxon texts; in A III 1:Men-Men-Derision bismer-words from Anglian and West Saxon texts, (h)leahter/hlehter and tāl only from West Saxon texts; in A III 2:Men-Men-Calumny hearmcwide/ -cwidolnes, scomu/sceomu, and tēlnis from Anglian, bismer-words, hosp, tēona, and tāl from West Saxon texts; in A III 3:Men-Men-Insult tēona and edwīt from Anglian, tēona and hosp from West Saxon texts; in B I: Misfortunes gedrēfednes/-nys from Anglian, gescendnes/-nys/etc., ge-drēfednes/-nys, and scamung from West Saxon texts; in B II:Unchastity scondlicnes/sceondlicnes/scandlicnes (only from Bede's History, p. 88), and a few instances each of gemang/gemeng/gemengnes/gemengednys, fȳlþ, sceamu, and hǣman (a verb!) from West Saxon texts; in B III:Misbehaviour scomu/sceomu from Anglian, gescendnes/-nys/etc., scamu/sceamu, scamung, and gedrēfednes/-nys from West Saxon texts.

Towards the end of the fourteenth century all the words above, apart from scamu, fȳlþ, and the simplex hearm, had disappeared or lost their importance. They had been replaced by mainly 15 French loan words, the Scandinavian loan word wrong, and the two new short-lived formations shenship and filthhed.

Fȳlþ, a late West Saxon word, is represented in my Old English material by only three instances, where it renders Latin turpitudo (B II:Unchastity). In the Middle English period filth (Old English fȳlþ) gained in importance. Together with filthhed it dominated almost completely as the translation of turpitudo (List ME 1:2).

Shenship, one of the two new formations, is the most frequent word in my Middle English material (List ME 3). It is also the only Middle English word of importance that occurs in both main Sense groups, A:Activity and B:State. The extension of its meaning to A:Activity, however, is temporary, in fact limited to texts written in the early fifteenth century containing parts of the Wyclif Bible (pp. 66-67). There it renders, besides ignominia, confusio, and dedecus (B:State), also opprobrium (A III 3:Men-Men-Insult). In AV the distinction between the two groups is reestablished. Reproach renders opprobrium but never ignominia, confusio, or dedecus.

The Middle English translations give evidence of the role Latin has played in the introduction and establishment of the Romance vocabulary in the English language. In my material the French derivatives of Latin words render, with only two exceptions, exclusively those Latin words from which they derive. The exceptions are the two derivatives of Latin scandalum, which render not only that word but also ignominia and infamia (p. 101). Middle English blasfemye/blasphemye (Latin blasphemia) is a conspicuous example of complete dependence on the Latin original. Normally blasphemia has the sense of A II:Men-God, but in some instances it has the sense of A III:Men-Men. The translators do not distinguish between the two senses when they render blasphemia but use invariably blasfemye/blasphemye. Latin contumelia, on the other hand, is not rendered by blasfemye/blasphemye in those instances where it really has the sense of A II:Men-God but by words of Sense group A III:Men-Men, where the instances of contumelia normally belong (p.105). Other examples are the translations of Latin calumnia and abominatio. In the later Middle English texts these words are rendered exclusively by their French derivatives, which in turn never render any other Latin words (p. 105). Compare also the words illusioun/illusion, confusioun/confusion, and injury/injurie, each one rendering only the Latin word from which it derives (pp. 105-106).

My last question on p. 7 reads: "How could words from a foreign vocabulary oust whole groups of old well-established words?" There seems to have been a break in the literary tradition of the English language. Middle English documents from the twelfth and thirteenth centuries are scarce (p. 14). During the first few centuries after the Norman Conquest (1066) English represented the culture of a socially and politically inferior group. French was the language of the ruling class in England and, apart from Latin, the language of learning and culture. The contribution of Latin to the establishment of the Romance vocabulary in the literary language has been discussed above. We have found little reason to explain the low rate of survival for the words in the relevant semantic field as a result of their liability to sound indecorous in the chivalrous society of the thirteenth and fourteenth centuries (p. 103) as the old words of the opposite field, that of ´honour, glory´, seem to have an even lower rate of survival (p. 104).   The prestige pertaining to the French language seems to have been the overriding factor. Most of the words in the two semantic fields cover highly abstract

senses, a fact which implies that they were more at home in literature
and among the upper classes than in ordinary conversation among the
common people.

During the second half of the fourteenth century the English language
began to prevail over French in England. The years 1349, 1362, and 1385
have been mentioned as important dates in the course of the reestablishment of the English language (p. 102). In manuscripts from this time
the French words are commonly used. As regards the semantic field of
shame/disgrace there are French words in two of my three texts from
the thirteenth century, it is true, but the old native words, which were
later ousted, dominate by far (see p. 101 as well as App. A, pp. 131 and
133). The instances given on pp. 101-102 seem to indicate that many of
the French words did not attain their dominant position in the English
literary vocabulary until the middle of the fourteenth century, some of
them even later.

Scandinavian influence on English vocabulary has been discussed on
pp. 99-101. Examples of Scandinavian loan words mentioned there are
wrong and ill. These words invaded or encroached upon the semantic area
of two of the seven old words which survived in Middle English, namely
tēona (Middle English tene) and yfel (Middle English yuel, see p. 97).
For the survival of Old English scamu (Middle English shame) I have suggested Scandinavian support or reinforcement (p. 99). Though Scandinavian loan words appear in the Old English vocabulary they do not seem
to have been generally used until the thirteenth or even the fourteenth
century (cf. the statement in Baugh, 1959, referred to on p. 66).

APPENDIX A. TEXTS

I. REGIONAL AND CHRONOLOGICAL ARRANGEMENT OF TEXTS

(Texts are identified and described below under II.)

1. Old English Texts

	Kentish	Mercian	Northumbrian	West Saxon
800– 899				
800– 849	Glosses:WW II	Glosses: Epinal, Erfurt, and Corpus MSS.		
875– 899		A:Vespasian Psalter		Alfred's PC (MSS. H20 and C)
900– 999				
Ca. 925		B:Junius Psalter Bede (MS. T)		Alfred's Or. (MS. L)
Ca. 950		Glosses: WW XI–XII	Gospels (MS.CND4)	D:Regius Psalter Alfred's Bo. (MS. C) Glosses: WW XI–XII
951– 999		L:Bosworth Psalter (A–type) Gospels (MS. Ru^1)	Gospels (MS. Ru^2) Dur.Ri.	L:Bosworth Psalter (D–type) Glosses: Aldhelm (Napier 4) Glosses: WW VI
1000–1099				
Ca. 1000				Gospels (MS. C) Bede (MS. O)
1000–1049		C:Cambridger Psalter (A–type)		I:Lambeth Psalter (Lambeth MS. 427) Hept. (MS. B) Alfred's Or. (MS. C) Rule S.B. (MS. A) Dialogues (MS. H) Glosses: Aldhelm (MS. H) Glosses: WW IV–V

	Kentish	Mercian	Northumbrian	West Saxon
Ca. 1050		P:Paris Psalter		Rule S.B. (MSS. W and CTA3) Bede (MS. B) Lib.Scint; De Vitiis MS. Arundel 155 Cons. (MS. CTA3) Glosses: Aldhelm (Napier 1: MS. Digby 146) Glosses: WW III (MS. CTA3)
1051-1099		J:Arundel Psalter (A-type) Dialogues (MS.C)		J:Arundel Psalter (D-type) Hept. (MS. L) Aelfric's Hom. Rule C Glosses: Aldhelm (Napier: 7, 8, 11, 18)
1100-1199				
Ca. 1100				K:Salisbury Psalter (D-type)
1100-1149				Alfred's Bo. (MS. B) Alfred's Sol.
Ca. 1150		E:Eadwine's Psalter (A-type)	E:Eadwine's Psalter	E:Eadwine's Psalter (D-type) Alcuin
1151-1199				Gospels (MS. H) Aelfric's Judith
1200-1249				Rule S.B. (MS. CCD3)

2. Middle English Texts

	N	NWM	SWM	SW	NEM	SEM
1200–1299						
Ca. 1225			St.Kath.			
1225–49			Ancr.R.			
late 13th c.	Surtees Psalter					
1300–1399						
1340–1350			Midland: London MS.			
Late 14th c.	Paues (MS. C)			Higd. Trev. (SW ?)		Wyclif Bible, EV 1, EV 2 (-Bar. 3,20) Chaucer's Boethius
1400–1499						
Ca. 1400	Castleford			Paues: (MS.S) Higd. Cott.		
1400–25					NPE	Wyclif Bible, EV 2 (Bar. 3,20 -), LV
Ca. 1450		Destr. Troy				
15th c.						Higd.Harl. (SEM ?)

II. DESCRIPTION OF TEXTS

The texts of the two periods, the Old English and the Middle English,
are ranged in two groups, Bible texts and non-Bible texts. The Bible
texts have yielded the larger crop for this investigation, and so they
form the first group. The non-Bible texts form the second group. The
texts of each group have been ordered according to the same principle.
King Alfred's four works (the Pastoral Care, Orosius, Boethius, and the
Soliloquies) form the first item in the enumeration of the Old English
non-Bible texts. For convenience I have placed them together, in spite
of the fact that two of them, viz. Boethius and the Soliloquies, are of
far less value for this investigation than many of the works which
follow in the enumeration. The texts (Appendices A II and C) appear
in the following order:

1. The Old English Bible Texts

    1.1. The Psalter
    1.2. The Gospels
    1.3. The Heptateuch
    1.4. Aelfric's Book Judith
    1.5. Biblical Quotations from Aelfric's Homilies

2. The Old English Non-Bible Texts

    2.1. King Alfred's Translations
    2.2. The Rule of St. Benedict
    2.3. Bede's History
    2.4. Liber Scintillarum; De Vitiis et Peccatis
    2.5. The Dialogues
    2.6. Alcuin's De Virtutibus et Vitiis
    2.7. The Durham Ritual
    2.8. Prayers from MS. Arundel 155
    2.9. A Prayer from MS. Lambeth 427
    2.10. De Consuetudine Monachorum
    2.11. The Rule of Chrodegang
    2.12. Vocabularies

3. The Middle English Bible Texts

    3.1. The Wyclif Bible
    3.2. The Surtees Psalter
    3.3. The Midland Prose Psalter
    3.4. Parts of the New Testament (Paues)
    3.5. The Epistles (NPE)

4. The Middle English Non-Bible Texts

    4.1. Higden's Polychronicon
    4.2. The Destruction of Troy
    4.3. The Ancrene Riwle
    4.4. Chaucer's Boethius

4.5. Thomas Castleford´s Chronicle
4.6. The Life of Saint Katherine

The dates and regions given refer to MSS., not to originals. MS.
dates not followed by references are those of the editors. For each
excerpted text an estimate has been made of the number of running words
it contains.

1. Old English Bible Texts

1.1. The Psalter

To identify the different versions I use the same letter for each
Psalter version as do Sisam (Salisbury Psalter), Wildhagen (Cambridger
Psalter), and Schabram (Superbia I).

A: Vespasian Psalter, MS. Cotton Vespasian **A 1,** ed. H. Sweet, Early
   English Text Society (henceforth EETS), 83 (1885), p. 183 f. -
   Ca. 875-900 (Sisam). - The Psalter contains about 32,500 words.
   The Hymns added to the Psalter have about 3,000 words.

B: Junius Psalter, **MS. Bodley Junius 27,** ed. E. Brenner,
   Anglistische Forschungen 23 (1908). - Ca. 925. - About 32,500
   words.

C: Cambridger Psalter, MS. Cambridge University Library. Ef. 1.23,
   ed. K. Wildhagen, Bibliothek der angelsächsischen Prosa (henceforth BdaP) 7 (1910). - Ca. 1025 (Sisam). - Psalter: about
   33,000 words; Hymns: about 3,000 words.

D: Regius Psalter, MS. Royal **2 B 5,** ed. F. Roeder, Studien zur
   englischen Philologie, H. 18 (1904). - Ca. 950 (Sisam). -
   Psalter: about 32,500 words; Hymns: about 3,000 words.

E: Eadwine´s Canterbury Psalter, MS. Trinity College, Cambridge,
   R. 17.1, ed. F. Harsley, EETS 92 (1889). - Ca. 1150 (Sisam). -
   Psalter: about 36,000 words; Hymns: about 4,000 words.

F: Stowe Psalter, MS. Stowe 2, ed. J. Spelman, Psalterium Davidis
   Latino-Saxonicum vetus, London 1640. - Ca. 1050-75 (Sisam). - The
   text was not available to me.

G: Vitellius Psalter, MS. Cotton Vitellius **E 18,** ed. J. L. Rosier,
   Cornell Studies in English 42, Ithaca-New York 1962 (Schabram,
   p. 22). - The text was not available.

H: Tiberius Psalter, MS. Cotton Tiberius **C 6,** not edited (Schabram, p. 22). - Ca. 1050-75 (Sisam). - The text was not available.

I: Lambeth Psalter, MS. Lambeth **Palace** (London) 427, ed. U. Lindelöf, Acta Societatis Scientiarum Fennicae, Tom. 35, No. 1,
   Helsingfors 1909. - Ca. 1025 (Sisam). - Psalter: about 38,000
   words; Hymns: about 4,000 words.

J: Arundel Psalter, MS. Arundel 60, ed. G. Oess, Anglistische
   Forschungen 30 (1910). - Ca. 1050-75 (Sisam). - Psalter: about
   32,500 words; Hymns: about 3,500 words.

K: Salisbury Psalter, MS. Salisbury Cathedral 150, ed. C. Sisam
   and K. Sisam, EETS 242 (1959). - Ca. 1100. - Psalter: about
   28,000 words; Hymns: about 3,000 words.

L: Bosworth Psalter, **MS. British Museum** A 37517, ed. U. Lindelöf,
   Mémoires de la Société néo-philologique de Helsingfors 5
   (1909), p. 143 f. - Ca. 975-1000. - Psalter: about 5,000 words;
   Hymns: about 900 words.

The oldest of the extant Old English Psalter glosses, the Vespasian
Psalter (A), is written in the Anglian dialect, or more accurately in
the Mercian dialect. The remaining eleven glosses are mainly West
Saxon.

Some of the West Saxon glosses, however, are directly or indirectly
dependent on the Vespasian Psalter (A). They reveal Anglian influence,
especially in the vocabulary. Cf. p. 15. The Vespasian Psalter (A)
together with the glosses dependent on it, form one group and are named
the glosses of A-type. The West Saxon glosses independent of the
Vespasian Psalter (A), form a second group and are named after their
oldest representative, which is the Regius Psalter (D). They are the
glosses of D-type. The arrangement is based on information given by
Lindelöf in Der Lambeth Psalter II, p. 19 f., and in Studien zu altenglischen Psalterglossen (Bonner Beiträge xiii, Bonn 1904). Other
scholars, e.g. Sisam (the Salisbury Psalter, App. II, p. 52 f.) and
Schabram (Superbia I, p. 23 f.), also refer to Lindelöf for information
about the relationship of the Old English Psalter glosses.

The two groups comprise the following glosses or parts of glosses:

A-type:
A, B, and C;
L: Psalms 50, 53, 63, 68, 101, 118-133, and 142;
J: Psalms 1-51 and 63-75.

D-type:
D, F, and K;
L: Psalms not depending on A, i.e. 40, 66, 69-70, 85, **and 139-140**;
J: "   "   "   " ", i.e. 42-62 and 76-150.

Two of the Psalter glosses, viz. the Lambeth Psalter (I) and
Eadwine's Canterbury Psalter (E), are not included in any of these

two groups.

The Lambeth Psalter (I) is a late West Saxon compilation. It is rich
in vocabulary and the glossator is considered to have been a learned
man. A Latin word is very often rendered by two or even three Old English words. Many of its renderings are found in no other extant Psalter
gloss.

Eadwine's Canterbury Psalter (E) is considered to be the youngest
and at the same time the most defective of the Old English Psalter
glosses. In the first 77 Psalms two layers of glossing have been dis-
cerned. The many corrections and additions represent a younger layer
which shows dependence on a source of D-type. The older original layer
of the first 77 Psalms as well as the glossing of the second part,
Psalms 78 onwards, which is free from corrections and additions, reveal
Anglian influence in the vocabulary. On account of this fact an Anglian
original, i.e. a source of A-type, has been postulated for the Psalter.
See Sisam, p. 57, and Schabram, p. 32.

A metrical version of Psalms 51-150 (ed. Krapp, the Anglo-Saxon Poetic Records V, London 1933) has also been included in my material. It
is part II of the so-called Paris Psalter (Bibliotèque Nationale, Paris,
MS. Fonds Latin 8824). Part I of the Paris Psalter, which contains a
prose version of Psalms 1-50 (ed. J.W. Bright and R.J. Ramsay, Liber
Psalmorum; The West Saxon Psalms, Boston-London 1907) was not available
to me. The metrical version has been dated "perhaps the latter ninth or
early tenth century" in Krapp's edition (p. xvii). Ker (No. 367), however, dates the text "Xl med." 'the middle of the eleventh century', and
Baugh (1967, p. 85) calls the Paris Psalter "an eleventh-century MS.".
The language is prevailingly West Saxon, but certain forms in it are
assumed to be of Anglian origin and to indicate that the translation was
originally made in the Anglian dialect (Krapp, p. xvii). My instances
from this text have been classified as Anglian. Latin opprobrium/in-
properium has been rendered by the Anglian word edwīt, and calumnia by
hearmcwide, which is also an Anglian word (see p. 62). The text contains rare words, e.g. hearmedwīt (Latin inproperium in Ps. 68,21/68,20),
hleorsceamu (p. 72), and ārscamu (pp. 6 and 11). The word ārscamu is
probably the result of a misinterpretation (Krapp, pp. 212-213), owing
to the mutilated state of the MS. (Baugh, 1967, p. 85), or the careless-
ness of the scribe. The letter P in Appendix C:Text Material refers to
the Paris Psalter.

The Old English Psalter glosses are based on two different versions
of Latin text, the "Roman" and the "Gallican". The "Roman" text prevailed in English church services until the late tenth century. Then,
after the Benedictine Reform, it was replaced by the "Gallican" text,
which is a revision made by Jerome of his earlier Old Latin version.
This revision was made on the basis of Hexapla, an edition of the Septua-
ginta with the Hebrew text and other translations in six parallel columns. The text, being used in Gaul, got the epithet "Gallican". It is
the text of the current (Clementine) Vulgate. (See Sisam, p. 47.) The
Old English Psalters A, B, C, D, E, and L, are glosses to the "Roman"
text, while F, I, J, and K, are glosses to the "Gallican" text.

I have compared the readings of a third Psalter text, the so-called
"Hebrew" Psalter, a final translation made by Jerome from the Hebrew.
(See pp. 71-72.) This text was not used in church services but was
studied by scholars and appears in early Bibles, notably in the Codex
Amiatinus, written at Jarrow or Wearmouth (Northumbria) about the year
700. In Biblia Sacra, Iuxta Vulgatam Versionem, Würtembergische Bibel-
anstalt, Stuttgart, 1969, the Latin text of the "Hebrew" Psalter occurs
together with the text of the current Vulgate, the "Gallican" Psalter.

1.2. The Gospels

The Holy Gospels in Anglo-Saxon, Northumbrian, and Old Mercian Versions,
ed. W.W. Skeat, Cambridge, 1871-1887:
MS. CND 4 (MS. Cotton Nero D 4, the Lindisfarne MS.), Northumbrian gloss.
         - Ca. 950. - Gospels: about 70,000 words; Prologue and Pre-
         faces: about 10,000 words.
MS. Ru^1 (MS. Rushworth), St. Matthew in Old Mercian dialect. - Latter
         part of tenth century.
MS. Ru^2 (MS. Rushworth), the three latter **Gospels** in Northumbrian dia-
         lect. - Latter part of tenth century. - **Ru^1 and Ru^2: about
         65,000 words.**
MS. C   (MS. Corpus Christi College, Cambridge, No. 140: CCCC 140),
         the West Saxon text in its earliest form. - Ca. 1000. - About
         70,000 words.
MS. H   (MS. Hatton 38, Oxford), the West Saxon text in its latest
         form. - Latter part of twelfth century. - About 70,000 words.

1.3. The Heptateuch (Hept.)

The Old English Version of the Heptateuch, ed. S.C. Crawford, EETS 160,
1922:
MS. B (MS. Cotton Claudius B 4). - Early eleventh century. - The first
       six Old Testament books. - About 57,000 words.
MS. L (MS. Bodley L 509). - Second half of eleventh century. - The
       seventh Old Testament book, the Judges. - About 2,500 words.

Älfrik de Vetere et Novo Testamento, Pentateuch, Iosua, Buch der Rich-
ter und Hiob, ed. Grein, Bibliothek der angelsächsischen Prosa (BdaP),
I, 1872. (The new Testament is missing.):

MS. L (MS.Bodley L 509).   - Second half of the eleventh century. -
    About 62,000 words.

The Old English Heptateuch consists of selections from the first
seven Old Testament books, i.e. the Pentateuch together with the books
of Joshua and Judges. It is mainly the work of the leading prose
writer of the classical period, Aelfric, who died ca. 1020. It is, however, assumed that a translation of the latter part of Genesis, perhaps
also of Exodus and Leviticus, existed when Aelfric set to work, and
that he incorporated the parts already translated into his own version
after having to some extent revised them (Baugh, 1967, p. 102). Others,
e.g. Schabram, regards not only the above-mentioned three books but also Numbers and Deuteronomy as older translations incorporated, at least
partly, by Aelfric in his version. As support for this supposition
concerning Deuteronomy Schabram offers three instances of ofermod-
(Lat. superbia, superbus, etc.), one instance in each of the three
books Leviticus, Exodus, and Deuteronomy. The type ofermod- is an
older West Saxon type used up to the middle of the tenth century.
Aelfric, on the other hand, used a younger West Saxon type of the word,
modi3- (Schabram, pp. 60 and 92).

1.4. Aelfric's Book Judith (Aelfric Judith)

Two fragments of MSS. from the twelfth century, ed. in Anglia 10, 1888,
pp. 87-104. - About 3,100 words.

1.5. Biblical Quotations from Aelfric's Homilies (Aelfric Hom.)

Biblical Quotations in Old English Prose Writers, ed. Albert S. Cook,
London, 1898.

2. Old English Non-Bible Texts

2.1. King Alfred's Translations

2.1.1. The Pastoral Care (PC)

King Alfred's West Saxon Version of Gregory's Pastoral Care, ed. H.
Sweet, EETS 45 (1871), 50 (1930):

MS. H20 (MS. Hatton 20). - 65 chapters. - About 83,000 words.
MS. C (MS. Cotton Tiberius B 11). - Only the first 49 chapters. -
    About 57,000 words.
Latin text: Cursus Completus, Series Latina 77.

    Both MSS. were written during the last decade of the ninth century,
i.e. during Alfred's reign. The translation was made by King Alfred himself with the aid of four scholars whom he names in his preface. The work
is a literal translation. It belongs to what has been called "the earlier
period of Alfred's literary career" (Baugh, 1967, p. 97).

2.1.2. Orosius (Or.)

King Alfred's Orosius, ed. H. Sweet, EETS O.S. 79 (1883):

MS. L (MS. Lauderdale: British Museum A 47967). - Ca. 925. -
    About 43,000 words.
MS. C (MS. Cotton Tib. B 1). - Early eleventh century. - About 3,600
    words (Sweet 18,2 - 42,25, the gap in the Lauderdale MS.).

    The work belongs to "the later period of Alfred's literary career"
(Baugh, 1967, p. 97). It shows less fidelity to the Latin original than
the Pastoral Care. In many places passages or even whole chapters have
been inserted.

2.1.3. Boethius (Bo.)

King Alfred's Old English Version of Boethius, De Consolatione Philosophiae, ed. Walter Sedgefield, Oxford 1899:

MS. C (MS. Cotton Otho A 6). - Ca. 960 ? (Sedgefield, p. xvii); Ker, No.
    167: X med. 'the middle of the tenth century'.
MS. B (MS. Bodley 180). - Ca. 1110 ? (Sedgefield, p. xvii); Ker: XII[1]
    'the middle of the first half of the twelfth century'. - The text
    from this MS. has been printed in italics instead of text illegible
    in MS. C.
Latin text: Boetii Philosophiae Consolatio, Libri Quinque, ed. R. Peiper,
1871.

    This translation was made after the translation of Orosius and it is
regarded to be the major of the two works from a literary point of view
(Baugh, 1967, p. 97). The work is a paraphrase rather than a translation, a circumstance which makes it less valuable for my investigation
than the other two. I have recorded ten instances from the prose part
(ca. 46,000 words), none from the metrical parts.

2.1.4. The Soliloquies (Sol.)

König Alfreds des Grossen Bearbeitungen der Soliloquien des Augustinus,
ed. W. Endter, BdaP 11(pp. 2-58), Hamburg 1922:
MS. C (MS. Cotton Vitellius A 15). - Second quarter of the twelfth centu-
    ry. - "Die Sprache selbst ist ein unreines spätes Westsächsisch."
    (Endter, p. xii). - About 12,000 words.

2.2. The Rule of St. Benedict (Rule S.B.)

2.2.1. Æthelwold's Translation

Die Angelsächsischen Prosabearbeitungen der Benedictinerregel, ed. A.
Schröer, BdaP 1-2, Kassel 1888:
MS. A (MS. Corpus Christi College, Cambridge, No. 178: CCCC 178). - Ca.
    1025 (Ker, No. 41B: XI^1). - About 18,000 words.
MS. W (Wells-Fragment). - Ca. 1050 (Ker, No. 395: XI med.). - About 3,900
    words.

Die Winteney-Version der Regula S. Benedicti, ed. A. Schröer, Halle 1888:
MS. CCD3 (MS. Cotton Claudius D 3). - The MS. was written in the first
    quarter of the thirteenth century. However, the Old English diph-
    thongs and case-suffixes are maintained, which indicates that the
    designation "Middle English version" (Schröer, p. ix) is applicable
    only to the time of its coming into existence, not of its language.
    See p. 22. - About 18,000 words.

2.2.2. The Interlinear Version

The Rule of S. Benet, Latin and Anglo-Saxon Interlinear Versi , ed. H.
Logeman, EETS O.S. 90 (1888):
MS. CTA3 (MS. Cotton Tiberius A 3). - Middle of the eleventh century. -
    About 18,000 words. - This version is said to have no connection
    whatever with the prose paraphrases of the Rule of St. Benedict
    edited by A. Schröer (2.2.1.). - The dialect is a mixture of West
    Saxon and Kentish, the present copy being a West Saxon copy of a
    Kentish copy of a West Saxon original (Schabram, p. 106).

2.3. Bede's History (Bede)

The Old English Version of Bede's Ecclesiastical History of the English
People, ed. Th. Miller, EETS O.S. 95 (1890), 96 (1891), 110 (1897), 111
(1898):
MS. T (MS. Tanner 10). - End of tenth century (according to the editor);
    ca. 925 (Ker, No. 351: X^1). - Anglian (Mercian) characteristics pre-
    served (see below). - About 82,000 words.

König Alfred's Übersetzung von Bedas Kirchengeschichte, ed. Jacob Schipper,
BdaP 4, Leipzig 1897:
MS. O (MS. Corpus Christi College, Oxford, No. 279: CCCO 279). - End of
    tenth or beginning of eleventh century. - About 67,000 words (pp.
    52-668 in Schipper's edition).
MS. B (MS. Corpus Christi College, Cambridge, No. 41: CCCC 41). - Middle
    of eleventh century (Schipper, p. xxvii); ca. 1025 (Ker, No. 32:
    XI^1). - About 82,000 words (pp. 7-701 in Schipper's edition).

    The Latin text in my lists is that which is printed on the lower part
of the pages in Schipper's edition.

This work was first ascribed to King Alfred, an opinion which had
remained undisputed until Miller in 1890 (EETS O.S. 95: Introduction)
showed that the translation was first made into the Mercian dialect
rather than into the West Saxon dialect of King Alfred. Scholars from
then onwards seem to agree about this. See Campbell (1951), pp. 349 f.,
Schabram (1965), p. 47, and Schipper's edition, pp. 40-41, where
it has been suggested that the translator might have been one of King
Alfred's Mercian assistants, as was for instance Waerferth (cf. below,
2.5.). Successive copying of the text by West Saxon scribes accounts
for the West Saxon character of the extant MSS. The Anglian (Mercian)
characteristics have been best preserved in MS. T, less in MS. O, and
least in MS. B (Schabram, 1965, p. 47 and Introduction of Schipper's
and Miller's editions).

2.4. Liber Scintillarum (Lib. Scint.); De Vitiis et Peccatis (De Vitiis)

Defensor's Liber Scintillarum with an Interlinear Anglo-Saxon Version,
ed. E.W. Rhodes, EETS 93 (1889):
MS. Royal 7C4. - Middle of the eleventh century. - Lib.Scint.: about
38,000 words; De Vitiis: about 2,300 words.

2.5. The Dialogues

Bischofs Waerferth von Worcester Übersetzung der Dialoge Gregors des
Grossen, ed. Hans Hecht, BdaP, 5 (1900), 2. Abteilung (1907):
MS. C (MS. Corpus Christi College, Cambridge, No. 322: CCCC 322). -
    Second half of the eleventh century. - About 79,000 words (pp.
    1-350 in Hecht's edition).- Concerning Anglian (Mercian) charac-
    teristics in this MS. see below!
MS. H (MS. Hatton 76,Oxford), a West Saxon remodelling of Waerferth's
    translation as represented in MS. C (Hecht's edition, part 2, p.
    130). It contains only the first two books of the Dialogues. -
    Ca. 1025. - About 25,500 words (pp. 1-174 in Hecht's edition).
Latin text: Fonti per la storia d'Italia, 57 (1924), Roma.

Waerferth (Werfrith), bishop of Worcester from the year 873 and one
of the Mercian scholars who assisted King Alfred (see above under 2.3.),
is believed to have translated the Dialogues in the period between 880
and 885 (Schabram, 1965, p. 42, and Hecht's edition, part 2, p. 22).

MS. C is considered to be descended from an Anglian (Mercian) original. An instance of a characteristically Anglian word from this MS. in
my material is fracod. "As a noun fracod/fracod 'insult, wickedness'
seems to be found only in Anglian, although the adjective is common Old
English." (Menner, 1948,p. 3).

2.6. Alcuin's De Virtutibus et Vitiis (Alcuin)

Übersetzung von Alcuin's De Virtutibus et Vitiis, ed. Assmann, Anglia
11 (1889), pp. 371-391, chapters 1-16. - About 5,400 words.
MS. Cotton Vespasian D 14. - Middle of **twelfth century** (Schabram, 1965,
p. 69). -   The MS. has also been edited by Warner in EETS O.S. 152,
1917, No. 35: Early English Homilies from the Twelfth Century MS. Vesp.
D. XIV, - My material is from Assmannn's edition.

Schabram (1965), pp. 69-70, has **found in** this text two instances of
the Anglian type oferhy3d- and nine instances of the West Saxon type
ofermod- as translations of Latin superbia. From this fact he concludes
that the text of the MS. represents a transformation of an original
Anglian text into the West Saxon dialect.

None of my seven instances from this text have Anglian words.

2.7. The Durham Ritual (Dur. Ri.)

Rituale Ecclesiae Dunelmensis. The Durham Collectar, ed. U. Lindelöf,
the Surtees Society 140 (1927):
MS. A.IV.19. - Second half of the tenth century. - About 23,200 words. -
Interlinear gloss in the Anglian (Northumbrian) dialect, free from West
Saxon intermixture (Schabram, 1965, p. 61). - The Lindisfarne Gospel
(MS. CND4) and the Durham Ritual were written by the same scribe (OEG,p.
5, note 3).

2.8. Prayers from MS. Arundel 155 (Arundel 155)

MS. Arundel 155, which contains Old English interlinear versions of
Latin prayers, has been edited in three parts:
(1) Anglo-Saxonica Minora, ed. Logeman, Anglia 11 (1889), pp. 111-120.
    - About 700 words (pp. 115-119).
(2) Altenglische Interlinearversionen Lateinischer Gebete und Beichten,
    ed. Holthausen, Anglia 65 (1941), pp. 231-254. - About 3,300 words.
(3) Prayers from MS. Arundel 155, ed. J.J. Campbell, Anglia 81 (1963),
    pp. 84-117. - About 3,200 words.

The MS. has been dated "middle of eleventh century" in Campbell's
edition as well as in Schabram (1965),p. 110, and in Ker, No. 135.
Holthausen, on the other hand, dates "tenth century" in his edition,
p. 230.

2.9. A Prayer from MS. Lambeth 427 (Lambeth 427)

Die Altenglischen Beigaben des Lambeth-Psalters, ed. M. Förster, Archiv
für das Studium der **neueren** Sprachen und Literaturen 132, pp. 328-331. -
About 200 words. - The **same** prayer also occurs as No. 19 in Holthausen's edition. **See above, 2.8.(2).** The Lambeth MS. is slightly
older than MS. Arundel 155. The translations in the two MSS. differ to
some extent in the vocabulary. See translations of blasphemia on p. 60.

2.10. De Consuetudine Monachorum (Cons.)

De Consuetudine Monachorum, ed. W.S. Logeman, Anglia 13 (1891), pp.
365-448, containing Aethelwold's translation into Old English (Baugh,
1967,p.18). - Introduction and corrections in Anglia 15 (1893), pp. 20-
40. (See Knowles, 1941, pp. 42-43: Regula Concordia.)

MS. Cotton Tiberius A 3. - Middle of the eleventh century. (See above 2.2.2. The Interlinear Version.) - About 10,700 words.

2.11. The Rule of Chrodegang (Rule C.)

The Old English **Version** of the Enlarged Rule of Chrodegang, ed. A.S. Napier, EETS O.S. 150 (1916):
MS. Corpus Christi College, Cambridge, No. 191: CCCC 191. - Second quarter of the eleventh century (Napier's edition, p. VII); third quarter of the eleventh century (Ker, No. 46). - The original transla-tion was presumably made in Winchester about the year 1000 (Schabram, 1965, p. 111). - About 18,000 words. - The dialect is "uncertain or mixed" (Campbell, 1951, p. 353).

2.12. Vocabularies

2.12.1. Aldhem's De Laude Virginitatis (Aldhelm)

Old English Glosses, Anecdota Oxoniensia, ed. A.S. Napier, Oxford
1900. The edition includes nineteen MSS. Only the following seven
contain material relevant to my investigation:

1 (MS. Digby 146). - Presumably late eleventh century (according to
  the editor); the middle of the eleventh century (Ker, No. 320).
2 (MS. Royal 6 B 7). - Early twelfth century.
4 ("   Corpus Christi College, Cambridge, No. 326: CCCC 326). - Tenth
  century.
7 (MS. Royal 6 A 6). - Late eleventh century.
8 ("   Royal 5 E 11). - Late eleventh century.
11 ("   Phillips 8071). - Eleventh century.
18 ("   Corpus Christi College, Cambridge, No. 285: CCCC 285). -
  Eleventh century.

Angelsächsische Glossen. B. Glossen in Aldhelm, ed. F.J. Mone, Quellen
und Forschungen zur Geschichte der teutschen Literatur und Sprache, I,
Aachen-Leipzig 1930 (p. 329 f.):
MS. H (MS. Brüssel 1650). - First half of the eleventh century (Schabram, 1965, p. 64, and Ker,No. 8).

Angelsächsische Glossen, ed. C.W. Bouterwek, Zeitschrift für deutsches
Altertum, 9 (1853), p. 403 f.:
MS. H (MS. Brüssel 1650). The edition is regarded to be in many respects
  defective (E. Hausknecht, Anglia 6, 1883, p. 96 f., and R. Dero-
  lez, Anglia 74, 1956, p. 153 f.).

From Bouterwek's edition I have recorded only those instances that
are missing in Mone's edition. When the spelling of an Old English word
differs in the two editions, I have put Bouterwek's spelling in brackets.
Instances in brackets are not recorded in the lists (OE 1-5)

2.12.2. Wright-Wülcker (WW)

Anglo-Saxon and Old English Vocabularies, ed. Thomas Wright; second
edition by R. Wülcker, London 1884:
II   (MS.Cotton Vesp. D 6). - First half of the ninth century. - Its
  dialect is that of Kent.
III (MS. Cotton Tiberius A 3). - Tenth or first half of eleventh century
  (according to the editor); the middle of the eleventh century (Ker,
  No. 186). Cf. 2.2.2. The Interlinear Version.
IV   (MS.Bodley Junius): Archbishop Alfric's vocabulary of the tenth
  century. - Eleventh century.
V   (MS. Bodley Junius): Supplement to Alfric's vocabulary. - Tenth or
  eleventh century.
VI   (MS. Harley 3376). - Tenth century.
X   (MS. Cotton Julius A 2). - Eleventh century.
XI   (MS. Cotton Cleopatra A 3). - The middle of the tenth century (Ker)
XII ("   "   "   "). - "   "   " "   "   "   (")

2.12.3. The Oldest Glossaries (Epinal, Erfurt, and Corpus)
The Oldest Glossaries, ed. Henry Sweet, EETS O.S. 83 (1885):
Epinal, Erfurt, and Corpus MSS. - Eighth or ninth century. - The dialect
is mainly Mercian (OEG, p. 7).

3. Middle English Bible Texts

3.1. The Wyclif Bible (WB)

3.1.1. Early Version 1 (EV 1)

MS.Bodley 959, Genesis-Baruch 3,20 in the Earlier Version of the
Wycliffite Bible, ed. Conrad Lindberg, Stockholm Studies in English,
Vol. 1-5 (1959-1969). - About 636,400 words.

According to the editor (Vol.5, p. 97) this version is not the ultimate original, but it may be an original copy of the ultimate original
of EV 1. The translator was probably Nicholas of Hereford, one of
Wyclif's disciples. The work was executed during the last two decades
of the fourteenth century (ca. 1385 according to the OED). The dialect
is mainly East Midland.

3.1.2. Early Version 2 (EV 2) and a Later Version (LV)

The Holy Bible Containing the Old and New Testaments, by John Wycliffe
and His Followers, ed. Forshall, J, and Madden, F, Oxford (1850), Vol.
1-4 (henceforth FM).

EV 2 in FM is based on five MSS., A, B, C, K, and M:

A (MS. CCCO 4): Genesis - III Kings; Ezekiel 1,26-32,23;
B ("   Bodley D 370): IV Kings - II Paralipomenon;
C ("   "   " 369, 1st part): I Esdras - Baruch 3,20;
 ("   "   "   ", 2nd part): Baruch 3,20 - Ezekiel 1,26;
                                          Ezekiel 32,23 - Acts 28,15;
M (" Old Royal Library I B 6): Acts 28,15 - end of New Testament.
MS. C is considered to be the oldest of these five MSS.

LV in FM is based on one MS., i.e. MS.Old Royal Library I C 8, dated
"Not later than 1420" (FM,Vol. 1, list of MSS.).

EV 2 and LV contain about 966,900 running words each.

As I have mentioned above Nicholas of Hereford is generally considered to be the original translator of the Old Testament books
Genesis - Baruch 3,20. According to Baugh (1967), p. 271, there is a
note in one of the manuscripts stating that Nicholas of Hereford translated about three quarters of the Old Testament. It is also known that
a revision of Nicholas of Hereford's translation was undertaken by John
Purvey, perhaps even before Wyclif's death. See Baugh (1967), p. 271,
footnote 28: "Purvey's part in the translation rests on strong evidence,
just short of proof." The revision, completed about 1395 was in every
way superior to the early version (Baugh, 1967, p. 271).

FM (Vol. 5, pp. 92 and 98) suggests that not only Genesis - Baruch
3,20 but probably also the rest of the Old Testament was translated by
Nicholas of Hereford, the New Testament,on the other hand, by Wyclif

himself. However, the **translations** of some of the Latin words in my
material, especially those of <u>calumnia</u> (p. 62), <u>opprobrium</u> (p. 67), and
<u>ignominia</u> (App. C, pp. 203 and 206), indicate a change of translators
at Baruch 3,20. From Baruch 3,20 to the end of the Old Testament (EV 2)
Middle English words other than those used before Baruch 3,20 (EV 2)
occur. For <u>calumnia</u> and <u>opprobrium</u> the Middle English words used after
Baruch 3,20 in EV 2 are the same as those used in LV throughout.

3.2. The Surtees Psalter (Surtees)

"Anglo-Saxon and Early English Psalter", Publications of the Surtees
Society, 16 (1843), 19 (1847):
MS. CVD7 (Cotton Vesp. D 7). - Late thirteenth century. - Of Northern or
          Midland origin (Severs II, p. 385 f.). - About 42,700 words.
MS. H   (MS. Harley 1770). - Late thirteenth century.
MS. E   (MS. Egerton 614). - Late thirteenth century.
          Readings from MS. H and MS. E, supplied in the edition, have
          been put in brackets in App. C. They are not included in the
          Lists (App. B).

   Certain peculiarities such as archaic diction, Latinized construc-
tions, and a relative rarity of French terms, indicate a source in an
earlier Latin Psalter with English glosses, i.e. a Psalter with Middle
English glosses, which was itself a modernized version of an Old English
glossed version. See. Severs II, p. 385 f. As far as my instances are
concerned only one French loan word **appears.** The word is <u>sclaundre/</u>
<u>sclaunder</u> (Lat. <u>scandalum</u>). See p. 101.

3.3. The Midland Prose Psalter (Midland)

The Earliest Complete English Prose Psalter, ed. Karl B. Bülbring, EETS
O.S. 97, Part I (1891):
London MS. (MS. **British Museum A** 17376). - Between the years 1340 and
          1350 (Paues, p. lvi). - Pure West Midland dialect (according
          to the editor). - About 40,000 words.
Dublin MS. (MS. Trinity College, Dublin, 69, A.4.4.). - Between 1375 and
          1425 (Severs II, p. 537).- **A revision of the text in the**
          London MS.; a help in emending the numerous senseless
          readings in the London MS. (Bülbring, p. **x**).

   This text cannot with certainty be designated the "Earliest" English
Prose Psalter. According to Paues (1902), p. lx, Rolle's version (see
p. 20) seems to be the older of the two. Paues, p. x, points out that
the <u>Midland Prose Psalter</u> (the <u>West Midland Psalter</u>) has a greater number of French loan words than Rolle's version. **A possible reason for**
this has also been mentioned. The English translator depended upon a
French glossed version. Many of the discrepancies between the Latin **text**
and **the** English rendering can be explained by reference to the French
version in Bibliothèque Nationale, <u>fr. 6260</u>, a MS. some hundred years

younger than the one which the English translator presumably used.

The London MS. is my earliest source for seven French loan words and my only source for one, viz. reproce/etc. (see p. 101).

Those readings of the Dublin MS. which occur in Bülbring's edition have been put in brackets in App. C. They are not included in the Lists (App. B).

3.4. Parts of the New Testament (Paues)

A fourteenth Century English Biblical Version, ed. A.C. Paues, Cambridge 1902, pp. 18-208. - About 68,200 words.
MS. S (MS. Selwyn College, Cambridge, 108). - Ca. 1400. - Dialect:mainly
    Southwestern (Severs II, p. 398). - Part of the Epistles and of
    the Gospel of St. Matthew.
MS. C (MS. University Library, Cambridge, Dd. XII.39). - The latter part
    of the fourteenth century. - The vocabulary is Northern in charac-
    ter. - The Acts.

3.5. The Epistles (NPE)

The Northern Pauline Epistles, ed. M.J. Powell, EETS E.S. 116 (1916).
MS. CCCC 32 (Corpus Christi College, Cambridge, No. 32). - Ca. 1400-
    1425 (Severs II, p. 546). - The dialect is mainly that of
    the North East Midlands in the late fourteenth century
    (NPE, pp. xci-xcii). - About 58,000 words.

4. Middle English Non-Bible Texts

4.1. Higden's Polychronicon

Polychronicon Ranulphi Higden, with English translation of John Trevisa
and of an unknown writer of the fifteenth century, ed. Babington and
Lumby, Rerum Britannicarum Medii Aevi Scriptores, Vol. 1-8 (1865-1882).
Higd.Trev. (Trevisa's translation, MS. H 1). - Only a few years younger
    than the original translation which was finished in 1387
    (Vol. 1, pp. 57-58). - About 320,000 words.
Higd.Harl. (MS. Harley 2261).   -   The translation of an unknown
    writer of the fifteenth century. - About 291,000 words.

Die Sprache des 'Polychronicon' John Trevisa's in der Hs. Cotton Tiberius D.7, ed. B. Pfeffer, Düren 1912. The text corresponds to the text
in Vol. 7, pp. 245-421 in Babington and Lumby's edition (see above).
Higd.Cott. (MS. Cotton Tiberius D 7). - Ca 1400 (Kjellmer, 1973, p.177).
    -    "Sie ist das letzte wichtige Werk in südwestlicher Mund-
    art." (Pfeffer, p. 111). - About 17,000 words.

4.2. The Destruction of Troy (Destr. Troy)

The "Gest Hystoriale" of the Destruction of Troy, "unique MS. in the
Hunterian Museum, University Glasgow", ed. G.A. Panton and D. Donaldson,
EETS O.S. 39 (1869), 56 (1874). Alliterative verse. - Ca. 1450. - North
West Midland dialect (Kjellmer, 1971, p. 120). - About 112,000 words
(14,000 lines). - Latin text: Guido de Columnis, Historia Destructionis
Troiae, ed. N.E. Griffin, Cambridge, 1936.

4.3. The Ancrene Riwle (Ancr.R.)

Ancrene Riwle, MS. Nero A. XIV, ed. Mabel Day, EETS 225 (1952). - 1225-
1249. - South West Midland dialect (Kjellmer, 1971, p. 118). - About
70,500 words. - Latin text ed. Charlotte d'Evelyn, EETS 216 (1944).

   The text has instances of Old English words which do not appear in
any of my later sources (cf. p. 20), i.e. wouh (OE wōh):injuria, hoker
(OE hocor):inrisio, and edwit (OE edwīt):exprobratio (Latin text, p.
32,21-22; English text, p. 47,28-29). It contains three French loan
words relevant to this investigation, i.e. schorn, schornung:derisus/
derisio, blasphemie:blasphemia, and scandle/schandle/schaundle:scandalum
(see p. 101).

4.4. Chaucer's Boethius

Chaucer's Translation of Boethius's "De Consolatione Philosophiae", EETS
E.S.5 (1968). - MS. British Museum A 10340,   supposed to be the oldest
extant MS. of the work.- The translation was made by Chaucer in the
early 1380's (Baugh, 1967, p. 255). - About 52,200 words.

4.5. Thomas Castleford's Chronicle (Castleford)

MS. Göttingen University Library Codex Hist. 740, ed. Frank Behre, Göte-
borgs Högskolas Årsskrift 46 (1940): 2, Göteborg, 1940. - End of fourteenth or beginning of fifteenth century. - The dialect is Northern
(Scottish). - The dialect of the original Northern, South-West Yorkshire
(Behre, pp. VIII-IX). - About 173,000 words (27,465 lines).

4.6. The Life of Saint Katherine (St. Kath.)

MS. Royal 17 A 27, ed. E. Einenkel, EETS 80 (1884).- South West Midland
dialect. - Ca. 1225 (Kjellmer, 1971, p. 126). - Alliterative verse. -
About 10,800 words (2,506 lines).

   The text contains only three instances relevant to this investigation,
viz. hokeres:blasphemias (one instance), and woh:injuria (two instances).
Cf. above, No. 4.3.

APPENDIX B. LISTS

List OE 1. Distribution of Old English Material over Latin Words

	bismer 1a	1b	1c	swic 2a	2b	hosp 3a	3b	costnunȝ 4	canc 5a	5b	scamu 6a	6b	6c	hleahter 7a	7c	tǣl 8a	8b	glīu 9a	9b	gānung 10	unhlīsa 11	edwīt 12a	12c	fraced 13a	13b	13c
1 inlusio	1	30	–	1	3	1	–	1	–	–	1	–	–	7	–	2	3	–	–	–	–	1	–	1	–	–
2 inrisio	–	3	–	–	–	–	–	–	–	–	–	–	–	–	–	–	–	–	–	–	–	–	–	–	–	–
3 ludibrium	4	2	–	–	–	–	–	–	1	–	–	–	–	–	–	–	–	–	–	–	–	–	–	–	–	–
4 derisus	–	10	–	–	–	–	–	–	–	2	–	–	–	–	1	–	–	–	–	–	–	–	–	–	–	–
5 gannatura	5	–	–	–	–	–	–	–	–	3	–	–	–	–	–	–	–	–	–	–	–	–	–	–	–	–
6 infamia	3	1	–	–	–	–	–	–	–	–	–	–	–	–	–	–	–	–	–	–	5	–	–	–	–	–
7 blasphemia	2	2	8	–	–	–	–	–	–	–	–	–	–	–	–	–	–	–	–	–	–	–	–	–	–	–
8 dedecus	4	–	–	–	–	–	–	–	–	–	–	–	–	–	–	2	2	–	–	–	–	–	–	2	2	–
9 subsannatio	2	–	–	–	–	–	–	–	–	–	–	–	–	2	–	2	–	–	–	–	–	–	–	–	2	–
10 contumelia	6	2	–	–	–	2	1	–	–	–	5	–	–	–	–	2	2	1	2	1	–	2	–	–	–	–
11 ignominia	2	1	–	–	–	–	–	–	–	–	–	1	–	–	–	–	1	–	–	–	–	–	–	–	–	1
12 calumnia	4	2	–	–	–	11	–	–	–	–	3	–	–	–	–	–	–	–	–	–	–	–	–	–	–	–
13 turpitudo	3	–	–	–	–	–	–	–	–	–	2	–	–	–	–	–	–	–	–	–	–	–	–	–	–	–
14 injuria	3	–	–	–	–	3	–	–	–	–	–	–	–	–	–	1	–	–	–	–	–	3	3	–	–	–
15 opprobrium	2	4	–	–	–	92	–	–	–	–	1	6	1	–	–	–	–	–	–	–	–	92	–	–	–	–
16 confusio	2	–	2	–	–	1	–	–	–	–	26	–	–	–	–	–	–	–	–	–	–	–	–	–	–	–
TOTAL	43	57	10	1	3	111	1	1	1	5	38	7	1	9	1	9	8	1	2	1	5	98	3	3	4	1

List OE 1(2)

	14 yfel			15 gylt		16 dysines	17 hyrwing	18 woffung	19 wiþersacung	20 unwlite		21 ungerisne (-nu)		22 scand			23 aepsenys	24 unweordscipe	25 golfetung	26 hlacerung	27 teona			28 orwyrd	29 grama	30 oretla
	a	b	c	a	b					a	b	a	b	a	b	c					a	b	c			
1 inlusio	-	-	-	-	-	-	-	-	-	-	-	-	-	-	-	-	-	-	-	-	-	-	-	-	-	-
2 inrisio	-	-	-	-	-	-	-	-	-	-	-	-	-	-	-	-	-	-	-	-	-	-	-	-	-	-
3 ludibrium	-	-	-	-	-	-	-	-	-	-	-	-	-	-	-	-	-	-	-	-	-	-	-	-	-	-
4 derisus	-	-	-	-	-	-	-	-	-	-	-	-	-	-	-	-	-	-	-	-	-	-	-	-	-	-
5 gannatura	-	-	-	-	-	-	-	-	-	-	-	-	-	-	-	-	-	-	-	-	-	-	-	-	-	-
6 infamia	-	-	-	-	-	-	-	-	-	-	-	-	-	-	-	-	-	-	-	-	-	-	-	-	-	-
7 blasphemia	-	1	21	-	2	2	2	2	1	3	2	2	1	1	-	-	1	1	1	1	-	-	-	-	-	-
8 dedecus	-	-	-	-	-	-	-	-	-	-	-	-	-	-	-	-	-	-	-	-	-	-	-	-	-	-
9 subsannatio	-	-	-	-	-	-	-	-	-	-	-	-	-	-	-	-	-	-	-	-	-	-	-	-	-	-
10 contumelia	1	-	-	-	-	-	-	-	-	-	-	1	-	6	-	-	-	-	-	-	25	-	1	3	-	-
11 ignominia	-	-	-	1	-	-	-	-	-	-	-	-	-	1	-	1	-	-	-	-	3	-	-	-	1	1
12 calumnia	-	-	-	-	-	-	-	-	-	-	-	-	-	-	14	-	2	1	-	-	10	3	-	2	2	-
13 turpitudo	2	-	-	-	-	-	-	-	-	-	-	-	-	2	-	-	-	-	-	-	38	-	5	-	-	-
14 injuria	2	-	-	-	-	-	-	-	-	-	-	-	-	-	-	-	-	-	-	-	-	-	-	-	-	-
15 opprobrium	-	-	-	-	-	-	-	-	-	-	-	-	-	-	-	-	-	-	-	-	-	-	-	-	-	-
16 confusio	-	-	-	-	-	-	-	-	-	-	-	-	-	4	35	-	-	-	-	-	-	-	-	-	-	-
TOTAL	5	1	21	1	2	2	2	2	1	3	2	3	1	14	49	1	3	2	1	1	76	3	6	5	3	1

List OE 1(3)

	unȝewiss	netenes	firenlust	unwitende	hearm		līcettan		lēas	hōltihte	yrmđu	fȳlþ	hǣman	wīte		lǣđo	demm	tȳnan	unriht	ābylgđ	baeligniso ?	**earfođe**	**trega**
	31	32	33	34	35		36		37	38	39	40	41	42		43	44	45	46	47	48	49	50
					a	c	a	b				b		a	b								
1 inlusio																							
2 inrisio																							
3 ludibrium																							
4 derisus																							
5 gannatura																							
6 infamia																							
7 blasphemia																							
8 dedecus																							
9 subsannatio																							
10 contumelia																							
11 ignominia	3	2	1	1																			
12 calumnia	-	-	-	-	2	5	1	2	3	2	1												
13 turpitudo	-	-	-	-	-	-	-	-	-	-	-	6	2										
14 **injuria**	-	-	-	-	-	-	-	-	-	-	-	-	-	1	4	3	2	2	2	1	1	1	1
15 opprobrium																							
16 confusio																							
TOTAL	3	2	1	1	2	5	1	2	3	2	1	6	2	1	4	3	2	2	2	1	1	1	1

List OE 1(4)

		51 unār	52 unēðnys	53 wraecsið	54 wraeððo	55 aeswicnes	56 gedroefnis	57 gemeng (a)(b)	58 āblysung	59 anddetnes	60 duolma	61 forwandung	62 wilnung	63 gewrixle	Most frequent translation	Number of instances of most frequent translation	bismer-words (tokens)	Percentage of occurrences of Latin words translated by bismer-words	Non-bismer-words (tokens)	Non-bismer-words (types)[1]	TOTAL
1	inlusio														bismer-words	31	31	(84%)	6	4	37
2	inrisio														bismer-words	3	3	(75%)	1	1	4
3	ludibrium														bismer-words	6	6	(67%)	3	2	9
4	derisus														bismer-words	10	10	(56%)	8	2	18
5	gannatura														bismer-words	5	5	(36%)	9	5	14
6	infamia														bismer-words	4	4	(36%)	7	3	11
7	blasphemia														unhlisa	22	12	(25%)	35	8	47
8	dedecus														ebolsung	4	4	(24%)	13	8	17
9	subsannatio														bismer-words	10	10	(15%)	54	15	64
10	contumelia														bismer-words/leahter/tal[2]	2	2	(22%)	7	5	9
11	ignominia														teona	10	3	(15%)	17	10	20
12	calumnia														bismer-words/teona/orwyrd[3]	3	6	(13%)	44	12	50
13	turpitudo					1									hosp	14	3	(10%)	28	6	31
14	injuria			1											scandlicnes	38	3	(4%)	80	23	83
15	opprobrium					1									hosp/edwit[4]	92	6	(3%)	193	7	199
16	confusio						21	3	6	1	1	1	1	1	gescendnes	35	2	(2%)	110	16	112
TOTAL		1	1	1	1	1	21	3	6	1	1	1	1	1			110	(15%)	615		725

[1] Each sub-category of List OE 1 has been counted as a type.

[2] Bismer-words, leahter, and tal are represented by 2 instances each.

[3] Bismer-words, teona, and orwyrd are represented by 3 instances each.

[4] Hosp and edwit are represented by 92 instances each.

List OE 2. Recorded Variants of Old English Head-Words

1 a bismer, bismor, bysmor, bysmur
  b bismerung, bismrung, gebismerung (gebismuᴣc);
     bismernis, bismernes, bysmyrnys, besmyrnes;
     bismrian, bysmrian (verb); bismerlecre daed
  c bismerspraec, -spaec, -speech, -spraech;
     woroldbismer, worldebismer/-uld-

2 a swic
  b swicung; big swic, biᴣ-swic

3 a hosp
  b hisping

4 costnunᴣ

5 a canc
  b gecanc, ᴣecanc; cancettan

6 a scamu, sceamu, scomu, sceomu (sceofmu)
  b scamung, sceamung; sceamian (verb)
  c hleorsceamu

7 a hleahter, leahter, hlehter
  c taelhlehter

8 a tael, tal
  b taelung; telnis, tellnis; taelice word, talliche word

9 a gliu
  b gliwung, ᴣliwunᴣ, gelivung

10 ganung

11 unhlisa

12 a edwit (edwid, aedwit)
  c edwitstaef; edwitspraec

13 a fraced, fraceþ, fraeced, fracebu
  b fracodne (-nes ?); fracodlic , fracudlic (word)
  c fracodword (-wyrd)

14 a yfel (noun), yfele word
  b eofolsan (verb)
  c ebolsung, -song, ebalsung, efolsung, -song, efulsung, efalsung,
     hefalsung, eofulsong, -sung, eofolsong; yfelsacunᴣ

15 a gylt
  b gyltlice spraec, gyltlice spaec

16 dysines , desynys (= dysignes)

17 hyrwing (hyrwincg, hyrwincᴣ)

18 woffung

19 wiþersacung

20 a unwlite
  b unwlitegian (verb)

List OE 2(2)

21 a   ungerisne, unȝerisne (HM: = -nu)
  b   unirisnys (= unge-)

22 a   scand, sceand, scond
  b   scandlicnes, scondlicnes, sceondlicnes; ȝescendd, ȝescentd; ȝescendnes, -nys, -nis, ȝescaendnys, ȝescindnes; forescending; āscyndnes; scyndan (verb)
  c   scondehlewung

23   aepsenys, aefesne (App. C, p. 187: aepsen?/-nes? or a̅ewiscnes?)

24 b   unweordscipe; anweardnys

25   golfetung (= gaffetung: see HM)

26   hlacerung

27 a   te̅o̅na, ti̅ona, te̅ana
  b   onte̅ona, onti̅ona, onti̅o̅nae (on te̅o̅na ?);
  c   teonword; teancuide; teonraeden, -re̅den; te̅onful (þing)

28   orwyrd, orwurd

29   grama

30   o̅retla

31   ungewiss, unȝewiss

32   netenes (= nytennes 'ignorance, ignominy': see HM)

33   firenlust

34   unwitende

35 a   hearm
  c   hearmcwide, -cwidolnes; hearmspra̅ec

36 a   li̅cettan (li̅cettende)
  b   li̅cettung, -unȝ

37   le̅as

38   ho̅ltihte

39   yrmdu

40 b   fy̅lþ; fu̅lnes, fo̅lnes

41   ha̅eman (verb)

42 a   wi̅te
  b   unricht wi̅tnung; wi̅tnan, -ian (verb)

43   lae̅do, lae̅ddo

44   demm

45   ty̅nan (verb)

46   unriht

47   a̅bylgd

48   baeligniso (bealu- ?)

49   earfode

50   trega

List OE 2(3)

51   unār

52   uneðnys

53   wraecsīð

54   wrāeððo

55   āeswicnes

56   gedrōefnis, gedrēfnes; gedrōefednis, -nes, gedrōfednes,
      gedrēfednes, ʒedrēfednys

57 a gemeng, ʒemanʒ
   b gemengung, -iung, gimaengiung; gemengnes, gemengednys

58   āblysunʒ

59   anddetnes

60   duolma

61   forwandung

62   wilnung

63   gewrixle

List OE 3. Distribution of Old English Material over Sense Groups

The number preceding each word refers to its number in Lists OE 1 and OE 2.

		A								B			
	I	II	III							I	II	III	TOTAL
			1a	1b	1c	2	3a	3b	3c				
12 edwit	-	-	-	-	-	-	53	26	21	1	-	-	101
1 bismer	29	12	16	2	2	6	17	3	1	7	2	2	99
3 hosp	1	-	1	-	-	4	49	22	20	1	-	-	98
27 teona	-	-	-	-	-	2	70	3	-	-	-	3	78
22 scand	-	-	-	-	-	-	8	-	-	14	15	24	61
6 scomu	-	-	-	1	-	3	5	-	-	8	2	27	46
14 yfel	-	22	-	-	-	-	3	-	-	-	-	2	27
56 gedroefnis	-	-	-	-	-	-	-	-	-	14	1	6	21
8 tal/tael	-	4	-	-	2	4	1	3	-	-	-	1	15
7 hlehter	-	-	8	1	-	-	-	-	-	-	-	-	9
13 fraced	-	-	-	-	-	-	5	-	-	-	-	2	7
28 orwyrd	-	-	-	-	-	-	2	-	-	-	-	3	5
25 hearm	-	-	-	-	-	5	-	-	-	-	-	-	5
42 wite	-	-	-	-	-	-	5	-	-	-	-	-	5
2 swic	4	-	-	-	-	-	-	-	-	-	-	-	4
57 gemeng	-	-	-	-	-	-	-	-	-	-	4	-	4
15 gylt	-	2	-	-	-	-	-	-	-	-	-	1	3
29 grama	-	-	-	-	-	-	3	-	-	-	-	-	3
31 unʒewiss	-	-	-	-	-	-	-	-	-	-	-	3	3
36 licettung	-	-	-	-	-	3	-	-	-	-	-	-	3
37 leas	-	-	-	-	-	3	-	-	-	-	-	-	3
40 fylþ	-	-	-	-	-	-	-	-	-	-	3	-	3
43 laedo	-	2	-	-	-	-	1	-	-	-	-	-	3
16 dysines	-	2	-	-	-	-	-	-	-	-	-	-	2
17 hyrwincg	-	2	-	-	-	-	-	-	-	-	-	-	2
18 woffung	-	2	-	-	-	-	-	-	-	-	-	-	2
20 unwlitegian	-	-	-	-	-	-	-	-	-	-	2	-	2
41 haeman	-	-	-	-	-	-	-	-	-	-	2	-	2
44 demm	-	-	-	-	-	-	2	-	-	-	-	-	2
45 tynan	-	-	-	-	-	-	2	-	-	-	-	-	2
24 anweardnys	-	-	-	-	-	-	1	-	-	-	-	1	2
4 costnung	1	-	-	-	-	-	-	-	-	-	-	1	2
19 wibersacung	-	1	-	-	-	-	-	-	-	-	-	-	1
21 ungerisne	-	-	-	-	-	-	1	-	-	-	-	-	1
23 aepsenys	-	-	-	-	-	-	-	-	-	-	-	1	1
25 golfetung	-	-	-	-	1	-	-	-	-	-	-	-	1
26 hlacerung	-	-	-	1	-	-	-	-	-	-	-	-	1
30 oretla	-	-	-	-	-	-	1	-	-	-	-	-	1
33 firenlust	-	-	-	-	-	-	-	-	-	-	1	-	1
34 unwitende	-	-	-	-	-	-	-	-	-	-	-	1	1
39 yrmdu	-	-	-	-	-	1	-	-	-	-	-	-	1
46 unriht	-	-	-	-	-	-	1	-	-	-	-	-	1
47 abylgd	-	-	-	-	-	-	1	-	-	-	-	-	1

List OE 3(2)

			A								B			TOTAL
	I	II				III					I	II	III	
			1a	1b	1c	2	3a	3b	3c					
	35	49	25	5	5	31	232	57	42		45	32	77	635
48 baeligniso	–	–	–	–	–	–	1	–	–		–	–	–	1
49 earfode	–	–	–	–	–	–	1	–	–		–	–	–	1
50 trega	–	–	–	–	–	–	1	–	–		–	–	–	1
51 unar	–	–	–	–	–	–	–	1	–		–	–	–	1
52 unednys	–	–	–	–	–	–	1	–	–		–	–	–	1
53 wraecsid	–	–	–	–	–	–	1	–	–		–	–	–	1
54 wraeddo	–	–	–	–	–	–	–	1	–		–	–	–	1
55 aeswicnes	–	–	–	–	–	–	1	–	–		–	–	–	1
58 ablysung	–	–	–	–	–	–	–	–	–		–	–	1	1
59 anddetnes	–	–	–	–	–	–	–	–	–		–	–	1	1
61 forwandung	–	–	–	–	–	–	–	–	–		1	–	–	1
62 wilnung	–	–	–	–	–	–	–	–	–		–	1	–	1
TOTAL	35	49	25	5	5	31	238	59	42		46	33	79	647

List OE 4. Distribution of Old English Material over Sense Groups and Centuries

The number in brackets after each word refers to its number in Lists OE 1 and OE 2.

Entire Corpus	A									B			TOTAL
	I	II	III							I	II	III	
			1a	1b	1c	2	3a	3b	3c				
800- 899	1	4	5	-	-	1	31	7	5	7	6	11	78
900- 999	7	20	6	-	-	10	53	18	8	16	6	18	162
1000-1099	25	15	11	3	5	17	109	22	19	15	19	36	296
1100-1199	1	10	3	2	-	3	35	13	9	8	2	12	98
1200-1299	1	-	-	-	-	-	9	-	1	-	-	2	13
TOTAL	35	49	25	5	5	31	237	60	42	46	33	79	647

bismer-words (1)	A									B			TOTAL
	I	II	III							I	II	III	
			1a	1b	1c	2	3a	3b	3c				
800- 899	1	-	5	-	-	-	9	2	-	-	2	2	21
900- 999	7	-	3	-	-	-	5	-	-	7	-	-	22
1000-1099	19	6	8	1	2	6	3	1	1	-	-	-	47
1100-1199	1	6	-	1	-	-	-	-	-	-	-	-	8
1200-1299	1	-	-	-	-	-	-	-	-	-	-	-	1
TOTAL	29	12	16	2	2	6	17	3	1	7	2	2	99

edwīt (12)	A									B			TOTAL
	I	II	III							I	II	III	
			1a	1b	1c	2	3a	3b	3c				
800- 899	-	-	-	-	-	-	10	5	5	-	-	-	20
900- 999	-	-	-	-	-	-	10	7	4	1	-	-	22
1000-1099	-	-	-	-	-	-	23	9	9	-	-	-	41
1100-1199	-	-	-	-	-	-	7	5	2	-	-	-	14
1200-1299	-	-	-	-	-	-	3	-	1	-	-	-	4
TOTAL	-	-	-	-	-	-	53	26	21	1	-	-	101

hosp (3)	A									B			TOTAL
	I	II	III							I	II	III	
			1a	1b	1c	2	3a	3b	3c				
800- 899	-	-	-	-	-	-	-	-	-	-	-	-	-
900- 999	-	-	-	-	-	1	11	7	4	-	-	-	23
1000-1099	1	-	1	-	-	2	24	7	9	1	-	-	45
1100-1199	-	-	-	-	-	1	12	8	7	-	-	-	28
1200-1299	-	-	-	-	-	-	2	-	-	-	-	-	2
TOTAL	1	-	1	-	-	4	49	22	20	-	-	-	98

List OE 4(2)

teona (27)	A									B			TOTAL
	I	II	III							I	II	III	
			1a	1b	1c	2	3a	3b	3c				
800- 899	-	-	-	-	-	-	2	-	-	-	-	-	2
900- 999	-	-	-	-	-	-	6	-	-	-	-	-	6
1000-1099	-	-	-	-	-	2	47	3	-	-	-	3	55
1100-1199	-	-	-	-	-	-	12	-	-	-	-	-	12
1200-1299	-	-	-	-	-	-	3	-	-	-	-	-	3
TOTAL	-	-	-	-	-	2	70	3	-	-	-	3	78

scand (22)	A									B			TOTAL
	I	II	III							I	II	III	
			1a	1b	1c	2	3a	3b	3c				
800- 899	-	-	-	-	-	-	8	-	-	2	2	1	13
900- 999	-	-	-	-	-	-	-	-	-	1	4	6	11
1000-1099	-	-	-	-	-	-	-	-	-	6	9	11	26
1100-1199	-	-	-	-	-	-	-	-	-	5	-	5	10
1200-1299	-	-	-	-	-	-	-	-	-	-	-	1	1
TOTAL	-	-	-	-	-	-	8	-	-	14	15	24	61

scomu (6)	A									B			TOTAL
	I	II	III							I	II	III	
			1a	1b	1c	2	3a	3b	3c				
800- 899	-	-	-	-	-	-	-	-	-	2	-	4	6
900- 999	-	-	-	-	-	3	5	-	-	2	-	6	16
1000-1099	-	-	-	-	-	-	-	-	-	3	2	15	20
1100-1199	-	-	-	1	-	-	-	-	-	1	-	1	3
1200-1299	-	-	-	-	-	-	-	-	-	-	-	1	1
TOTAL	-	-	-	1	-	3	5	-	-	8	2	27	46

yfel (14)	A									B			TOTAL
	I	II	III							I	II	III	
			1a	1b	1c	2	3a	3b	3c				
800- 899	-	-	-	-	-	-	-	-	-	-	-	-	-
900- 999	-	20	-	-	-	-	2	-	-	-	-	1	23
1000-1099	-	2	-	-	-	-	1	-	-	-	-	-	3
1100-1199	-	-	-	-	-	-	-	-	-	-	-	1	1
TOTAL	-	22[1]	-	-	-	-	3	-	-	-	-	2	27

[1] All these instances in A II:Men-God have _ebolsung_/etc. (14 c, see List OE 2:1).

List OE 4(3)

g̅edroe fnis (56)	I	II	A							B I	II	III	TOTAL
			III 1a	1b	1c	2	3a	3b	3c				
800- 899	-	-	-	-	-	-	-	-	-	3	-	1	4
900- 999	-	-	-	-	-	-	-	-	-	5	-	1	6
1000-1099	-	-	-	-	-	-	-	-	-	5	1	3	9
1100-1199	-	-	-	-	-	-	-	-	-	1	-	1	2
TOTAL	-	-	-	-	-	-	-	-	-	14	1	6	21

t̄al (8)	I	II	1a	1b	1c	2	3a	3b	3c	I	II	III	TOTAL
800- 899	-	2	-	-	-	-	-	-	-	-	-	-	2
900- 999	-	-	-	-	-	2	-	2	-	-	-	1	5
1000-1099	-	1	-	-	2	1	-	1	-	-	-	-	5
1100-1199	-	1	-	-	-	1	-	-	-	-	-	-	2
1200-1299	-	-	-	-	-	-	1	-	-	-	-	-	1
TOTAL	-	4	-	-	2	4	1	3	-	-	-	1	15

hlehter (7)	I	II	III 1a	1b	1c	2	3a	3b	3c	I	II	III	TOTAL
800- 899													
900- 999	-	-	3	-	-	-	-	-	-				3
1000-1099	-	-	2	1	-	-	-	-	-				3
1100-1199	-	-	3	-	-	-	-	-	-				3
TOTAL	-	-	8	1	-	-	-	-	-				9

fraced (13)	I	II	III 1a	1b	1c	2	3a	3b	3c	I	II	III	TOTAL
800- 899	-	-	-	-	-	-	-	-	-	-	-	2	2
900- 999	-	-	-	-	-	-	1	-	-	-	-	-	1
1000-1099	-	-	-	-	-	-	3	-	-	-	-	-	3
1100-1199	-	-	-	-	-	-	1	-	-	-	-	-	1
TOTAL	-	-	-	-	-	-	5	-	-	-	-	2	7

List OE 5. Distribution of Old English Material over Dialects and Centuries

The number in brackets after each word refers to its number in
Lists OE 1 and OE 2.

Entire Corpus	Kentish	Anglian	West Saxon	TOTAL
800- 899	3	37	45	85
900- 999	-	99	80	179
1000-1099	-	98	251	349
1100-1199	-	26	73	99
1200-1299	-	-	13	13
TOTAL	3	260	462	725

bismer-words (1)	Anglian	West Saxon	TOTAL
800- 899 (a)bismer	-	15	15
(b)bismerung	3	-	3
bismernis	1	-	1
(c)woroldbismer	-	2	2
900- 999 (a)bismer	-	13	13
(b)bismerung	8	1^1	9
bismernes	1	-	1
bismerlecre dǣd	-	1	1
1000-1099 (a)bismer	-	13	13
(b)bismerung	11	20	31
gebismerung	-	2	2
bysmyrnys/besmyrnes	2	-	2
bismrian	1	3	4
(c)bismerspraec	-	4	4
1100-1199 (a)bismer	-	2	2
(b)bismerung	-	2	2
(c)bismerspraec	-	4	4
1200-1299 (b)gebismerung	-	1	1
TOTAL	27	83	110

[1]This instance of bismerung is from the Regius Psalter (D) dated
ca. 950.

List OE 5(2)

edwīt (12)		Anglian	West Saxon	TOTAL
800- 899	(a) edwīt	18	2	20
900- 999	(a) edwīt	21	1	22
1000-1099	(a) edwīt	31	7	38
	(c) edwītstaef/-spraēc	3	-	3
1100-1199	(a) edwīt	12	2	14
1200-1299	(a) edwīt	-	4	4
TOTAL		85	16	101

hosp (3)		Anglian	West Saxon	TOTAL
800- 899	(a)hosp	-	-	-
900- 999	(a)hosp	4	19	23
	(b)hisping	-	1	1
1000-1099	(a)hosp	8	50	58
1100-1199	(a)hosp	3	25	28
1200-1299	(a)hosp	-	2	2
TOTAL		15	97	112

tēona (27)		Anglian	West Saxon	TOTAL
800- 899	(a)tēona	2	-	2
900- 999	(a)tēona	3	2	5
	(b)ontēona (on tēona ?)	-	1	1
	(c)teancuide	1	-	1
1000-1099	(a)tēona	9	49	58
	(b)ontēona (on tēona ?)	-	1	1
	(c)teonraeden	-	2	2
	teonword	1	-	1
1100-1199	(a)tēona	-	10	10
	(b)ontēona (on tēona ?)	-	2	2
1200-1299	(a)tēona	-	1	1
	(b)tēonfull (þing)	-	1	1
	(c)teonreden	-	1	1
TOTAL		16	70	86

List OE 5(3)

scand (22)		Anglian	West Saxon	TOTAL
800- 899	(a)scand/scond	-	10	10
	(b)scondlicnes/sceond-	-	2	2
	gescendd	1	-	1
900- 999	(a)scond	-	1	1
	(b)scondlicnes/sceond-	4	-	4
	gescyndnis/-nes	-	4	4
	forescending	2	-	2
	gescentd	1	-	1
	(c)scondehlewung	-	1	1
1000-1099	(a)scand/sceand	1	2	3
	(b)gescendnes/-nys/-scind-	4	12	16
	scondlicnes/scand-	-	8	8
1100-1199	(b)gescindnes/-sciend-	6	3	9
	scyndan (verb)	-	1	1
1200-1299	(b)ascyndnes	-	1	1
TOTAL		19	45	64

scomu (6)		Anglian	West Saxon	TOTAL
800- 899	(a)scomu/scamu	2	4	6
900- 999	(a)scomu/sceomu/scamu	13	1	14
	(b)scamung/sceamung	-	2	2
1000-1099	(a)scomu/-eo-/scamu/-ea-	7	9	16
	(b)scamung/sceamung	-	2	2
	sceamian (verb	1	-	1
	(c)hleorsceamu	1	-	1
1100-1199	(a)sceamu	-	1	1
	(b)sceamung/scaemung	-	2	2
1200-1299	(a)sceamu	-	1	1
TOTAL		24	22	46

yfel (14)		Anglian	West Saxon	TOTAL
800- 899		-	-	-
900- 999	(a)yfel	-	3	3
	(b)ebolsung/efulsung/etc.	19	-	19
	efolsian	1	-	1
1000-1099	(a)yfele word	-	1	1
	(b)yfelsacung	1	1	2
1100-1199	(a)yfel	-	1	1
TOTAL		21	6	27

List OE 5(4)

gedroefnis (56)		Anglian	West Saxon	TOTAL
800- 899	gedroefnis/-ed-	3	-	3
900- 999	gedroefednis,gedroefednes/-ō-	3	-	3
	gedrefnes,gedrefednis/-nes	2	2	4
1000-1099	gedrēfydnys/-ednes/-ednys	6	3	9
1100-1199	gedrēfednes/-nys	-	2	2
TOTAL		14	7	21

tāl (8)		Anglian	West Saxon	TOTAL
800- 899	(a) tael	-	2	2
900- 999	(b) telnis/tellnis	5	-	5
1000-1099	(a) tāl	-	6	6
	(b) tallice word	-	1	1
1100-1199	(a) tāl	-	1	1
	(b) talliche word	-	1	1
1200-1299	(b) taelung	-	1	1
TOTAL		5	12	17

hlehter (7)		Anglian	West Saxon	TOTAL
800- 899		-	-	-
900- 999	(a)hleahter	-	3	3
1000-1099	(a)leahter	2	-	2
	hleahter	-	1	1
	(c)taelhlehter	-	1	1
1100-1199	(a)hleahter	-	1	1
	leahter/hlehter	2	-	2
TOTAL		4	6	10

fraced (13)		Anglian	West Saxon	TOTAL
800- 899	(b)fracodlic/fracudlic	-	2	2
900- 999	(a)fraeced/fracepu	2	-	2
1000-1099	(a)fracep	1	-	1
	(b)fracodlic wyrd (word)	1	-	1
	(c)fracodword	1	-	1
1100-1199	(b)fracodne	-	1	1
TOTAL		5	3	8

List OE 5(5)

gemeng (57)		Anglian	West Saxon	TOTAL
800- 899 (b)	gimengiung/gemengiung	3	-	3
900- 999 (a)	ʒemanʒ	-	1	1
(b)	gemengung	1	-	1
	gemengnes	-	1	1
1000-1099 (a)	ʒemanʒ	-	1	1
(b)	gemengednys	-	1	1
1100-1199 (a)	gemeng	-	1	1
TOTAL		4	5	9

hearm (25)		Anglian	West Saxon	TOTAL
800- 899 (a)	hearm	1	-	1
900- 999 (c)	hearmcwide	2	-	2
	hearmspraec	-	1	1
1000-1099 (a)	hearm	-	1	1
(c)	hearmcwide	1	-	1
1100-1199 (c)	hearmcwidolnes	1	-	1
TOTAL		5	2	7

fȳlþ (40)		Kentish	Anglian	West Saxon	TOTAL
800- 899 (b)	fōlnes	1	-	-	1
1000-1099 (b)	fȳlþ	-	-	3	3
	fulnes,fūlnys	-	-	2	2
TOTAL		1	-	5	6

orwyrᵭ (28)		Anglian	West Saxon	TOTAL
800- 899	orwyrᵭ	1		1
900- 999	orwyrᵭ	1		1
1000-1099	orwyrᵭ, orwurᵭ	3		3
TOTAL		5		5

wīte (42)		Anglian	West Saxon	TOTAL
900- 999 (a)	wīte		1	1
(b)	wītnung; wītnan/wītnian		4	4
TOTAL			5	5

unwlite (20)		Anglian	West Saxon	TOTAL
800- 899 (b)	unwlitegian (verb)		2	2
900- 999 (a)	unwlite		3	3
TOTAL			5	5

List OE 5(6)

In List OE 5(6-7) the instances of those words which are represented
by less than five instances each in my material are placed together
under the centuries from which their respective sources derive.

			Kentish	Anglian	West Saxon	TOTAL
800- 899	(9a)	glīu	-	1	-	1
	(32)	netenes (= nytennes)	2	-	-	2
	(43)	laeddo		-	2	2
	(44)	demm		-	2	2
	(60)	duolma		1	-	1
900- 999	(5b)	cancettan (verb)		-	1	1
	(10)	ganung		-	1	1
	(11)	unhlīsa		-	2	2
	(15)	gylt		-	1	1
	(31)	unȝewiss		-	1	1
	(36)	līcettung		1	-	1
	(37)	lēas		1	-	1
	(38)	hōltihte		-	1	1
	(43)	laeđo		1	-	1
	(46)	unriht		-	2	2
	(47)	ābylgd		-	1	1
	(48)	baeligniso (bealu- ?)		1	-	1
	(49)	earfođe		-	1	1
	(51)	unār		-	1	1
	(53)	wraecsīd		-	1	1
	(54)	wraeddo		1	-	1
1000-1099	(2a)	swic		-	1	1
	(2b)	big swic/biȝ-swic(be-)		-	2	2
		swicung		-	1	1
	(4)	costnung		-	1	1
	(5a)	canc		-	1	1
	(5b)	ȝecanc		-	4	4
	(9b)	glīwung/gelīvung		-	2	2
	(11)	unhlīsa		-	2	2
	(15)	gyltlice spraec		-	1	1
	(16)	dysines		-	1	1
	(17)	hyrwincg		-	2	2
	(18)	woffung		-	1	1
	(19)	wiþersacung		-	1	1
	(21)	ungerisne (-nu)		-	2	2
		unirisnys (unge-)		-	1	1
	(23)	aepsenys		-	1	1
		aefesne (aepsen/-es ?)		-	2	2
	(25)	golfetung		-	1	1
	(26)	hlacerung		-	1	1
	(29)	grama		-	3	3
	(30)	ōretla		1	-	1
	(31)	ungewiss		-	1	1
	(33)	firenlust		-	1	1
	(36)	līcettan (verb)		-	1	1
		līcettunȝ		-	1	1

List OE 5(7)

			Kentish	Anglian	West Saxon	TOTAL
			2	8	52	62
1000-1099	(37)	lēas		–	2	2
	(38)	holtihte		–	1	1
	(39)	yrmþu		1	–	1
	(41)	haēman (verb)		–	2	2
	(45)	tȳnan (verb)		–	2	2
	(50)	trega		–	1	1
	(55)	aeswicnes		–	1	1
	(58)	ablysung		–	1	1
1100-1199	(11)	unhlīsa		–	1	1
	(15)	ʒyltlice spaec		–	1	1
	(16)	desynes		–	1	1
	(18)	woffung		–	1	1
	(21)	unʒerisne (-nu)		–	1	1
	(24)	unweordscipe		–	1	1
		anweardnys		–	1	1
	(31)	ungewiss		–	1	1
	(34)	unwītende		1	–	1
	(52)	unednys		–	1	1
	(59)	anddetnes		1	–	1
	(61)	forwandung		–	1	1
	(62)	wilnung		–	1	1
TOTAL			2	11	73	86

List ME 1. Distribution of Middle English Material over Latin Words

	1 scorn a	1 scorn b	2 illusion	3 desceit	4 bygile	5 hethyng	6 bismer	7 hoker	8 repref a	8 repref b	9 dispit a	9 dispit b	10 dispisyng	11 vilenye	12 rebuke	13 derision	14 yuel fame a	14 yuel fame b	15 evel loos	16 sclaundre	17 evel deed	18 trespas	19 blasfemye	20 schame	21 dishonour	22 schenschipe b	23 gram	24 cowardise	25 unworschippe	26 trowble
1 inlusio	2	–	6	3	2	–	2	–	–	–	–	–	–	–	–	1	–	–	–	–	–	1	–	–	–	–	–	–	–	–
2 inrisio	–	6	–	–	–	1	–	–	–	–	–	–	–	–	–	–	–	–	–	–	–	–	–	–	–	–	–	–	–	–
3 ludibrium	1	8	–	–	–	1	–	1	–	–	–	–	–	–	–	–	–	–	–	–	–	–	–	–	–	–	–	–	–	–
4 derisus	22	15	–	–	–	1	2	1	2	–	1	1	–	1	–	1	–	1	2	1	1	1	–	8	4	4	1	1	1	1
5 gannatura	–	–	–	–	–	–	–	–	–	–	–	–	–	–	–	–	–	–	–	–	–	–	–	–	–	–	–	–	–	–
6 infamia	–	–	–	–	–	–	–	–	–	–	–	–	–	–	–	–	–	–	–	–	–	–	–	–	–	–	–	–	–	–
7 blasphemia	–	–	–	–	–	1	–	–	–	–	3	–	–	1	–	–	–	1	2	1	1	1	88	–	–	–	1	1	1	1
8 dedecus	–	–	–	–	–	1	–	–	–	1	1	–	–	6	–	–	–	–	–	–	–	1	–	8	4	4	–	–	–	–
9 subsannatio	–	9	–	–	–	4	–	–	–	–	–	–	–	–	–	–	–	–	–	–	–	1	–	–	1	–	–	–	–	–
10 contumelia	1	–	–	–	–	–	–	–	4	3	21	–	18	1	1	–	–	–	–	5	–	–	–	6	–	97	–	–	–	–
11 ignominia	–	–	–	–	–	1	–	1	–	–	1	–	–	1	–	–	29	–	1	–	–	–	–	1	–	–	–	–	–	–
12 calumnia	–	–	–	–	–	–	–	–	–	–	–	1	–	–	–	–	–	–	–	–	–	–	–	–	1	–	–	–	–	–
13 turpitudo	–	–	–	–	–	–	–	–	–	–	–	–	–	1	–	–	–	–	–	–	–	–	–	1	1	1	1	2	–	–
14 injuria	–	–	–	–	–	4	–	–	–	–	1	–	–	–	–	–	–	–	–	–	–	1	–	–	1	–	1	–	–	–
15 opprobrium	–	–	–	–	–	–	–	–	128	–	–	1	–	–	–	–	–	–	–	–	–	–	–	21	–	115	1	–	–	–
16 confusio	–	–	–	–	–	–	–	–	–	–	–	–	–	1	–	–	–	–	–	–	–	–	–	–	–	52	–	–	–	–
TOTAL	26	40	6	3	2	7	3	2	134	3	26	2	21	10	1	1	33	1	3	6	1	2	88	37	5	268	3	3	1	1

List ME 1(2)

	27 a	27 b	28	29	30	31 a	31 b	32 a	32 b	33	34 a	34 b	35 a	35 b	36	37	38	39	40	41	42	43	44	45 a	45 b	46	47	48
	mouwing		snering	undernyming	wrong	strif		blame		turmenten	þet fule		iniury		missiggen	saye after pleasure	contek	destroyen	flytyng	dishese	chiding	outerage	sunne	filth/-hed		mescheef	seoruwe	unworþy
1 inlusio	–	–	–	–	–	–	–	–	–	–	–	–	–	–	–	–	–	–	–	–	–	–	–	–	–	–	–	–
2 inrisio	–	–	–	–	–	–	–	–	–	–	–	–	–	–	–	–	–	–	–	–	–	–	–	–	–	–	–	–
3 ludibrium	–	–	–	–	–	–	–	–	–	–	–	–	–	–	–	–	–	–	–	–	–	–	–	–	–	–	–	–
4 derisus	–	–	–	–	–	–	–	–	–	–	–	–	–	–	–	–	–	–	–	–	–	–	–	–	–	–	–	–
5 gannatura	–	–	–	–	–	–	–	–	–	–	–	–	–	–	–	–	–	–	–	–	–	–	–	–	–	–	–	–
6 infamia	–	–	–	–	–	–	–	–	–	–	–	–	–	–	–	–	–	–	–	–	–	–	–	–	–	–	–	–
7 blasphemia	–	–	–	–	–	–	–	–	–	–	–	–	–	–	–	–	–	–	–	–	–	–	–	–	–	–	–	–
8 dedecus	–	–	–	–	–	–	–	–	–	–	–	–	–	–	–	–	–	–	–	–	–	–	–	–	–	–	–	–
9 subsannatio	7	5	3	2	–	–	–	–	–	–	–	–	–	–	–	–	–	–	–	–	–	–	–	–	–	–	–	–
10 contumelia	–	–	–	2	19	13	1	–	9	4	1	2	–	1	1	1	1	1	1	1	1	1	2	1	–	1	1	1
11 ignominia	–	–	–	–	–	–	–	–	–	–	–	–	–	–	–	–	–	–	–	–	–	–	–	–	–	–	–	–
12 calumnia	–	–	–	–	–	–	–	2	1	–	2	–	–	–	–	–	–	–	–	–	–	–	3	–	–	–	–	–
13 turpitudo	–	–	–	–	–	–	–	–	–	–	–	–	–	–	–	–	–	–	–	–	–	–	–	48	57	–	–	–
14 **injuria**	–	–	–	–	–	–	–	–	–	–	–	–	18	–	–	–	–	–	–	–	–	–	–	–	–	–	–	–
15 opprobrium	–	–	–	–	124	–	–	–	–	–	–	–	–	–	1	–	–	–	–	–	–	–	–	–	–	1	–	–
16 confusio	–	–	–	–	–	–	–	–	–	–	–	–	–	–	–	–	–	–	–	–	–	–	–	–	–	–	–	–
TOTAL	7	5	3	4	143	13	1	2	10	4	3	2	18	1	2	1	1	1	1	1	1	1	5	49	57	2	1	1

List ME 1(3)

#		49a chalenge	49b	50 craving	51 eny thynge ...	52a harm	52b	53 woh/wouh	54 unright	55 greuans	56 hardlaike	57 damage	58 hurtys	59 tene	60 gilt	61 derf word	62 redur	63 mysse	64a obbrayd/-ing	64b	65a reproce/-ing	65b	66 opprobry	67 confusioun	68 bimased	69 scheding	70 spreding	TOTAL
1	inlusio																											21
2	inrisio																											3
3	ludibrium																											18
4	derisus																											38
5	gannatura																											-
6	infamia																											9
7	blasphemia																											90
8	dedecus																											28
9	subsannatio																											26
10	contumelia																											109
11	ignominia																											146
12	calumnia	75																										82
13	turpitudo																											113
14	injuria		2	1	1	10	1	9	6	3	2	1	1	1	1	1	1	1	1	18	9	6	2					189
15	opprobrium																							150				285
16	confusio																								2	2	1	230
	TOTAL	75	2	1	1	10	1	9	6	3	2	1	1	1	1	1	1	1	1	18	9	6	2	150	2	2	1	1387

List ME 1(4)

	Most frequent translation	Number of instances of most frequent translation	Middle English equivalents (types)[1]	Middle English equivalents (tokens)
1 inlusio	scornyng/illusion[2]	6	7	21
2 inrisio	scornyng	2	2	3
3 ludibrium	scornyng	8	9	18
4 derisus	scorn	22	3	38
5 gannatura	—	—	—	—
6 infamia	yuel fame	3	6	9
7 blasphemia	blasfemye	88	3	90
8 dedecus	shame	8	10	28
9 subsannatio	scornyng	9	5	26
10 contumelia	dispit	21	24	109
11 ignominia	shenship	97	12	146
12 calumnia	chalenge	75	6	82
13 turpitudo	filthhed	57	6	113
14 injuria	wrong	124	21	189
15 opprobrium	repref	128	11	285
16 confusio	confusioun	150	8	230
TOTAL				1387

[1] Each sub-category of List ME 1 has been counted as a type.

[2] Scornyng and illusion are represented by 6 instances each.

List ME 2. Recorded Variants of Middle English Head-Words

1 a scorn, schorn, scoorn, scorne, scoorne

   b scornyng, scornung; byskorn (by skorn ?); scornen (verb)

2   illusioun, illusion

3   desceit, deseit, deceyt

4   bygile, bigile

5   hethyng, heþing

6   bismer

7   hoker

8 a repref, reproof, repreef, reprof, repreue, reproue, reprofe, reprove, reproef, repreff

   b reprouyng, repreuyng

9 a dispit, dispite, spite

   b dispitousness; dispitous word

10   dispisyng, dispising, dispysing, dyspysyng, despisynge

11   vilenye, vylenye, vilenie, vilonye, velany

12   rebuke

13   derision

14 a yuel fame, ylle fame, fame (losen), fame (of filth)

   b diffamynge

15   evel loos; wicked los; lose (losen)

16   sclaundre, sclaundir, sclaundrith, schaundre (**sclaundre** ?)

17   evel deed

18   trespas

19   blasfemye, blasphemye, **blasfeme, blasfemy, blasphemie,** blasphemy

20   schame, shame, schome, scheome

21   dishonour, dyshonour, dyshoner; miserable honoure

22 b schenschipe, schenschip, shenshipe, shenship, shendship, senship, schendship, schendschip, shendshipe, schenschype, schenschyp, shenshype, shenshepe; schendnes; schendfulness; schendlac; schendfule word

23   gram, grem

24   schame of cowardise; (a signe of **a**) **cowarde,** (accounted **a**) **coward**

25   unworschippe

26   trowble

27 a mouwing, mouwyng, mowyng, mowynge

   b undermouwing, undirmouwing, undirmouwyng, undermouwyng

28   snering, sneryng, sneringe

List ME 2(2)

29   undernyming, undernymyng

30   wrong, wronge, wrang, wrange

31 a strif, strijf

   b striuyng word

32 a blame

   b blamyng, blamynge, blamenge

33   turmenten

34 a þet fule, fyle, foyle

   b defoul; defilen (verb)

35 a iniury, iniurie, iniurye

   b iniuryos word

36   missiggen, mysseien (verb)

37   saye after theire pleasure

38   contek

39   destroyen (verb)

40   flytyng

41   dishese

42   chiding

43   word of outerage

44   synne, sunne

45 a filth, filþ, fulþ, (fame of) filth, filþ (of synne)

   b filthhed, filthehed, filtheheed, fulþhed

46   mescheef, meschif

47   seoruwe

48   unworþy

49 a chalenge, chaleng, chalange, caleng, calenge

   b chalengyng, chalaynge

50   craving

51   eny thynge to be discussed afterwarde

52 a harm

   b harmen (verb)

53   woh, wouh

54   unright; unri3twisness; unri3tfulness; nat ry3t

55   greuans, greuaunce; greuen (verb)

56   hardlaike

List ME 2(3)

57   damage
58   hurtys
59   tene
60   gilt
61   derf word
62   redur
63   mysse
64 a obbrayd
   b upbraidyng, upbraiding, upbradeing
65 a reproce, repruse, repruce
   b reproceing, reproceyng, reprusyng, repruseyng
66   opprobry
67   **confusioun,** **confusion,** confucioun, confisioun
68   bimased (past part.)
69   schedyng
70   spreding

List ME 3. Distribution of Middle English Material over Sense Groups

The number preceding each word refers to its number in Lists ME 1 and ME 2.

	A									B			TOTAL
	I	II				III				I	II	III	
			1a	1b	1c	2	3a	3b	3c				
22 schenschipe	-	-	-	-	-	-	42	54	19	30	45	78	268
67 confusioun	-	-	-	-	-	-	-	-	-	20	9	114	143
30 wrong	-	3	-	-	-	-	138	2	-	-	-	-	143
8 repref	-	2	2	-	-	-	39	73	21	-	-	-	137
45 filth/-hed	-	-	-	-	-	-	-	-	-	-	104	2	106
19 blasfemye	-	76	-	-	-	-	7	3	2	-	-	-	88
49 **chalenge**	-	-	-	-	-	77	-	-	-	-	-	-	77
1 scorn/-yng	1	3	24	27	10	-	1	-	-	-	-	-	66
20 schame	-	-	-	-	-	-	1	-	-	10	5	21	37
14 yuel fame	-	-	-	-	-	-	-	-	-	2	13	19	34
9 dispit	-	5	1	-	-	-	16	5	-	1	-	-	28
10 dispisyng	-	1	1	-	-	-	14	4	-	1	-	-	21
35 iniury	-	-	-	-	-	-	19	-	-	-	-	-	19
64 obbrayd/-ing	-	-	-	-	-	-	7	4	8	-	-	-	19
65 reproce/-ing	-	-	-	-	-	-	8	1	6	-	-	-	15
31 strif	-	-	-	-	-	-	12	2	-	-	-	-	14
27 mouwing	-	-	3	3	6	-	-	-	-	-	-	-	12
32 blame/-ng	-	-	-	-	-	3	7	2	-	-	-	-	12
52 harm	-	-	-	-	-	-	11	-	-	-	-	-	11
11 vilenye	-	-	1	-	-	-	2	-	-	-	2	5	10
53 woh/wouh	-	-	-	-	-	-	8	1	-	-	-	-	9
5 hethyng	-	-	-	-	2	-	4	-	-	1	-	-	7
2 illusioun	2	-	4	-	-	-	-	-	-	-	-	-	6
16 sclaundre	-	-	-	-	-	-	-	-	-	-	2	4	6
54 unright	-	-	-	-	-	-	6	-	-	-	-	-	6
21 dishonour	-	-	-	-	-	-	1	-	-	3	-	1	5
34 þet fule	-	-	-	-	-	-	1	1	-	-	1	2	5
44 sunne	-	-	-	-	-	-	-	-	-	-	2	3	5
29 undernyming	-	-	1	-	1	-	2	-	-	-	-	-	4
33 turmenten	-	-	-	-	-	-	4	-	-	-	-	-	4
3 desceit	2	-	-	-	1	-	-	-	-	-	-	-	3
6 bismer	1	-	1	-	1	-	-	-	-	-	-	-	3
15 evel loos	-	-	-	-	-	-	-	-	-	-	1	2	3
23 gram/grem	-	-	-	-	-	-	2	-	-	1	-	-	3
24 cowardise	-	-	-	-	-	-	-	-	-	-	-	3	3
28 snering	-	-	1	-	2	-	-	-	-	-	-	-	3
55 greuans	-	-	-	-	-	-	3	-	-	-	-	-	3
4 bygile	2	-	-	-	-	-	-	-	-	-	-	-	2
7 hoker	-	1	1	-	-	-	-	-	-	-	-	-	2
18 trespas	-	-	-	-	-	-	1	-	-	-	1	-	2
36 missiggen	-	-	-	-	-	-	2	-	-	-	-	-	2
46 mescheef	-	-	-	-	-	-	1	-	-	1	-	-	2
56 hardlaike	-	-	-	-	-	-	2	-	-	-	-	-	2
66 opprobry	-	-	-	-	-	-	2	-	-	-	-	-	2
12 rebuke	-	-	1	-	-	-	-	-	-	-	-	-	1
13 derision	-	-	-	1	-	-	-	-	-	-	-	-	1
17 evel deed	-	-	-	-	-	-	-	-	-	-	-	1	1
25 unworschippe	-	-	-	-	-	-	-	-	-	-	-	1	1
26 trowble	-	-	-	-	-	-	-	-	-	-	-	1	1

List ME 3(2)

		A									B			TOTAL
	I	II	III							I	II	III		
			1a	1b	1c	2	3a	3b	3c					
	8	91	41	31	23	80	363	152	56	70	185	257		1357
37 saye ...	–	–	–	–	–	–	1	–	–	–	–	–		1
38 contek	–	–	–	–	–	–	1	–	–	–	–	–		1
39 destroyen	–	–	–	–	–	–	1	–	–	–	–	–		1
40 flytyng	–	–	–	–	–	–	1	–	–	–	–	–		1
41 dishese	–	–	–	–	–	–	1	–	–	–	–	–		1
42 chiding	–	–	–	–	–	–	1	–	–	–	–	–		1
43 outerage	–	–	–	–	–	–	1	–	–	–	–	–		1
47 seoruwe	–	–	–	–	–	–	–	–	–	–	–	1		1
48 unworby	–	–	–	–	–	–	–	–	–	–	–	1		1
50 craving	–	–	–	–	–	1	–	–	–	–	–	–		1
51 eny thynge	–	–	–	–	–	1	–	–	–	–	–	–		1
57 damage	–	–	–	–	–	–	1	–	–	–	–	–		1
58 hurtys	–	–	–	–	–	–	1	–	–	–	–	–		1
59 tene	–	–	–	–	–	–	1	–	–	–	–	–		1
60 gilt	–	–	–	–	–	–	1	–	–	–	–	–		1
61 derf word	–	–	–	–	–	–	1	–	–	–	–	–		1
62 redur	–	–	–	–	–	–	1	–	–	–	–	–		1
63 mysse	–	–	–	–	–	–	1	–	–	–	–	–		1
TOTAL	8	91	41	31	23	82	377	152	56	70	185	259		1375

List ME 4. Distribution of Middle English Material over Sense Groups and Centuries

The number in brackets after each word refers to its number in Lists ME 1 and ME 2.

Entire Corpus	I	II	A							B I	B II	B III	TOTAL
			1a	1b	1c	2	3a	3b	3c				
1200-1299	1	2	5	-	4	1	20	3	7	6	2	17	68
1300-1399	5	21	21	15	13	44	162	79	27	34	88	127	636
1400-1499	2	68	15	16	6	37	195	70	22	30	95	115	671
TOTAL	8	91	41	31	23	82	377	152	56	70	185	259	1375

shenship (22)	I	II	A							B I	B II	B III	TOTAL
			1a	1b	1c	2	3a	3b	3c				
1200-1299										4	-	4	8
1300-1399										13	20	33	66
1400-1499							41	54	19	12	25	35	186
shendnes (22)													
1200-1299										-	-	3	3
1300-1399										-		1	1
1400-1499										-	-	-	-
schendlac (22)													
1200-1299										1	-	2	3
1300-1399										-	-	-	-
1400-1499										-	-	-	-
schendful word (22)													
1200-1299						1	-	-	-	-	-	-	1
TOTAL							42	54	19	30	45	78	268

confusion (67)	I	II	A							B I	B II	B III	TOTAL
			1a	1b	1c	2	3a	3b	3c				
1200-1299										-	-	-	-
1300-1399										15	1	77	93
1400-1499										5	8	37	50
TOTAL										20	9	114	143

List ME 4(2)

wrong (30)	I	II		A			III				B			TOTAL
			1a	1b	1c	2	3a	3b	3c		I	II	III	
1200-1299														
1300-1399		-						75	2						77
1400-1499		3						63	-						66
TOTAL		3						138	2						143

repref (8)	I	II					III				I	II	III	TOTAL
			1a	1b	1c	2	3a	3b	3c					
1200-1299														
1300-1399	2	2						35	69	20					128
1400-1499	-	-						1	4	1					6

reprouyng(8)														
1400-1499	-	-						3	-	-					3
TOTAL	2	2						39	73	21					137

filth (45)	I	II					III				I	II	III	TOTAL
			1a	1b	1c	2	3a	3b	3c					
1200-1299													1	-	1
1300-1399													9	1	10
1400-1499													38	1	39

filthhed (45)														
1300-1399													52	-	52
1400-1499													4	-	4
TOTAL													104	2	106

blasfemye (19)	I	II					III				I	II	III	TOTAL
			1a	1b	1c	2	3a	3b	3c					
1200-1299		1						-	-	-					1
1300-1399		16						2	2	-					20
1400-1499		59						5	1	2					67
TOTAL		76						7	3	2					88

List ME 4(3)

chalenge (49)	I	II				III				I	II	III	TOTAL
			1a	1b	1c	2	3a	3b	3c				
1200-1299													
1300-1399						**41**							41
1400-1499						**34**							34

chalengyng(49)													
1300-1399						2							2
TOTAL						77							77

scorn (1)	I	II				III				I	II	III	TOTAL
			1a	1b	1c	2	3a	3b	3c				
1200-1299			2	-	-	-							2
1300-1399			3	6	3	1							13
1400-1499			1	9	1	-							11

scornyng (1)													
1200-1299	-	-	1	-	-	-							1
1300-1399	-	2	4	8	3	-							17
1400-1499	1	1	8	4	3	-							17

scornen (1)													
1300-1399	-	-	2	-	-	-							2
1400-1499	-	-	2	-	-	-							2

byskorn (1)													
1300-1399	-	-	1	-	-	-							1
TOTAL	1	3	24	27	10		1						66

schame (20)	I	II				III				I	II	III	TOTAL
			1a	1b	1c	2	3a	3b	3c				
1200-1299						-				1	1	4	6
1300-1399						1				4	-	3	8
1400-1499						-				5	4	14	23
TOTAL						1				10	5	21	37

List ME 4(4)

yuel fame (14)	A I	II	III 1a	1b	1c	2	3a	3b	3c	B I	II	III	TOTAL
1200-1299											-	-	
1300-1399											-	-	
1400-1499										2	13	16	31
fame(losen)													
1400-1499										-	-	1	1
fame(of filth)													
1400-1499										-	-	1	1
diffamyng													
1300-1399										-	-	1	1
TOTAL										2	13	19	34

dispit (9)	I	II	III 1a	1b	1c	2	3a	3b	3c	I	II	III	TOTAL
1300-1399		-	-				4	-		-			4
1400-1499		5	1				10	5		-			21
spite													
1400-1499		-	-				-	-		1			1
dispitousnes													
1400-1499		-	-				1	-		-			1
dispitous(word)													
1300-1399		-	-				1	-		-			1
TOTAL		5	1				16	5		1			28

dispisyng (10)	I	II	III 1a	1b	1c	2	3a	3b	3c	I	II	III	TOTAL
1300-1399		1	-				-			-			1
1400-1499		-	1				14	4		1			20
TOTAL		1	1				14	4		1			21

List ME 4(5)

iniury (35)	I	II					A III				B I	II	III	TOTAL
			1a	1b	1c	2	3a	3b	3c					
1300-1399							1							1
1400-1499							17							17
iniurious word														
1300-1399							1							1
TOTAL							19							19

obbrayd (64)	I	II					III				I	II	III	TOTAL
			1a	1b	1c	2	3a	3b	3c					
1400-1499							-	1	-					1
upbraiding(64)														
1200-1299							7	2	7					16
1300-1399							-	1	1					2
TOTAL							7	4	8					19

reproce (65)	I	II					III				I	II	III	TOTAL
			1a	1b	1c	2	3a	3b	3c					
1300-1399							4	1	4					9
reproceing(65)														
1300-1399							4	-	2					6
TOTAL							8	1	6					15

strif (31)	I	II					III				I	II	III	TOTAL
			1a	1b	1c	2	3a	3b	3c					
1300-1399							11	2						13
striuyng word														
1300-1399							1	-						1
TOTAL							12	2						14

List ME 4(6)

mouwing (27)	I	II	A III							B I	II	III	TOTAL
			1a	1b	1c	2	3a	3b	3c				
1300-1399			-	-	2								2
1400-1499			1	2	2								5
undermouwing													
1300-1399			2	-	2								4
1400-1499			-	1	-								1
TOTAL			3	3	6								12

blame (32)	I	II	III							I	II	III	TOTAL
			1a	1b	1c	2	3a	3b	3c				
1300-1399						1	-	-					1
1400-1499						1	-	-					1
blamyng (32)													
1300-1399						-	6	2					8
1400-1499						1	1	-					2
TOTAL						3	7	2					12

harm (52)	I	II	III							I	II	III	TOTAL
			1a	1b	1c	2	3a	3b	3c				
1300-1399							2						2
1400-1499							8						8
harmen (52)											.		
1400-1499						1							1
TOTAL						11							11

vilenye (11)	I	II	III							I	II	III	TOTAL
			1a	1b	1c	2	3a	3b	3c				
1300-1399			1			1					2	4	8
1400-1499			-			1					-	1	2
TOTAL			1			2					2	5	10

List ME 4(7)

			A							B			
woh/wouh(53)	I	II	III							I	II	III	TOTAL
			1a	1b	1c	2	3a	3b	3c				
1200-1299						8	1						9

						III							
hethyng (5)	I	II								I	II	III	TOTAL
			1a	1b	1c	2	3a	3b	3c				
1200-1299					2								2
1300-1399					-		-			-			-
1400-1499					-		4			1			5
TOTAL					2		4			1			7

illusion (2)	I	II								I	II	III	TOTAL
			1a	1b	1c	2	3a	3b	3c				
1300-1399	1		4										5
1400-1499	1		-										1
TOTAL	2		4										6

						III							
sclaundre(16)	I	II								I	II	III	TOTAL
			1a	1b	1c	2	3a	3b	3c				
1300-1399											1	-	1
1400-1499											1	4	5
TOTAL											2	4	6

						III							
unright (54)	I	II								I	II	III	TOTAL
			1a	1b	1c	2	3a	3b	3c				
1200-1299						1							1

unrigtwisnes

1200-1299						1							1
1300-1399						2							2

unri3tfulnes

1400-1499						1							1

nat ry3t

1300-1399						1							1
TOTAL						6							6

List ME 4(8)

In List ME 4(8-9) the instances of those words which are represented by less than five instances each in my material are placed together under the centuries from which their respective sources derive.

word	ref	A‑I	A‑II	1a	1b	1c	2	3a	3b	3c	B‑I	B‑II	B‑III	TOTAL
1200–1299														
þet fule	(34)	-	-	-	-	-	-	-	-	-	-	-	1	1
sunne	(44)	-	-	-	-	-	-	-	-	-	-	-	2	2
bismer	(6)	1	-	-	-	-	-	-	-	-	-	-	-	1
gram	(23)	-	-	-	-	-	1	-	-	-	-	-	-	1
snering	(28)	-	-	1	-	2	-	-	-	-	-	-	-	3
hoker	(7)	-	1	1	-	-	-	-	-	-	-	-	-	2
missiggen	(36)	-	-	-	-	-	1	-	-	-	-	-	-	1
seoruwe	(47)	-	-	-	-	-	-	-	-	-	-	-	1	1
craving	(50)	-	-	-	-	-	1	-	-	-	-	-	-	1
1300–1399														
dishonour	(21)	-	-	-	-	-	-	-	-	-	1	-	-	1
fule/foyle	(34)	-	-	-	-	-	-	-	-	-	-	1	1	2
synne	(44)	-	-	-	-	-	-	-	-	-	-	1	1	2
undernyming	(29)	-	-	1	-	1	-	2	-	-	-	-	-	4
desceit	(3)	2	-	-	-	1	-	-	-	-	-	-	-	3
bismer	(6)	-	-	1	-	1	-	-	-	-	-	-	-	2
evel loos	(15)	-	-	-	-	-	-	-	-	-	-	1	-	1
wicked los	(15)	-	-	-	-	-	-	-	-	-	-	-	1	1
cowardise	(24)	-	-	-	-	-	-	-	-	-	-	-	1	1
greuaunce	(55)	-	-	-	-	-	-	1	-	-	-	-	-	1
bygile	(4)	2	-	-	-	-	-	-	-	-	-	-	-	2
trespas	(18)	-	-	-	-	-	-	1	-	-	-	-	-	1
mysseien	(36)	-	-	-	-	-	-	1	-	-	-	-	-	1
meschif	(46)	-	-	-	-	-	-	1	-	-	1	-	-	2
derision	(13)	-	-	-	1	-	-	-	-	-	-	-	-	1
evel deed	(17)	-	-	-	-	-	-	-	-	-	-	-	1	1
unworschippe	(25)	-	-	-	-	-	-	-	-	-	-	-	1	1
destroyen	(39)	-	-	-	-	-	-	1	-	-	-	-	-	1
outerage	(43)	-	-	-	-	-	-	1	-	-	-	-	-	1
unworþy	(48)	-	-	-	-	-	-	-	-	-	-	-	1	1
damage	(57)	-	-	-	-	-	-	1	-	-	-	-	-	1
1400–1499														
dishonour	(21)	-	-	-	-	-	-	1	-	-	2	-	-	3
... honoure	(21)	-	-	-	-	-	-	-	-	-	-	-	1	1
defoul	(34)	-	-	-	-	-	-	-	1	-	-	-	-	1
defilen	(34)	-	-	-	-	-	-	1	-	-	-	-	-	1
synne	(44)	-	-	-	-	-	-	-	-	-	-	1	-	1
lose(losen)	(15)	-	-	-	-	-	-	-	-	-	-	-	1	1
turmenten	(33)	-	-	-	-	-	-	4	-	-	-	-	-	4
grem	(23)	-	-	-	-	-	-	1	-	-	1	-	-	2
coward	(24)	-	-	-	-	-	-	-	-	-	-	-	2	2
greuans	(55)	-	-	-	-	-	-	1	-	-	-	-	-	1

Columns I, II and 1a–3c are grouped under **A**; columns I, II, III are grouped under **B**.

List ME 4(9)

		A									B			TOTAL
		I	II				III				I	II	III	
				1a	1b	1c	2	3a	3b	3c				
		5	1	4	1	5	1	19	1	-	5	4	15	61
1400-1499														
greuen	(55)	-	-	-	-	-	-	1	-	-	-	-	-	1
trespas	(18)	-	-	-	-	-	-	-	-	-	-	1	-	1
hardlaike	(56)	-	-	-	-	-	-	2	-	-	-	-	-	2
opprobry	(66)	-	-	-	-	-	-	2	-	-	-	-	-	2
rebuke	(12)	-	-	1	-	-	-	-	-	-	-	-	-	1
trowble	(26)	-	-	-	-	-	-	-	-	-	-	-	1	1
saye ...	(37)	-	-	-	-	-	-	1	-	-	-	-	-	1
contek	(38)	-	-	-	-	-	-	1	-	-	-	-	-	1
flytyng	(40)	-	-	-	-	-	-	1	-	-	-	-	-	1
dishese	(41)	-	-	-	-	-	-	1	-	-	-	-	-	1
chiding	(42)	-	-	-	-	-	-	1	-	-	-	-	-	1
eny thynge	(51)	-	-	-	-	-	1	-	-	-	-	-	-	1
hyrtys	(58)	-	-	-	-	-	-	1	-	-	-	-	-	1
tene	(59)	-	-	-	-	-	-	1	-	-	-	-	-	1
gilt	(60)	-	-	-	-	-	-	1	-	-	-	-	-	1
derf word	(61)	-	-	-	-	-	-	1	-	-	-	-	-	1
redur	(62)	-	-	-	-	-	-	1	-	-	-	-	-	1
mysse	(63)	-	-	-	-	-	-	1	-	-	-	-	-	1
TOTAL		5	1	5	1	5	2	35	1	-	5	5	16	81

APPENDIX C. TEXT MATERIAL

Appendix C contains the whole corpus of collected instances with references to the excerpted sources (App. A, pp. 118-133). To save space I have, where this was possible, written two or even three instances on the same line, e.g. "Gospels: (MS. CND4), Matt. 15,19; 26,65" under "TEXT" and "ebolsung; efolsung" under "ENGLISH WORD" (p. 176, SENSE GR. A II, blasphemia). This means that the Latin word blasphemia in Matt. 15,19 has been rendered by ebolsung, in Matt. 26,65 by efolsung. When references to two different pages, as e.g. under "Bede I, 27,9" (p. 176, SENSE GR. A I, inlusio), have been made, the first one, "p. 92,3", refers to the Latin text, the second one, "MS. T, p. 84,21", to the English text.

Instances in brackets are not included in the Lists, App. B. See for instance p. 188, A I, inlusio: (heþing) and inlusio: (heving). The two words in brackets, heþing and heving, are quoted for comparison. They derive from two MSS., H and E, whose texts are not given in full in my source, the Surtees Psalter (App. A, p. 131). Cf. also p. 23 where instances in brackets have been discussed.

A different spelling of a word given in brackets after that word indicates that the spelling in question is uncommon but that it is the one which occurs in my source. See for instance p. 178, A III 3a, contumelia:sceomu (sceofmu). Sceofmu is the spelling in the source referred to, i.e. Gospels (MS. CND4), Mark 12,4, in Skeat's edition (App. A, p. 122).

Inflected forms in brackets after a word are the forms which occur in the excerpted sources, as e.g. in the instance inlusio: bigile (be bigiled) on p. 188.

Instances are arranged by Sense groups and within Sense groups in accordance with the order of the Latin words which they render (see Lists OE 1 and ME 1). The order of the sources has been described in Appendix A, pp. 118-119.

Appendix C contains five sections which have the following headings:
1. Classified Old English Material
2. Unclassified Old English Material
3. Classified Middle English Material
4. Unclassified Middle English Material
5. Notes to Classified Middle English Material

The footnotes to the Old English Material have been placed at the bottom of the relevant pages, whereas the footnotes to the Middle English material have been placed at the end of the Appendix under a separate heading (5. Notes to Classified Middle English Material). The reason for this discrepancy is that most of the footnotes to the Middle English material, unlike those to the Old English material, apply to more than one page. Compare e.g. footnote 1, which applies to pp. 189, 191, 192, 194, and 199.

1. Classified Old English Material

TEXT	LATIN WORD	ENGLISH WORD	SENSE GR.
Psalter A,Ps. 37,8	inlusio	bismernis	A I
" B," " (A-type)	"	bismernes	"
" C," " (")	"	bysmyrnys	"
" D," "	"	bysmrun3	"
" E," " (D-type)	"	bysmrung	"
" I," "	"	bismrung, hosp	"
" J," " (A-type)	"	besmyrnes	"
Rule S.B.(MS.A),p. 83,8	"	3ebysmerun3	"
" " (" W)," 82,8	"	costnun3	"
" " (" CCD3),p.107,2	"	3ebismerung	"
" " (" CTA3)," 88,4	"	swīcuncg	"
Bede I, 27,9:			
p. 92,3; (MS.T),p. 84,21	"	bysmrung	"
" 93,5; (" ")," 86,4	"	bysmrung	"
" 93,9; (" ")," 86,9	"	bysmrung	"
" 94,3; (" ")," 86,11	"	bysmrung	"
" 95,1; (" ")," 86,20	"	bysmrung	"
" 92,3; (" O)," 92,2074	"	bysmrun3	"
" 93,5; (" ")," 94,2106	"	bysmrun3	"
" 93,9; (" ")," 94,2116	"	bysmrun3	"
" 94,3; (" ")," 94,2121	"	bysmrun3	"
" 95,1; (" ")," 95,2139	"	bysmrun3	"
" 92,3; (" B)," 92,2074	"	bysmrun3	"
" 93,5; (" ")," 94,2106	"	bysmrun3	"
" 93,9; (" ")," 94,2117	"	bysmrun3	"
" 94,3; (" ")," 94,2122	"	bysmrun3	"
" 95,1; (" ")," 95,2139	"	bysmrun3	"
Dialogues IV,50:			
p. 309,5-; (MS.C),p. 339,4	"	bysmrun3	"
(" ")," 339,6	"	bysmrun3	"
(" ")," 339,9	"	bysmrun3	"
" 310,13; (" ")," 339,17	"	bysmrun3	"
" 310,16; (" ")," 339,19	"	þam fulan bysmriendan	"
Arundel 155 (1),p. 118,56	"	big swic	"
" " (2)," 235(12,6)	"	bi3-swic	"
Cons. (MS.CTA3),p. 396,441	"	swic	"
Gospels:			
(MS.CND4),p. 19,4	blasphemia	ebolsung	A II
(" "),Matt. 12,31	"	ebolsung	"
(" "), " "	"	ebolsung/efalsong	"
(" "), " 15,19; 26,65	"	ebolsung; efolsung	"
(" "),Mark 3,28; 7,22	"	ebolsung; efolsung	"
(" "), " 14,64	"	ebolsung	"
(" "),p. 3,2	"	ebolsong	"
(" "),Luke 5,21	"	ebolsong	"
(" "),John 10,33	"	ebolsong	"
(" Ru¹),Matt. 12,31	"	efulsung; efalsung	"
(" "²)," 15,19; 26,65	"	hefalsung; efalsung	"
(" Ru²),Mark 3,28; 14,64	"	eofolsan; eofulsung	"
(" "),John 10,33	"	eofolsong__	"
(" C),Matt. 12,31	"	bysmur-spaec	"
(" "), " "	"	bysmur-spaec	"

TEXT	LATIN WORD	ENGLISH WORD	SENSE GR.
(MS. C),Matt. 15,19	blasphemia	tallice word__	A II
(" "), " 26,65	"	gyltlice spraec,	"
		bysmor-spraec	"
(" "),Mark 3,28	"	bysmorung	"
(" "), " 7,22	"	dysines	"
(" "), " 14,64	"	bysmer	"
(" "),Luke 5,21	"	woffung __	"
(" "),John 10,33	"	bysmor-spaec	"
(" H),Matt. 12,31	"	bismer-spraec	"
(" "), " "	"	bysmer-spraec	"
(" "), " 15,19	"	talliche word	"
(" "), " 26,65	"	gyltlice spaec,	"
		bysmere-spaech	"
(" "),Mark 3,28	"	bismerung	"
(" "), " 7,22	"	desynys	"
(" "), " 14,64	"	bismer	"
(" "),Luke 5,21	"	woffung __	"
(" "),John 10,33	"	bismere-spraech	"
PC(MS. C), p. 222,9; 222,12	"	tael; tael	"
Lib.Scint.,p. 102,16	"	wiþersacung	"
" " ," 137,14	"	hyrwincg	"
Dialogues IV,41:			
p. 296,14; (MS.C),p. 328,7	"	yfelsacun3	"
Dur.Ri.,p. 12,18-19	"	ebolsung	"
Arundel 155 (2),p.246(19,17)	"	hyrwinc3	"
Lambeth 427,p. 331	"	yfelsacun3	"
PC(MS.H20),p. 339,8	injuria	laeddo	"
" (" C)," 338,8	"	laeddo	"
Dialogues:			
I,1, p.18,2;(MS.C),p. 11,26	inrisio	bysmerun3	A III la
" , " 18,5;(" ")," 11,29	"	bysmrun3	"
III,1," 136,9;(MS.C),p.180,8	"	bysmrun3	"
PC(MS. H20),p. 205,12	ludibrium	bismer	"
" (" C)," 204,12	"	bismer	"
Psalter:			
A,Ps. 34,16; 43,14	derisus	bismerung; bismerung	"
"," 78,4	"	bismerung	"
B," 34,16; 43,14 (A-type)	"	bismrun3; bismrun3	"
"," 78,4 (")	"	bismrun3	"
C," 34,16; 43,14 (")	"	bysmrun3; bysmrun3	"
"," 78,4 (")	"	bysmrun3	"
D," 34,16; 43,14	"	hleahter; hleahter	"
"," 78,4	"	hleahter	"
E," 34,16; (D-type)	"	hleahter	"
"," 43,14; 78,4 (A-type)	"	leahter; hlehter	"
J," 43,14 (")	"	bismrung (bismrum)	"
I," 34,16	subsannatio	bismer, hosp	"
J," 34,16; 43,14	"	leahter; leahter	"

TEXT	LATIN WORD	ENGLISH WORD	SENSE GR.
Psalter J,Ps. 78,4 (D type)	inlusio	bismer	A III 1b
Sol.,p. 11,35;(MS.C),p.11,21- " ," " ;(" ")," 12,1	ludibrium "	bysmor sceamu	" "
Psalter I,Ps. 43,14	derisus	hleahter	"
" "," "	subsannatio	hlacerung	"
Psalter I, Ps. 78,4	inlusio	gebismerung	A III 1c
" ", " 43,14	subsannatio	tāl, bysmur	"
" ", " 78,4	"	tāl, golfetung	"
Psalter A,Ps. 118,134	calumnia	hearm	A III 2
" B," " (A-type)	"	hearmcwide	"
" C," " (")	"	yrmðu	"
" D," "	"	hosp	"
" E," " (A-type)	"	hearmcwidolnes	"
" I," "	"	hosp, teona	"
" J," " (D-type)	"	hosp	"
" K," " (")	"	hosp	"
" L," " (A-type)	"	hearmcwide	"
" P," "	"	hearmcwide	"
Gospels(MS.CND4),Luke 3,14	"	telnis, sceomu	"
" (" Ru2), " "	"	tellnis, scomu	"
" (" C), " "	"	tāl	"
" (" H), " "	"	tāl	"
Hept.(MS.B),Lev. 19,13	"	bysmrian	"
" (" "),Deut. 28,29; 28,33	"	bysmor; bysmor	"
" (" L),Lev. 19,13	"	bysmrian	"
" (" "),Deut. 28,29; 28,33	"	bysmor; bismor	"
Bede,V,19: p.668,9; (MS.T),p.460,29	"	līcettung, lēas	"
" " ; (" O)," 668,2724	"	līcettunȝ, lēas	"
" " ; (" B)," 668,2724	"	līcettende, lēas	"
De Vitiis, p. 224,18	"	teona	"
Dur.Ri., p. 102,6-7	"	sceomu	"
Gospels(MS.CND4),Matt. 22,6	contumelia	fraeced	A III 3a
" (" "),Mark 12,4	"	sceomu (sceofmu)	"
" (" "2),Luke 11,45;20,11	"	sceomu; teancuide	"
" (" Ru2),Mark 12,4	"	scomu	"
" (" "),Luke 11,45	"	scomu	"
" (" C), Matt. 22,6	"	teona	"
" (" "), Mark 12,4	"	teona	"
" (" "), Luke 11,45; 20,11	"	teona; teona	"
" (" H), Matt. 22,6	"	teona	"
" (" "), Mark 12,4	"	teone	"
" (" "), Luke 11,45; 20,11	"	teona; teone	"
Aelfric's Hom.,p. 165	"	teona	"
PC(MS.C),p. 60,10	"	worldebismer/-uld-	"
" (" ")," 166,12	"	edwit	"
" (" ")," 224,16; 226,1	"	scand; scand	"
" (" ")," 224,25	"	scond	"

TEXT	LATIN WORD	ENGLISH WORD	SENSE GR.
PC(MS. C),p. 226,10; 226,23	contumelia	bismer; bismer	A III 3a
" (" H2O),p. 61,10; 227,10	"	woroldbismer; bismer	"
" (" ")," 167,12	"	edwīt	"
" (" ")," 225,16; 225,25	"	scand; scand	"
" (" ")," 227,1	"	scand	"
" (" ")," 227,23; 423,34	"	bismer; bismer	"
Or. (MS.L),p. 280,14	"	bismer	"
Bo. (" C)," 45,5-6	"	bismrian	"
" (" ")," 45,12	"	hisping	"
Lib.Scint., p. 9,5-6; 12,14	"	grama; grama	"
" " , " 9,18; 11,17	"	teona; teona	"
" " , " 12,15-16; 19,4	"	teona; teona; teona	"
" " , " 40,9; 82,12	"	teona; teona	"
" " , " 119,19	"	teona	"
De Vitiis, p. 225,5	"	teona	"
Dialogues:			
I,2, p. 24,17; (MS.C),p.21,34	"	fraceþ	"
I,5, " 41,18; (" ")," 47,9	"	teona	"
II,8, " 96,14; (" "),"122,15	"	teona	"
II,23, " 114,21; (" "),"152,6	"	teona, orwyrd	"
II,23, " 114,21; (" "),"152,7	"	fracodword	"
III,14," 165,4 ; (" "),"200,16	"	oretla, bysmrian	"
III,17," 183,14; (" "),"218,10	"	teona	"
III,37," 218,19; (" "),"251,1	"	orwyrd,fracodlic word	"
I,2, " 24,17; (" H)," 21,32	"	teona	"
II,23, " 114,21; (" "),"152,4-6	"	teona, yfel word	"
Alcuin, p. 381,235-236	"	fracodne, unзerisne	"
Dur.Ri., p. 107,15	"	sceomu	"
Or. (MS.L),p. 146,33	(ignominia)	bismer	"
" (" C)," 30,34	(")	bysmrung	"
" (" L)," 64,9	(turpitudo)	bismer	"
Psalter:			
A,Ps. 102,6; 145,7	injuria	tīona; teona	"
B," 102,6 (A-type)	"	teona	"
C," 102,6; 145,7 (")	"	teona; teona	"
D," 102,6; 147,7	"	onteona(on t.?);teona	"
E," 102,6; 145,7 (A-type)	"	ontīona (on t.?)	"
I," 102,6; 145,7	"	teona; teona	"
J," 102,6; 145,7 (D-type)	"	onteona(on t.?);teona	"
K," 102,6; 145,7 (")	"	teona; teona	"
P," 102,6; 145,7	"	teona; teona	"
Gospels:			
(MS.CNDᴣ),Matt. 20,13	"	laedo, baeligniso	"
(" Ruᴸ), " "	"	teane	"
(" C), " "	"	teona	"
(" H), " "	"	teone	"
Hept.,(MS.B),Gen. 50,15	"	teona	"
" ,(" "),Lev. 19,18	"	tynan	"
" ,(" L),Gen. 50,15	"	teona	"
" ,(" "),Lev. 19,18	"	tynan	"
PC(MS. C),p.226,3; 226,16	"	scand; demm, bismer	"
" (" H2O),p.227,3; 227,16	"	scand; demm, bismer	"

TEXT	LATIN WORD	ENGLISH WORD	SENSE GR.
Or.(MS.L),p. 154,12-13	injuria	ābylgd; bismer _	A III 3a
Bo.(" C)," 22,10-11	"	earfode, wraecsid	"
" (" ")," 117,2	"	unriht	"
" (" ")," 122,18-19	"	witnan, witnian	"
" (" ")," 122,28-30	"	witnan, wite (þolan)	"
" (" ")," 123,1	"	yfel _	"
" (" ")," 123,2-4	"	unriht witnung, yfel	"
Rule S.B:			
(MS.A), p. 17,11	"	teona__	"
(" ")," 27,1; 27,21	"	teonraeden; teonraeden	"
(" ")," 97,7	"	hosp, edwit	"
(" W)," 96,6-7	"	hosp, edwit _	"
(" CCD3),p. 23,26; 37,1	"	teone; teonreden	"
(" ")," 37,20	"	teonful þing	"
(" ")," 115,26	"	hosp, edwit	"
(" CTA3)," 20,10	"	trega _	"
(" ")," 32,3;32,12	"	teona; teona	"
(" ")," 95,14	"	teona	"
Bede III,22:			
p. 295,7; (MS.T),p. 228,3	"	teona	"
" " ; (" O)," 296,2465	"	teona	"
" " ; (" B)," 296,2465	"	teona	"
Lib.Scint.,p. 8,20; 9,7-8	"	teona; teona	"
" " ," 10,13; 11,15	"	teona; teona	"
" " ," 69,9	"	teona	"
" " ," 212,4	"	grama	"
Dialogues I,2:			
p. 24,10; (MS.C),p. 21,11	"	teona	"
" " ; (" H)," 21,12	"	teona	"
Dialogues III,37:			
p. 218,14; (MS.C),p. 250,20	"	teonword	"
Alcuin, p. 379,187-188	"	teona	"
" , " 379,204-205	"	teona	"
" , " 379,207-380,209	"	unednys, anweardnys	"
" , " 380,212	"	teona	"
Psalter:			
A,Ps. 14,3; 56,4; 68,8	opprobrium[1]	edwit; edwit; edwit	"
"," 68,10-11; 77,66	"	edwit; edwit; edwit	"
"," 88,51; 122,4	"	edwit; edwit	"
B," 14,3;56,4;68,8 (A-type)	"	edwit; edwit; edwit	"
"," 68,10 (")	"	hosp	"
"," 68,11; 77,66 (")	"	edwit; edwit	"
"," 88,51; 122,4 (")	"	edwit; edwit	"
C," 14,3;56,4;68,8 (")	"	edwit; edwit; edwit	"
"," 68,10-11 (")	"	edwit; edwit	"
"," 77,66 (")	"	hosp	"
"," 88,51; 122,4 (")	"	edwit; edwit, hosp	"
D," 14,3;56,4;68,8	"	hosp; hosp; hosp	"
"," 68,10-11; 77,66	"	hosp; hosp; hosp	"
"," 88,51; 122,4	"	hosp; hosp	"

---

[1]Ps.68,8 has inproperium in the "Roman" text, opprobrium in the "Gallican".

TEXT	LATIN WORD	ENGLISH WORD	SENSE GR.
E, Ps. 14,3; 68,8 (D-type)	opprobrium	edwīt, hosp; hosp	A III 3a
", " 56,4; 68,8 (A-type)	"	edwīt; edwīt	"
", " 68,10-11 (")	"	edwīt; edwīt	"
", " 68,10 (D-type)	"	hosp	"
", " 77,66 (A-type)	"	edwīt	"
", " 88,51 (")	"	hosp	"
", " 122,4 (")	"	edwit (edwīd)	"
I, " 14,3	"	hosp, bysmerung	"
", " 56,4;68,8;77,66	"	hosp; hosp; hosp	"
", " 68,10-11; 88,51	"	hosp; hosp; hosp	"
", " 122,4	"	aeswicnes, hosp	"
J, " 14,3; 68,8 (A-type)	"	hosp; hosp, edwit	"
", " 56,4; 77,66 (D-type)	"	hosp; hosp	"
", " 68,10-11 (A-type)	"	hosp, edwit; edwīt	"
", " 88,51; 122,4 (D-type)	"	hosp; hosp	"
K, " 14,3;56,4;68,8 (")	"	hosp; hosp; hosp	"
", " 68,10-11; 88,51 (")	"	hosp; hosp; hosp	"
", " 77,66; 122,4 (")	"	hosp; hosp	"
L, " 68,8; 122,4 (A-type)	"	edwit; edwit	"
", " 68,10-11 (")	"	hosp; edwīt	"
P, " 56,4(56,3);68,8; 77,66	"	edwīt; edwīt; edwīt	"
", " 68,10(68,9);68,11(68,10)	"	edwīt; edwit	"
", " 122,4 (122,5)	"	edwīt	"
", " 88,51(88,44)	"	edwitspraec	"

Dialogues I,1:

TEXT	LATIN WORD	ENGLISH WORD	SENSE GR.
p.18,5; (MS.C),p. 11,29	"	edwīt	"

Rule S.B.(MS.A),p.3,21-22

TEXT	LATIN WORD	ENGLISH WORD	SENSE GR.
" " (" ")," 97,18	"	hosp, edwīt	"
" " (" W)," 96,18	"	hosp, edwit (wīt)	"
" " (" CTA3),p.4,5-6;96,6	"	hosp; hosp	"
" " (" CCD3)," 7,4	"	hosp, edwit (edwt)	"
" " (" ")," 117,5	"	taelung, edwīt	"

TEXT	LATIN WORD	ENGLISH WORD	SENSE GR.
Lib.Scint., p. 174,7	contumelia	teona	A III 3b
Or.(MS.L),p. 240,9	**injuria**	unār	"

Dialogues I,4:

TEXT	LATIN WORD	ENGLISH WORD	SENSE GR.
p.34,4; (MS.C),p.35,27	"	teona	"
p. " ; (" H)," 35,29	"	teona	"
Dur.Ri., p.105,5	"	wraeddo	"

Psalter:

TEXT	LATIN WORD	ENGLISH WORD	SENSE GR.
A,Ps. 43,14; 88,42	opprobrium	edwīt; edwīt	"
", " 118,22; 118,39	"	edwīt; edwīt	"
",Hymn 1,11 (Cant. 16,8)	"	edwīt	"
B,Ps. 43,14; 78,4 (A-type)	"	edwīt; edwīt	"
", " 88,42; 118,22 (")	"	edwīt; edwīt	"
", " 118,39 (")	"	edwīt	"
C, " 43,14; 78,4 (")	"	edwīt; edwīt	"
", " 88,42;118,22 (")	"	edwīt; edwīt	"
", " 118,39 (")	"	edwit	"
D, " 43,14; 78,4; 88,42	"	hosp; hosp; hosp	"
", " 118,22; 118,39	"	hosp; hosp	"

TEXT		LATIN WORD	ENGLISH WORD	SENSE GR.
E,Ps. 43,14; 78,4	(A-type)	opprobrium	edwīt; edwīt	A III 3b
",". 88,42	(")	"	hosp	"
",". 118,22	(")	"	edwīt	"
",". 118,39	(")	"	edwīt (edwīd)	"
",Cant. 16,8	(")	"	edwīt (aedwīt)	"
I,Ps. 43,14; 78,4; 88,42		"	hosp; hosp; hosp	"
",". 118,22;118,39		"	hosp,bysmerung;hosp	"
J," 118,22	(D-type)	"	hosp	"
",". 118,39	(")	"	edwit	"
K," 43,14; 78,4	(")	"	hosp; hosp	"
",". 118,22;118,39	(")	"	hosp; hosp	"
L," 118,22	(A-type)	"	edwīt, hosp	"
",". 118,39	(")	"	hosp, edwīt	"
P," 88,42 (88,35)		"	edwīt	"
",". 118,22;118,39		"	edwīt; edwīt	"

Gospels:

(MS.CND4), Luke 1,25		"	telnis	"
(" Ru²), " "		"	telnis	"
(" C), " "		"	hosp	"
(" H), " "		"	hosp	"

Aelfric's Judith 5,18; 5,25		"	hosp; hosp	"

PC(MS.H20),p. 207,12		"	bismer	"
" (" C),p. 206,12		"	bismer	"
Lib.Scint., p. 177,4		"	tal	"

Psalter:

A,Ps. 21,7; 30,12; 38,9		opprobrium	edwīt; edwīt; edwīt	A III 3c
",". 78,4; 108,25		"	edwīt; edwīt	"
B," 21,7; 30,12	(A-type)	"	edwīt; edwīt	"
",". 38,9; 108,25	(")	"	edwīt; edwīt	"
C," 21,7; 30,12	(")	"	edwīt; edwīt	"
",". 38,9; 108,25	(")	"	edwīt; edwīt	"
D," 21,7; 30,12; 38,9		"	hosp; hosp; hosp	"
",". 108,25		"	hosp	"
E," 21,7	(D-type)	"	edwīt (aedwīt),hosp	"
",". 30,12	(")	"	hosp	"
",". 38,9	(A-type)	"	hosp	"
",". 108,25	(")	"	edwīt (edwīd)	"
I," 21,7		"	bysmerung, hosp	"
",". 30,12; 38,9		"	hosp; hosp	"
J," 21,7; 30,12	(A-type)	"	hosp; hosp	"
",". 38,9	(")	"	hosp, edwīt	"
",". 78,4; 88,42	(D-type)	"	edwīt; hosp	"
",". 43,14	(A-type)	"	edwīt	"
",". 108,25	(D-type)	"	hosp	"
K," 21,7; 30,12	(")	"	hosp; hosp	"
",". 38,9; 88,42	(")	"	hosp; hosp	"
P," 78,4; 108,25(108,24)		"	edwītstaef;edwītstaef	"

Rule S.B. (MS.A),p. 29,13		"	hosp	"
" " ("CCD3),p. 39,18		"	edwīt	"

TEXT	LATIN WORD	ENGLISH WORD	SENSE GR.
Or.,p. 83,34;(MS.L),p. 82,34	infamia	edwīt	B I
" ," 121,21;(" ")," 120,21	"	bismer	"
" ," 123,22;(" ")," 122,22	"	bismer	"
" ," 217,15;(" ")," 216,15-	"	bismer (hit)[1]_	"
" ," 221,18;(" ")," 220,20-	"	bismerlecre daed (yfelan friþ)	"
" ," 121,27;(" ")," 122,1	dedecus	bismer, bismer	"
" ," 123,4 ;(" ")," 122,8	ignominia	bismer	"
Psalter:			
A,Ps. 43,16	confusio	gedroefednis	"
"," 68,20	"	gedroefnis	"
"," 88,46	"	gedroefednis	"
B," 43,16; 68,20 (A-type)	"	ʒedrefednes; ʒedrefnes	"
"," 88,46 (")	"	ʒedroefednes	"
C," 43,16 (")	"	ʒedrefydnys	"
",", 68,20 (")	"	ʒedrefydnys	"
",", 88,46 (")	"	ʒedrefydnys	"
D," 43,16	"	ʒescyndnis	"
",", 68,20	"	scamunʒ	"
",", 88,46	"	ʒedrefednis	"
E," 43,16; 68,20 (A-type)	"	gescindnes; gescindnes	"
",", 88,46 (")	"	gescindnes	"
I," 43,16	"	hosp, gescyndnys	"
",", 68,8	"	gescyndnes	"
",", 68,20	"	gescaendnys, sceamung	"
",", 88,46	"	gescaendnys	"
J," 43,16 (A-type)	"	gedrefednes	"
",", 68,8; 68,20 (")	"	gescindnes; gescindnes	"
",", 88,46 (D-type)	"	gedrefednes	"
K," 43,16 (")	"	ʒescyndnes	"
",", 68,8 (")	"	forwandunʒ	"
",", 68,20 (")	"	scaemunʒ	"
",", 88,46 (")	"	gedrefednes	"
L," 68,20 (A-type)	"	gedrefednes	"
P," 68,8	"	hleorsceamu	"
",", 88,46 (88,39)	"	sceamu	"
Aelfric's Judith 14,15	"	scyndan	"
PC(MS. H20),p. 207,11	"	scamu, scand	"
" (" C),p. 206,11	"	scamu, scand	"
(Bo.,p.129,89-91;(MS.C), p. 142,21 or p.142,23)	"	gedrefednes	"
Dur.Ri.,p. 27,15-17	"	sceomu	"
PC(MS. Cl),p. 72,10	dedecus	unwlitegian	B II
" (" H20),p. 73,10	"	unwlitegian	"
Or.,p. 31,29;(MS.C),p.30,3	ignominia	firenlust	"

---

[1]Or.,p.217,14-15: ... quasi pro abolenda superiore macula turpiorem
ipse auxit infamiam:
(MS.L),p.216,15-16: ... & þohte þaet he Romana bismer gewrecan
sceolde, ac he hit on þaem faerelte geīecte swiþor, &
uneaþe self com āweg.

TEXT		LATIN WORD	ENGLISH WORD	SENSE GR.
Hept. (MS.B),Ex. 20,26		turpitudo	sceamu	B II
" (" "),Lev. 18,16		"	haeman	"
" (" L),Ex. 20,26		"	sceamu	"
" (" "),Lev. 18,16		"	haeman	"
PC(MS. H2O), p. 73,4; 73,12		"	scondlicnes; bismer	"
" (" C), p. 72,4; 72,12		"	sceondlicnes; bismer	"
Bede I,27,5:				
p.69,4; (MS.T),p.70,8		"	scondlicnes	"
" 69,8; (" ")," 70,14		"	scondlicnes	"
" 70,2; (" ")," 70,17		"	sceondlicnes	"
" 70,3; (" ")," 70,18		"	scondlicnes	"
" 69,4; (" O)," 69,1540		"	sceondlicnes	"
" 69,8; (" ")," 69,1552		"	sceondlicnes	"
" 70,2; (" ")," 70,1558		"	scandlicnes	"
" 70,3; (" ")," 70,1561		"	scondlicnes	"
" 69,4; (" B)," 69,1540		"	scandlicnes	"
" 69,8; (" ")," 69,1554		"	scandlicnes	"
" 70,2; (" ")," 70,1559		"	scandlicnes	"
" 70,3; (" ")," 70,1562		"	scandlicnes	"
Lib.Scint., p.144,1-3; 177,1		"	fȳlþ; fȳlþ	"
De Vitiis, p. 225,5		"	fȳlþ	"
Psalter:				
C,Hymn 15,36	(A-type)	confusio	ȝedrēfydnys	"
D, " " (11,36)		"	ȝemanȝ	"
E, " "	(D-type)	"	gemeng	"
I, " "		"	gemengednys	"
J, " "		"	gescindnes	"
K, " "	(D-type)	"	wilnunȝ	"
L, " " (2,51)		"	gemengnes	"
PC(MS. H2O),p. 45,14		dedecus	fracodlic	B III
" (" C),p. 44,15		"	fracudlic	"
Bo.(MS.B),p. 61,27		"	unweordscipe	"
Lib.Scint.,p. 174,9		"	aepsenys	"
Psalter:				
A,Ps. 82,17		ignominia	orwyrd	"
B," "	(A-type)	"	orwyrd	"
C," "	(")	"	orwurd	"
D," "		"	unȝewiss	"
E," "	(A-type)	"	unwitende	"
I," "		"	teona	"
J," "	(D-type)	"	ungewiss	"
K," "	(")	"	ungewiss	"
P," " (82,12)		"	sceamian	"
Or.,p. 141,16; MS.L),p.140,16		"	gylt	"
Lib.Scint., p. 158,12		"	teona	"
" " , " 113,16(Prov.13,18)		"	teona	"
Bo.,p.104,122;(MS.C),p.123,4		turpitudo	yfel	"
Sol.,p.5,29; (MS.C),p. 5,11		"	yfel	"
Psalter:				
A,Ps. 39,16		confusio	scomu	"

TEXT		LATIN WORD	ENGLISH WORD	SENSE GR.
A,Ps. 70,13		confusio	gedroefednis	B III
",\" 108,29		"	gescendd	"
",\" 131,18		"	scomu	"
B," 39,16	(A-type)	"	scamu	"
",\" 70,13	(")	"	ȝedrofednes	"
",\" 108,29	(")	"	ȝescentd	"
",\" 131,18	(")	"	scomu	"
C," 39,16	(")	"	scomu	"
",\" 70,13	(")	"	ȝedrefydnys	"
",\" 108,29;131,18	(")	"	sceomu; sceamu	"
D," 39,16; 70,13		"	ȝescyndnes;ȝescyndnis	"
",\" 108,29		"	scamu	"
",\" 131,18		"	sceamunȝ	"
E," 39,16; 70,13	(A-type)	"	gesciendnes;gescindnes	"
",\" 108,29	(")	"	gescindnes	"
",\" 131,18	(")	"	anddetnes	"
I," 34,26		"	sceamu, gescaendnes	"
",\" 39,16		"	sceamu, gescendnes	"
",\" 70,13		"	gedrefednys	"
",\" 108,29		"	sceamu	"
",\" 131,18		"	gescendnes	"
J," 34,26	(A-type)	"	gescildnes(-scind-?)	"
",\" 39,16	(")	"	scamu	"
",\" 70,13	(")	"	gescindnes	"
",\" 108,29	(D-type)	"	scamu	"
",\" 131,18	(")	"	scamung	"
K," 39,16; 70,13	(")	"	gescyndnes; ȝescyndnes	"
",\" 131,18	(")	"	sceamung	"
L," 70,13	(")	"	gescyndnes	"
",\" 131,18	(A-type)	"	scomu	"
P," 70,13 (70,12)		"	scand	"
",\" 108,29 (108,28)		"	sceamu	"
",\" 131,18 (131,19)		"	sceamu	"
Gospels:				
(MS.CND4),Prol., p. 3,11		"	sceomu, telnis	"
(" "₂),Luke 21,25		"	forescending	"
(" Ru²), " "		"	forscending	"
(" C), " "		"	gedrefednes	"
(" H), " "		"	gedrefednys	"
Aelfric´s Hom.(i 604),p.248		"	gescyndnys	"
PC(MS.C),p. 208,19		"	scamu	"
" (" "),\" 316,23		"	bismer	"
" (" H20),p. 209,19		"	scamu	"
" (" "),\" 317,23		"	bismer	"
Rule S.B.(MS.A),p. 133,11		"	sceamu, ablysunȝ	"
" (" CCD3),p. 147,13		"	sceamu, ascyndnes	"
" (" CTA3),\" 118,11		"	scamu, gescyndnys	"
Lib.Scint.,p. 94,16		"	gescyndnys	"
" " ,\" 96,18		"	sceamu	"
" " ,\" 174,8		"	sceand	"
De Vitiis,p. 224,1		"	gescyndnys	"

2. Unclassified Old English Material

LATIN WORD	ENGLISH WORD	VOCABULARIES
2 inrisio	canc	Aldhelm(MS.H),Bouterwek,p.510
3 ludibrium	bismerung	" (" "),Mone, no. 4323
"	gecanc	" (" "),Bouterwek,p.441
"	3ecanc	" (" 1),Napier, no. 1473
"	gebismrung (gebismu3c)	" (" 11), " " 181
"	bysmer	WW, XI, col. 431,24
4 derisus	taelhlehter	" , V , " 172,4
5 gannatura	tāl, glīwung	Aldhelm(MS.H),Mone, no. 1489
	(tāl, gelīvung)	" (" "),Bouterwek,p.441
"	gecanc	" (" "),Mone, no. 4514
"	bismer	" (" "), " , " 4779
"	bismer	" (" "), " , " 6261
"	tāl, 3līwun3	" (" 1),Napier,no.1472
"	bysmer	" (" "), " ," 4757
"	bysmer	" (" "), " ," 5230
"	3ecanc	" (" "), " ," 4504
"	glīu	Corpus MS.,Sweet, no. 948
"	cancettende	" ,XI, " 412,32
"	bysmir	" ,XII, " 509,28
"	ganung	" , " , " 476,9
6 infamia	unhlīsa	Aldhelm(MS.4),Napier,no. 55
"	unhlīsa	WW, IV, col. 116,15
"	unhlīsa	" , X , " 315,36
"	unhlīsa	" , XI, " 420,14
"	fracebu	" , " , " 429,23
"	unhlīsa	" ,XIII, " 542,3
8 dedecus	bismer, ungerisne	Aldhelm(" H),Mone, no. 4315
"	unirisnys	" (" "), " , " 4331
"	ungerisne, bismer	" (" 1),Napier, no. 4309
"	unwlite	WW, XI, col. 387,32
"	unwlite, scond	" , " , " 388,30
"	unwlite	" , XII, " 508,26
10 contumelia	hosp	Aldhelm(MS.H),Mone, no. 4270
"	hosp	" (" 1),Napier, no.4268
11 ignominia	netenes	WW, II, col. 68,15
"	netenes	" , " , " 72,27
"	scondehlēwung	" , XI, " 429,23
"	scand	" , IV, " 116,14
12 calumnia	hosp	Aldhelm(MS.H),Mone,no. 541
"	hosp	" (" "), " ," 1293
"	tēona, hosp	" (" "), " ," 4206
"	tēona	" (" "), " ," 4269
"	tēona	" (" "), " ," 4713
"	hosp	" (" 1),Napier,no. 471
"	hosp	" (" "), " ," 1261
"	tēona, hosp	" (" "), " ," 4207
"	tēona	" (" "), " ," 4267
"	tēona	" (" "), " ," 4690
"	holtihte, tēona	WW, IV, col. 116,25
"	hosp,hearmspraec,holtihte	" , VI, " 198,2

LATIN WORD	ENGLISH WORD	VOCABULARIES
12 calumnia	tēona	WW, XI, col. 383,28
"	hearm	Aldhelm(MS. 8),Napier,no.233
13 turpitudo	aefesne, fūlnes	" (" H),Bouterwek,p.492
"	fūlnys, aefesne[1]	" (" 1),Napier,no.3674
	(HM: "= aepsen?")[2]	
"	fōlnes	WW, II, col. 60,21
14 injuria	unriht	" , XI, " 429,19
15 opprobrium	hosp	Aldhelm(MS.H),Mone, no. 6259
"	hosp	" (" "),Bouterwek,p.436
"	bismerung	" (" "), " ,p.507
"	hosp	" (" 1),Napier,no. 471
"	hosp	" (" "), " ," 1261
"	hosp	" (" "), " ," 5228
16 confusio	gimaengiung	Epinal MS,Sweet,no.203
"	gemengiung	Erfurt " , " ," "
"	gemengiung	Corpus " , " ," 522
"	duolma	" " , " ," 457
"	ȝemanȝ	Aldhelm(MS.18),Napier,no.12
"	gemengung	WW, XI, col. 365,3

[1] ..., "in all probability, corrupted f. āewiscnes (w and f are easily confused, and c could fall out between consonants)." (Napier, no.3674, footnote 1)

[2] = aepsenes/-nys? (cf. App. C, p. 184: dedecus)

3. Classified Middle English Material

TEXT	LATIN WORD	ENGLISH WORD	SENSE GR.
WB,EV 1,Ps. 37,8	inlusio	deseit	A I
" ,EV 2," "	"	deceyt	"
" ,LV ," "	"	scornyng	"
Surtees (MS.CVD7),Ps. 37,8	"	bismer	"
" (" H)," "	"	(heþing)	
" (" E)," "	"	(heving)	
Midland (London MS.),Ps. 37,8(37,7)	"	illusioun	"
Higd.Trev., Vol. 2,pp.430-431	"	bygile (verb)	"
" Harl., " "," "	"	illusion (of the (deuelle)	"
" Trev., " "," 210-211	"	bigile (be bigiled)	"
WB,EV 1,4(2) Kings 19,3	blasphemia	blasfemye	A II
" , " ,2 Par.(Chron.) 32,17	"	blasfemye	"
" , " , " " 32,20	"	blasfemye	"
" , " ,2 Esr. (Neh.) 9,18	"	blasfemye	"
" , " , " (") 9,26	"	blasfeme	"
" , " , Tob. 1,21	"	blasfemye	"
" , " ,Job 34,37	"	blasfemye	"
" , " ,Isaiah 37,3	"	blasfemye	"
" ,EV 2,4(2) Kings 19,3	"	blasfemye	"
" , " ,2 Par.(Chron.) 32,17	"	blasfemy	"
" , " , " " 32,20	"	blasfemye	"
" , " ,2 Esr. (Neh.) 9,18	"	blasfemy	"
" , " , " (") 9,26	"	blasfemy	"
" , " , Tob. 1,21	"	blasfemye	"
" , " ,Job 34,37	"	blasfemye	"
" , " ,Isaiah 37,3	"	blasfemye	"
" , " , Daniel 3,96	"	blasfeme	"
" , " ,1 Mcc. 7,38	"	blasfemye	"
" , " ,2 Mcc. 8,4	"	blasfemye	"
" , " ,Matt. 12,31	"	blasfemye,blasfemye	"
" , " , " 15,19	"	blasfemye	"
" , " , " 26,65	"	blasfemye	"
" , " ,Mark 3,28	"	blasphemye	"
" , " , " 7,22	"	blasphemye	"
" , " , " 14,64	"	blasphemye	"
" , " ,Luke 5,21	"	blasphemye	"
" , " ,John 10,33	"	blasphemye	"
" , " ,Jude 9 (cf.2 Peter, 2,11)	"	blasfemye	"
" , " ,Ephes. 4,31	"	blasphemye	"
" , " ,Col. 3,8	"	blasfemye	"
" , " ,1 Tim. 6,4	"	blasfemye	"
" , " ,Acts 6,11	"	blasfemye	"
" , " ,Apc. 13,1; 13,5	"	blasfemye;blasfemye	"
" , " , " 13,6; 17,3	"	blasfemye;blasfemye	"
" ,LV ,4(2) Kings 19,3	"	blasfemye	"
" , " ,2 Par.(Chron.) 32,17	"	blasfemye	"
" , " , " " 32,20	"	blasfemye	"
" , " ,2 Esr. (Neh.) 9,18	"	blasfemye	"
" , " , " (") 9,26	"	blasfemye	"
" , " , Tob. 1,21	"	blasfemye	"

TEXT	LATIN WORD	ENGLISH WORD	SENSE GR.
WB,LV,Job 34,37	blasphemia	blasfemye	A II
" ," ,Isaiah 37,3	"	blasfemye	"
" ," ,Daniel 3,96	"	blasfemye	"
" ," ,1 Mcc. 7,38	"	blasfemye	"
" ," ,2 Mcc. 8,4	"	blasfemye	"
" ," ,Matt. 12,31	"	blasfemye,blasfemye	"
" ," , " 15,19; 26,65	"	blasfemye;blasfemye	"
" ," ,Mark 3,28; 7,22	"	blasfemye;blasfemye	"
" ," , " 14,64	"	blasfemye	"
" ," ,Luke 5,21	"	blasfemye	"
" ," ,John 10,33	"	blasfemye	"
" ," ,Jude 9 (cf.2 Peter 2,11)	"	blasfemye	"
" ," ,Ephes. 4,31	"	blasfemye	"
" ," ,Col. 3,8	"	blasfemye	"
" ," ,1 Tim. 6,4	"	blasfemye	"
" ," ,Acts 6,11	"	blasfemye	"
" ," ,Apc. 13,1; 13,5	"	blasfemye;blasfemye	"
" ," , " 13,6; 17,3	"	blasfemye;blasfemye	"
Paues (MS.S),Jude 9	"	blasphemye	"
" (" "),Ephes. 4,31	"	blasphemye	"
" (" "),Col. 3,8	"	blasphemye	"
" (" "),1 Tim. 6,4	"	blasphemye	"
" (" C),Acts 6,11	"	blaspheme	"
NPE, Ephes. 4,31	"	blasphemye	"
" , Col. 3,8	"	blasphemye	"
" , 1 Tim. 6,4	"	blasphemy	"
Higd.Trev., Vol.7,pp.464-465	"	despisyng	"
" Harl., " "," "	"	blasphemy	"
Ancr.R., p. 68,18; p.88,14	"	blasphemie	"
St.Kath., p. 22; 1.419	"	hoker	"
WB,EV 1,Sir.Eccl. 34,21	subsannatio	scornyng	"
" ,EV 2, " "	"	scornyng	"
" ,LV , " "	"	scornyng	"
" ,EV 2,2 Mcc. 8,17	contumelia	dispite	"
" , " ,Hebr. 10,29	"	wrong, dispit[1]	"
" ,EV 1,Jer. 14,21	"	repref	"
" ,EV 2, " "	"	repref	"
" ,LV ,2 Mcc. 8,17	"	dispit	"
" ," ,Hebr. 10,29	"	dispit	"
" ," ,Jer. 14,21	"	dispite	"
Paues (MS.S),Hebr. 10,29	"	wrong	"
NPE, Hebr. 10,29	"	wrong	"
WB,EV 1,Sir.Eccl. 27,31	inlusio	illusioun, scoorne[1]	A III la
" , " ,Isaiah 66,4	"	illusioun	"
" ,EV 2,Sir.Eccl. 27,31	"	illusioun,scorne[1]	"
" , " ,Isaiah 66,4	"	illusioun	"
" ,LV ,Sir. Eccl. 27,31	"	scornyng	"
" , " ,Isaiah 66,4	"	scornyng	"

TEXT	LATIN WORD	ENGLISH WORD	SENSE GR.
Ancr.R., p. 64,5; p. 83,10-11	irrisio	hoker	A III la
WB,EV 1,Sap.(Wisdom) 12,26	ludibrium	repref	"
" ,EV 2, "	"	repref	"
" , " ,2 Mcc. 8,17	"	scornyng	"
" , " ,Hebr. 11,36	"	scornyng	"
" ,LV , Sap.(Wisdom) 12,26	"	scornyng	"
" , " ,2 Mcc. 8,17	"	scornyng	"
" , " ,Hebr. 11,36	"	scornyng	"
Paues (MS.S), Hebr. 11,36	"	dyspysyng	"
NPE, Hebr. 11,36	"	despyt	"
Higd.Trev., Vol.3, pp.388-389	"	scornen (verb), vilonye	"
" " , " 1, " 178-179	"	byskorn, bysmer	"
" " , " 5, " 430-431	"	scorn	"
" " , " ", " 356-357	"	scornen (verb)	"
" Harl., " 3, " 388-389	"	rebuke	"
WB,EV 1,Jer. 20,8	derisus	scornyng	"
" ,EV 2, " "	"	scornyng	"
" , " ,2 Mcc. 7,39	"	scornen (verb)	"
" ,LV ,Jer. 20,8	"	scorn	"
" , " ,2 Mcc. 7,39	"	scornen (verb)	"
Ancr.R.,p. 32,22; p. 47,29	"	schorn	"
" ," 70,12; " 89,15	"	schornung	"
" ," 132,33; " 155,22	"	schorn	"
WB,EV 1,Ps. 34,16	subsannatio	undirmouwing	"
" , " ,Sir.Eccl. 11,35	"	scorning	"
" ,EV 2,Ps. 34,16	"	undermouwing	"
" , " ,Sir.Eccl. 11,35	"	scornyng	"
" ,LV ,Ps. 34,16	"	mowyng	"
" , " ,Sir.Eccl. 11,35	"	scornyng	"
Surtees (MS.CVD7),Ps. 34,16	"	snering	"
Midland			
(London MS.),Ps.34,16(34,19)	"	undernyming	"
(Dublin ")," " (")	"	(scornyng)	"
WB,EV 1, Sap.(Wisdom) 12,25	derisus	scorn	A III lb
" , " ,Jer. 20,8; 48,26	"	scornyng; scornyng	"
" , " , " 48,39	"	scornyng	"
" , " , " 20,7	"	scorn	"
" , " ,Lam. 3,14	"	scorn	"
" , ,Sap.(Wisdom) 12,25	"	scorn	"
" , " ,Jer. 20,8	"	scornyng	"

TEXT	LATIN WORD	ENGLISH WORD	SENSE GR.
WB,EV 2,Jer. 20,7	derisus	scorn	A III 1b
" , " , " 48,26-27	"	scornyng; scornyng	"
" , " , " 48,39	"	scornyng	"
" , " ,Ez. 23,32	"	scornyng	"
" , " ,1 Mcc. 10,70	"	scoorn	"
" , " ,Lam. 3,14	"	scorn	"
" ,LV ,Sap.(Wisdom) 12,25	"	scorn	"
" , " ,Jer. 20,7-8	"	scorn; scorn	"
" , " , " 48,26-27	"	scorn; scorn	"
" , " , " 48,39	"	scorn	"
" , " ,Ez. 23,32	"	scornyng	"
" , " ,1 Mcc. 10,70	"	scorn	"
" , " ,Lam. 3,14	"	scorn	"
Higd.Harl.,Vol.5, pp.356-357	ludibrium	derision	"
WB,EV 2, Ez. 23,32	subsannatio	undirmouwyng	"
" , " ,Os.(Hosea) 7,16	"	mowyng, scornyng[1]	"
" ,LV , Ez. 23,32	"	mouwyng	"
" , " , Os. (Hosea) 7,16	"	scornyng	"
WB,EV 1,Ps. 78,4	inlusio	scornyng	A III 1c
" ,EV 2," "	"	scornyng	"
" ,LV ," "	"	scornyng	"
Surtees (MS.CVD7),Ps.78,4[2]	"	hebing	"
" (" E)," "	"	(bismer)	"
Midland (London MS.),Ps.78,4	"	desceit	"
WB,EV 2,Ez. 22,4	inrisio	scornyng	"
" ,LV ," "	"	scornyng	"
Higd.Trev.,Vol. 5,pp.356-357	ludibrium	bismer	"
WB,EV 1,Ps. 43,14	derisus	scorn	"
" ,EV 2," "	"	scorn	"
" ,LV ," "	"	scorn	"
Surtees (MS.CVD7),Ps.43,14[3]	"	hebing	"
Midland (London MS.), Ps. 43,14 (43,16)	"	scorne	"
WB,EV 1,Ps. 43,14	subsannatio	undermouwyng	"
" , " ," 78,4	"	mouwing	"
" ,EV 2," 43,14	"	undermouwing	"
" , " ," 78,4	"	mouwing	"
" ,LV ," 43,14	"	mouwyng	"
" , " ," 78,4	"	mowynge	"
Surtees (MS.CVD7),Ps.43,14[3]	"	sneringe	"
" (" ")," 78,4[2]	"	sneryng	"
" (" H)," "	"	(swering)	"
Midland (London MS.) Ps. 43,14 (43,16)	"	undernymyng	"
" (London MS.),Ps. 78,4	"	scornynge	"

TEXT	LATIN WORD	ENGLISH WORD	SENSE GR.
WB, EV 1, Ps. 118,134	calumnia	chaleng	A III 2
" , " , Gen. 43,18	"	chalengyng	"
" , " , Lev. 6,2	"	wrong chalenge	"
" , " , " 19,13	"	wrong chalenge	"
" , " , Deut. 28,29	"	wrong chalenge	"
" , " , " 28,33	"	wrong chaleng	"
" , " , Prov. 28,16	"	chalenge	"
" , " , Eccl. 4,1	"	**chaleng**	"
" , " , " 5,7	"	wrong[1] chaleng	"
" , " , Sir.Eccl. 26,7	"	chaleng	"
" , " , Isaiah 23,12	"	chaleng	"
" , " , " 30,12	"	wronge[1] chalenge	"
" , " , " 33,15	"	wronge[1] chalenge	"
" , " , " 54,14	"	wronge[1] chalenge	"
" , " , " 59,13	"	wrong[1] chalenge	"
" , " , Jer. 7,6	"	wrong[1] chalenge	"
" , " , " 22,17	"	chalange	"
" , " , " 50,33	"	wronge[1] chalenge	"
" , EV 2, Ps. 118,134	"	chaleng	"
" , " , Gen. 43,18	"	chalengyng	"
" , " , Lev. 6,2	"	wrong chalenge	"
" , " , " 19,13	"	wronge chalenge	"
" , " , Deut. 28,29	"	wrong chalenge	"
" , " , " 28,33	"	wronge chaleng	"
" , " , Prov. 28,16	"	chalenge	"
" , " , Eccl. 4,1	"	chalenge	"
" , " , " 5,7	"	wronge chaleng	"
" , " , Sir.Eccl. 26,7	"	chaleng	"
" , " , Isaiah 23,12	"	chaleng	"
" , " , " 30,12	"	wronge chaleng	"
" , " , " 33,15	"	wrong chaleng	"
" , " , " 54,14	"	chalenge	"
" , " , " 59,13	"	wrong chalenge	"
" , " , Jer. 7,6	"	wrong chaleng	"
" , " , " 22,17	"	wronge chalenge	"
" , " , " 50,33	"	chalenge	"
" , " , Ez. 22,29	"	fals chalenge	"
" , " , Os. (Hosea) 5,11	"	fals chalenge	"
" , " , " (") 12,7	"	fals chalenge	"
" , " , Amos 3,9	"	fals chalenge	"
" , " , " 4,1	"	fals chalenge	"
" , " , Luke 3,14	"	fals chaleng	"
" , LV , Ps. 118,134	"	chaleng	"
" , " , Gen. 43,18	"	chalenge	"
" , " , Lev. 6,2	"	fals chaleng	"
" , " , " 19,13	"	fals chalenge	"
" , " , Deut. 28,29	"	fals chaleng	"
" , " , " 28,33	"	fals chaleng	"
" , " , Prov. 28,16	"	fals chalenge	"
" , " , Eccl. 4,1	"	fals chaleng	"
" , " , " 5,7	"	fals chaleng	"
" , " , Sir.Eccl. 26,7	"	fals chaleng	"
" , " , Isaiah 23,12	"	caleng	"
" , " , " 30,12	"	fals caleng	"

TEXT	LATIN TEXT	ENGLISH TEXT	SENSE GR.
WB,LV, Isaiah 33,15	calumnia	false calenge	A III 2
" ," , " 54,14	"	fals caleng	"
" ," , " 59,13	"	fals caleng	"
" ," , Jer. 7,6	"	fals caleng	"
" ," , " 22,17	"	fals caleng	"
" ," , " 50,33	"	fals caleng	"
" ," , Ez. 22,29	"	fals caleng	"
" ," , Os. (Hosea) 5,11	"	fals **chalenge**	"
" ," , " (") 12,7	"	fals caleng	"
" ," , Amos 3,9	"	fals calenge	"
" ," , " 4,1	"	fals caleng	"
" ," , Luke 3,14	"	fals chalange	"
Surtees (MS.CVD7),Ps. 118,134	"	craving	"
Midland (London MS.),Ps. 118,134	"	chalange	"
Higd.Trev., Vol. 4,pp.450-451	"	chalange	"
" " , " 6," 46-47	"	chalenge, blame	"
" " , " 7," 272-273	"	(cause of)chalenge	"
" " , " 7," 274-275	"	chalange	"
" " , " 7," 312-313	"	chalange	"
" " , " 7," 370-371	"	chalange	"
" Harl., " 6," 46-47	"	blamenge	"
" " , " 7," 274-275	"	eny thynge to be discussed afterwarde	"
" " , " 7," 312-313	"	blame	"
" Cott., Pfeffer, p. 105	"	(a cause of) chalange	"
" " , " , " 106	"	chalaynge	"
" " , " , " 116	"	chalange	"
" " , " , " 131	"	chalange	"
WB,EV 1, Isaiah 51,7	blasphemia	blasfeme	A III 3a
" ,EV 2, " "	"	blasfeme	"
" , " , 2 Mcc. 10,35	"	blasfeme	"
" , " , So. (Zeph.) 2,8	"	blasfemye	"
" ,LV , Isaiah 51,7	"	blasfemye	"
" ," , 2 Mcc. 10,35	"	blasfemye	"
" ," , So. (Zeph.) 2,8	"	blasfemye	"
WB,EV 1, 1 Par. (Chron.) 19,5	contumelia	despit	"
" , " , Esther 13,12	"	strijf	"
" , " , Prov. 10,18	"	wrongful blamyng	"
" , " , " 11,2	"	wrongful blamynge	"
" , " , " 20,3	"	wronge blamyng	"
" , " , Sap. (Wisdom) 2,19	"	wrong vndernymyng	"
" , " , Sir.Eccl. 5,17; 10,8	"	strijf; strif	"
" , " , " 21,27; 26,11	"	strijf; strijf	"
" , " , " 22,30; 29,9	"	wrong; wrong	"
" ,EV 2, 1 Par. (Chron.) 19,5	"	despyte	"
" , " , Esther 13,12	"	strif	"
" , " , Prov. 10,18	"	wrongful blamyng	"
" , " , " 11,2	"	wrongful blamyng	"
" , " , " 20,3	"	wrong blamyng	"
" , " , Sap. (Wisdom) 2,19	"	wrong vndernymyng	"
" , " , Sir.Eccl. 5,17; 10,8	"	strif; strif	"

TEXT	LATIN WORD	ENGLISH WORD	SENSE GR.
WB,EV 2,Sir.Eccl. 21,27; 26,11	contumelia	strif; strif	A III 3a
" , " , " 22,30; 29,9	"	wrong; wrong	"
" , " ,Ez. 22,7	"	wrong	"
" , " ,Micha 7,6	"	wronge	"
" , " ,Naum 3,6	"	dispit	"
" , " ,2 Mcc. 1,28	"	dispite	"
" , " ,Matt. 22,6	"	contek	"
" , " ,Mark 12,4	"	chiding, reprouyng[1]	"
" , " ,Luke 11,45	"	dispit	"
" , " , " 20,11	"	dispising	"
" , " ,Rom. 1,24	"	wrong, dispit[1]	"
" , " ,1 Thess. 2,2	"	wrong,fals reprouyng[1]	"
" , " ,Acts 5,41	"	dispysing, wrong	"
" , " , " 14,5	"	dispising,fals blamyng[1]	"
" ,LV ,1 Par.(Chron.) 19,5	"	dispit	"
" , " ,Esther 13,12	"	dispit	"
" , " ,Prov. 10,18; 11,2	"	dispising; dispising	"
" , " , " 20,3	"	dispisyng	"
" , " ,Sap.(Wisdom) 2,19	"	dispisyng	"
" , " ,Sir.Eccl. 5,17; 10,8	"	dispisyng; dispisyng	"
" , " , " 21,27; 26,11	"	dispisyng; dispisyng	"
" , " , " 22,30; 29,9	"	dispisyng; dispisyng	"
" , " ,Ez. 22,7	"	wrong	"
" , " ,Micha 7,6	"	wrong	"
" , " ,Naum 3,6	"	dispit	"
" , " ,2 Mcc. 1,28	"	dispit	"
" , " ,Matt. 22,6	"	turmenten(verb)	"
" , " ,Mark 12,4	"	turmenten(verb)	"
" , " ,Luke 11,45	"	dispit	"
" , " , " 20,11	"	turmenten(verb)	"
" , " ,Rom. 1,24	"	wrong	"
" , " ,1 Thess. 2,2	"	wrong, fals repreuyng[1]	"
" , " ,Acts 5,41	"	dispisyng	"
" , " , " 14,5	"	turmenten (verb)	"
Paues (MS.S),1 Thess. 2,2	"	dishese	"
" (" C),Acts 5,41	"	strif, schame	"
" (" "), " 14,5	"	iniuryos word	"
NPE, Rom. 1,24	"	wrong	"
" , 1 Thess. 2,2	"	wrong	"
Higd.Trev.,Vol. 1,pp.240-241	"	dispitous word	"
" " , " 2," 70-71	"	destroyen (verb)	"
" " , " 3," 80-81	"	mysseien (þerfore)	"
" " , " 5," 364-365	"	dispitous scorn	"
" Harl., " 1," 240-241	"	saye after pleasure	"
" " , " 2," 70-71	"	defilen (verb)	"

TEXT	LATIN WORD	ENGLISH WORD	SENSE GR.
Destr.Troy, p. 157,9; 1. 7658	contumelia	flytyng	A III 3a
Chaucer, p. 46,64-65; 1. 1583	"	striuyng word	"
" , " 46,70; 1. 1592-3	"	word of outerage	"
WB,EV 1, Gen. 50,15	injuria	wronge	"
" , " , Ex. 2,13	"	wrong	"
" , " , Lev. 19,18	"	wroong	"
" , " , 1 Kings (Sam.), Prol. (III,63,90)	"	harm	"
" , " , 2 Kings(Sam.) 19,19	"	wrong	"
" , " , " " (") 19,43	"	wrong	"
" , " , 1 Par.(Chron.) 19,6	"	wrong	"
" , " , Esther, Prol.(IV,114)	"	wrong; wrong	"
" , " , Prov. 9,7	"	wrong	"
" , " , Sir.Eccl. 4,9; 9,17	"	wrong; wrong	"
" , " , " 7,3	"	vnri3twisnes	"
" , " , " 10,6	"	wrong; wrong	"
" , " , " 10,8; 21,5	"	wrong; wrong	"
" , " , Ps. 102,6; 145,7	"	wrong; wrong	"
" ,EV 2, Gen. 50,15; Ex. 2,13	"	wrong; wrong	"
" , " , Lev. 19,18	"	wronge	"
" , " , 1 Kings (Sam.),Prol.	"	harme	"
" , " , 2 " (") 19,19	"	wrong	"
" , " , " " (") 19,43	"	wronge	"
" , " , 1 Par.(Chron.) 19,6	"	wrong	"
" , " , Esther, Prol.	"	wrong; wrong	"
" , " , Prov. 9,7	"	wrong	"
" , " , Sir.Eccl. 4,9; 9,17	"	wrong; wrong	"
" , " , " 7,3	"	vnri3twisnes	"
" , " , " 10,6	"	wrong; wrong	"
" , " , " 10,8; 21,5	"	wrong; wrong	"
" , " , Ps. 102,6; 145,7	"	wrong; wrong	"
" , " , Bar. 6,53; Ez. 18,17	"	wronge; wroong	"
" , " , 2 Mcc. 8,17	"	wronge	"
" , " , Matt. 20,13	"	wrong	"
" , " , 2 Peter 2,7	"	wrong	"
" , " , 1 Cor. 6,7; 6,8	"	wrong; wrong	"
" , " , Col. 3,25	"	iniurie, wrong	"
" , " , 2 Cor. 7,12; 12,13	"	iniurie; wrong	"
" , " , Acts 7,24; 7,27	"	wrong; wrong; wrong	"
" , " , " 27,10; 27,21	"	wrong; wrong	"
" ,LV , Gen. 50,15; Ex. 2,13	"	wrong; wrong	"
" , " , Lev. 19,18	"	wrong	"
" , " , 1 Kings (Sam.),Prol.	"	dispitousnes	"
" , " , 2 " (") 19,19	"	wrong	"
" , " , " " (") 19,43	"	wrong	"
" , " , 1 Par.(Chron.) 19,6	"	wrong	"
" , " , Prov. 9,7	"	wrong	"
" , " , Sir.Eccl. 4,9; 9,17	"	wrong; wrong	"
" , " , " 7,3	"	vnri3tfulnes	"
" , " , " 10,6	"	wrong; wrong	"
" , " , " 10,8; 21,5	"	wrong; wrong	"
" , " , Ps. 102,6; 145,7	"	wrong; wrong	"
" , " , Bar. 6,53	"	**wrong**	"
" , " , Ez. 18,17	"	wrong	"

TEXT	LATIN WORD	ENGLISH WORD	SENSE GR.
WB, LV, 2 Mcc. 8,17	injuria	wrong	A III 3a
" ", Matt. 20,13	"	wrong	"
", ", 2 Peter 2,7	"	wrong	"
", ", 1 Cor. 6,7; 6,8	"	wrong; wrong	"
", ", Col. 3,25	"	iniurie	"
", ", 2 Cor. 7,12	"	iniurie	"
", ", " 12,13	"	wrong	"
", ", Acts 7,24; 7,27	"	wrong; wrong; wrong	"
", ", " 27,10; 27,21	"	wrong; wrong	"
Paues (MS.S), 2 Peter 2,7	"	iniurye	"
" (" "), 1 Cor. 6,7; 6,8	"	wrong; wrong	"
" (" "), Col. 3,25	"	wrong	"
" (" C), Acts 7,24; 7,27	"	wrong; wrong; wrong	"
" (" "), " 27,10	"	iniurye	"
Surtees (MS.CVD7), Ps. 102,6	"	un-right	"
" (" "), " 145,7	"	unrightwisnes	"
Midland (London MS.),Ps.102,6	"	wrong	"
" (" ")," 145,7	"	wrong	"
NPE, Col.3,25; 1 Cor. 6,7	"	wrong; wrong	"
", 1 Cor. 6,8	"	iniurye	"
", 2 Cor. 7,12; 12,13	"	wrong; wrong	"
Higd.Trev., Vol. 2, pp.404-405	"	wrong	"
" " , " ", " 406-407	"	trespas	"
" " , " ", " 410-411	"	wrong	"
" " , " 3, " 472-473	"	wrong	"
" " , " 4, " 216-217	"	wrong	"
" " , " ", " 282-283	"	wrong	"
" " , " ", " 328-329	"	wrong	"
" " , " ", " 330-331	"	damage, wrong	"
" " , " ", " 452-453	"	meschif	"
" " , " 7, " 174-175	"	wrong	"
" " , " ", " 138-139	"	wrong	"
" " , " ", " 218-219	"	wrong	"
" " , " 8, " 94-95	"	wrong	"
" " , " ", " 138-139	"	wrong	"
" " , " ", " 148-149	"	wrong	"
" Harl., " 2, " 404-405	"	wronge	"
" " , " ", " 406-407	"	iniurye	"
" " , " ", " 410-411	"	iniurye	"
" " , " 3, " 472-473	"	iniury	"
" " , " 4, " 282-283	"	iniury	"
" " , " ", " 328-329	"	iniury	"
" " , " ", " 330-331	"	iniury	"
" " , " 7, " 174-175	"	iniury	"
" " , " ", " 138-139	"	iniury	"
" " , " ", " 218-219	"	iniury	"
" " , " 8, " 138-139	"	iniury	"
" " , " ", " 148-149	"	iniury	"
Destr.Troy,p. 32,28-;1.1005-6	"	dyshoner,derf word	"
" " ," 43,13-;" 1424	"	harme	"
" " ," 51,7- ;" 1717-9	"	harm	"
" " ," 51,33-;" 1753-4	"	harme (hethyng)[4]	"
" " ," 52,28-;" 1799	"	harm	"

TEXT	LATIN WORD	ENGLISH WORD	SENSE GR.
Destr.Troy,p.56,15-;1.2033	injuria	tene (torfor)[5]	A III 3a
" " ,p.59,16-;1.2211-	"	hardlaike (shame);	"
		wrange;harme,hethyng,	"
		hurtys; mysse[6]	"
" " ,p.57,22;1.2110	"	wronge	"
" " ,p.61,7-8;1.2324	"	harmen (verb)	"
" " ,p.65,12-;1.2586-	"	greuen(verb); hethyng	"
" " ,p.68,2-3;1.2769	"	velany (grem);hardlaike[7]	"
1.2779	"	wrange (wrathe)[7]	"
" " ,p.81,11-;1.3612-3	"	harme, hethyng	"
" " ,p.104-5; 1.4854-5	"	harm, grem, hethyng	"
" " ,p.107,32;1.5034	"	gilt, greuans	"
" " ,p.109,16;1.5129	"	redur	"
" " ,p.143,5-6;1.6944	"	harme (malis)[8]	"
Ancr.R.,p.64,16-17	"	wouh	"
" ,p.68,22; 88,19	"	wouh (wowes)	"
" ,p.107,23; 128,23	"	wouh	"
" ,p.137,8-9; 160,2	"	wouh (wowes)	"
" ,p. 51,25-26;71,1-2	"	wouh	"
" ,p. 60,33-34;80,2	"	wouh	"
Chaucer,p.12,32; 1.294	"	wronge	"
" ,p.12,35; 1.300	"	wrong	"
" ,p.27,31; 1.875	"	wronge	"
" ,p.32,17; 1.1030	"	wrong	"
" ,p.46,68; 1.1589	"	wronge	"
" ,p.56,17; 1.1910	"	wrong, greuaunce	"
" ,p.88,7 ; 1.3089	"	wronge	"
" ,p.100,1; 1.3519	"	nat ry3t	"
" ,p.103,109;1.3682-3	"	wrong, wrong	"
" ,p.104,117;1.3693	"	wronge, wronge	"
" ,p.104,118-9;1.3696-8	"	wrong, wrong	"
" ,p.104,122-3;1.3702-4	"	wrong, wrong, wronge	"
" ,p.135,112; 1.4822	"	wronge	"
" ,p.144,129; 1.5157	"	wronge	"
Castleford, p.65; 1. 21521	"	wrange	"
St.Kath.,p. 56; 1.1189	"	woh	"
" ,p. "; 1.1193	"	woh	"
WB,EV 1,Ps. 14,3;56,4;68,8	opprobrium	reproof;reproof;reproof	"
" , " ," 68,10-11;122,4	"	reprooue;reproof;reprof	"
" , " ," 77,66;88,51;	"	reproof; reproof	"
" , " ,2 Esr.(Neh.) 4,4	"	repref	"
" , " ,Prov. 18,3	"	reproof	"
" , " ,Sir.Eccl. 41,9	"	reproof	"
" , " ,Isaiah 51,7	"	repref	"
" , " ,Jer. 6,10;20,8;51,51	"	repref;repref;repref	"
" , " ,Lam. 3,30; 3,61	"	repreue; repreue	"
" ,EV 2,Ps. 14,3; 56,4	"	reprof; reprof	"
" , " ," 68,8;68,10-11	"	repref;repreue;repref	"
" , " ," 77,66;88,51;122,4	"	repref;repref;repref	"
" , " ,2 Esr.(Neh.) 4,4	"	repref	"
" , " ,Prov. 18,3	"	repreff	"
" , " ,Sir.Eccl. 41,9	"	repref	"
" , " ,Isaiah 51,7	"	repref	"
" , " ,Jer. 6,10; 20,8;51,51	"	repref; repref; repref	"

TEXT	LATIN WORD	ENGLISH WORD	SENSE GR
WB,EV 2,Lam. 3,30; 3,61	opprobrium	repreue; repreue	A III 3a
" , " ,Bar. 6,72	"	shenship	"
" , " ,Ez. 21,28; 36,30	"	shenship; shenship	"
" , " ," 34,29; 35,12	"	shendship; shendship	"
" , " ," 36,3; 36,15	"	shendship; shendshipe	"
" , " ,Daniel 11,18	"	shendship	"
" , " ,Os.(Hosea) 12,14	"	shenship	"
" , " ,Micha 6,16	"	shenship	"
" , " ,So. (Zeph.) 2,8	"	shenshipe	"
" , " ,Hebr. 10,33	"	schenschip	"
" ,LV ,Ps. 14,3; 56,4	"	schenschip; schenschip	"
" , " ," 68,8; 68,10	"	schenschipe; schenschip	"
" , " ," 68,11; 77,66	"	schenschip; schenschipe	"
" , " ," 88,51; 122,4	"	schenschipe;schenschipe	"
" , " ,2 Esr.(Neh.) 4,4	"	schenschip	"
" , " ,Prov. 18,3	"	schenschip	"
" , " ,Sir.Eccl. 41,9	"	schenschipe	"
" , " ,Isaiah 51,7	"	schenschipe	"
" , " ,Jer. 6,10	"	dispit	"
" , " , " 20,8; 51,51	"	schenschip; schenschipe	"
" , " ,Lam. 3,30; 3,61	"	schenschip; schenschip	"
" , " ,Bar. 6,72	"	schenschip	"
" , " ,Ez. 21,28; 34,29	"	schenschipe; schenschip	"
" , " ," 35,12; 36,3	"	schenschip; schenschipe	"
" , " ," 36,15; 36,30	"	schenschipe;schenschipe	"
" , " ,Daniel 11,18	"	schenschipe	"
" , " ,Os.(Hosea) 12,14	"	schenschipe	"
" , " ,Micha 6,16	"	schenschipe	"
" , " ,So.(Zeph.) 2,8	"	schenschip	"
" , " ,Hebr. 10,33	"	schenschip	"
Surtees (MS.CVD7),Ps. 14,3	"	gram	"
" (" ")," 56,4	"	up-braidinge	"
" (" ")," 68,8	"	up-braidinge	"
" (" ")," 68,10	"	up-braidinge	"
" (" ")," 68,11	"	up-braidinge	"
" (" ")," 77,66	"	up-braidynge	"
" (" ")," 88,51	"	up-braidinge	"
" (" ")," 122,4	"	up-braiding	"
Midland			
(London MS.),Ps. 14,3 (14,4)	"	reprusynge	"
(Dublin ")," " (")	"	(reprofe)	
(London ")," 56,4	"	reproceinge	"
(Dublin ")," "	"	(reproue)	
(London ")," 68,8 (68,10)	"	reproce	"
(Dublin ")," " (")	"	(reproue)	
(London ")," 68,10(68,12)	"	repruce	"
(Dublin ")," " (")	"	(reproue)	
(London ")," 68,11(68,13)	"	reproceing	"
(Dublin ")," " (")	"	(reproue)	
(London ")," 77,66(77,72)	"	repruce	"
(Dublin ")," " (")	"	(reproue)	
(London ")," 88,51(88,49)	"	repruce	"
(Dublin ")," " (")	"	(reproue)	
(London ")," 122,4(122,5)	"	reprucynge	"
NPE,Hebr. 10,33	"	reproue	"

TEXT	LATIN WORD	ENGLISH WORD	SENSE GR.
Higd.Trev., Vol. 3,pp.388-389	opprobrium	despite	A III 3a
" " , " 4," 364-365	"	despite	"
" " , " 7," 176-177	"	reprove	"
" " , " 8," 298-299	"	vilenye	"
" Harl., " 4," 364-365	"	opprobry	"
" " , " 8," 298-299	"	obprobry	"
Ancr.R., p. 51,22; p. 69,33	"	schendfule word	"
" , " 51,27; " 70,2-3	"	missiggen (verb)	"
WB,EV 1,Isaiah 43,28	blasphemia	blasfemye	A III 3b
" ,EV 2, " "	"	blasfemye	"
" ,LV , " "	"	blasfemye	"
" ,EV 1,Sap.(Wisdom) 4,19	contumelia	wrong blamyng	"
" , " ,Sir.Eccl. 6,1	"	strijf	"
" , " , " 3,12	"	wrong	"
" , " , " 22,4	"	repref	"
" ,EV 2,Sap.(Wisdom) 4,19	"	wrong blamyng	"
" , " ,Sir.Eccl. 6,1	"	strif	"
" , " , " 3,12	"	wrong	"
" , " , " 22,4	"	repref	"
" , " ,Rom. 9,21	"	dispyt	"
" , " ,2 Tim. 2,20	"	dispit	"
" ,LV ,Sap.(Wisdom) 4,19	"	dispisyng	"
" , " ,Sir.Eccl. 6,1; 3,12	"	dispisyng; dispisyng	"
" , " , " 22,4	"	dispisyng	"
" , " ,Rom. 9,21	"	dispit	"
" , " ,2 Tim. 2,20	"	dispit	"
Paues (MS.S),2 Tim. 2,20	"	defoul	"
NPE,Rom. 9,21	"	despyt	"
" ,2 Tim. 2,20	"	vilenye	"
Ancr.R., p. 138,5-6; p.161,3	**injuria**	wouh	"
WB,EV 1,Ps. 118,22; 118,39	opprobrium	reproof; reproof	"
" , " ,Gen. 30,23	"	reproue	"
" , " ,Joshua 5,9	"	repreef	"
" , " ,1 Kings(Sam.) 17,26	"	reproof	"
" , " ," " (") 25,39	"	reproef	"
" , " ,2 " (") 13,13	"	reproef	"
" , " ,2 Esr.(Neh.) 1,3	"	repref	"
" , " ,Judith 5,18; 5,25	"	repref; repref	"
" , " ,Job 19,5	"	repreue	"
" , " ,Prov. 6,33	"	reproof	"
" , " ,Sir.Eccl. 20,26;41,40	"	wicke reproof;reproof	"
" , " , " 42,11;42,14	"	reprof; reproof	"
" , " , " 47,4	"	repref	"
" , " ,Isaiah 4,1; 25,8	"	reprof; reprof	"
" , " , " 30,5;47,3;54,4	"	repref;repref;repref	"
" , " ,Jer. 14,21; 20,11;23,40	"	repref;repref;repref	"
" , " , " 24,9; 29,18; 31,19	"	repref;repref;repref	"
" , " , " 42,18; 49,13	"	repreef; repreef	"
" , " , " 44,8; 44,12	"	repref; repref	"
" , " ,Lam. 2,6; 5,1	"	repref; repref	"
" ,EV 2,Ps. 118,22; 118,39	"	repref; repref	"
" , " ,Gen. 30,23	"	reprofe	"

TEXT	LATIN WORD	ENGLISH WORD	SENSE GR.
WB,EV 2,Joshua 5,9	opprobrium	reproof	A III 3b
" , " ,1 Kings (Sam.) 17,26	"	reprofe	"
" , " ," " (") 25,39	"	reproof	"
" , " ,2 " (") 13,13	"	reproof	"
" , " ,2 Esr.(Neh.) 1,3	"	repref	"
" , " ,Judith 5,18; 5,25	"	repref; repref	"
" , " ,Job 19,5	"	repreue	"
" , " ,Prov. 6,33	"	repref	"
" , " ,Sir.Eccl. 20,26	"	wicke repref	"
" , " , " 41,10; 42,11	"	repref; repref	"
" , " , " 42,14; 47,4	"	repref; repref	"
" , " ,Isaiah 4,1;25,8;30,5	"	repref;repref;repref	"
" , " , " 47,3; 54,4	"	repreef; repref	"
" , " ,Jer. 14,21;20,11;23,40	"	repref;repref;repref	"
" , " , " 24,9; 29,18;31,19	"	repref;repref;repref	"
" , " , " 42,18; 49,13	"	repref; repref	"
" , " , " 44,8; 44,12	"	repref; repref	"
" , " ,Lam. 2,6; 5,1	"	repref; repref	"
" , " ,Bar. 6,47	"	shenshipe	"
" , " ,Ez. 5,14; 16,57	"	shenship; shenship	"
" , " ,Daniel 9,16	"	shenshipe	"
" , " ,Joel 2,17	"	schendship	"
" , " ,1 Mcc. 1,41; 4,45	"	shenship; shenship	"
" , " , " 4,58; 10,70	"	shenship; shenship	"
" , " ,Luke 1,25	"	schenschip	"
" , " ,1 Tim. 3,7	"	schenschip, reprof	"
" ,LV ,Ps. 118,22; 118,39	"	schenschipe;schenschip	"
" , " ,Gen. 30,23	"	schenschipe	"
" , " ,Joshua 5,9	"	schenschip	"
" , " ,1 Kings (Sam.) 17,26	"	schenschip	"
" , " ," " (") 25,39	"	schenschip	"
" , " ,2 " (") 13,13	"	schenschip	"
" , " ,2 Esr.(Neh.) 1,3	"	schenschip	"
" , " ,Judith 5,18; 5,25	"	schenschip;schenschip	"
" , " ,Job 19,5	"	schenschip	"
" , " ,Prov. 6,33	"	schenschip	"
" , " ,Sir.Eccl. 20,26	"	wickid schenschip	"
" , " , " 41,10; 47,4	"	schenschip; schenschip	"
" , " , " 42,11; 42,14	"	schenschipe;schenschipe	"
" , " ,Isaiah 4,1; 30,5	"	schenschip; schenschip	"
" , " , " 25,8; 47,3	"	schenschipe;schenschipe	"
" , " , " 54,4	"	schenschipe	"
" , " ,Jer. 14,21; 20,11	"	schenschip; schenschip	"
" , " , " 23,40; 24,9	"	schenschipe;schenschipe	"
" , " , " 29,18; 31,19	"	schenschipe;schenschipe	"
" , " , " 42,18; 44,8	"	schenschipe;schenschipe	"
" , " , " 44,12; 49,13	"	schenschipe;schenschipe	"
" , " ,Lam. 2,6; 5,1	"	schenschipe;schenschipe	"
" , " ,Bar. 6,47	"	schenschipe	"
" , " ,Ez. 5,14; 16,57	"	schenschip; schenschip	"
" , " ,Daniel 9,16	"	schenschipe	"
" , " ,Joel 2,17	"	schenschipe	"
" , " ,1 Mcc. 1,41; 4,45	"	schenschip; schenschip	"
" , " , " 4,58; 10,70	"	schenschipe;schenschip	"
" , " ,Luke 1,25	"	repreef	"
" , " ,1 Tim. 3,7	"	repreef	"

TEXT	LATIN WORD	ENGLISH WORD	SENSE GR.
Surtees (MS.CVD7), Ps. 118,22	opprobrium	up-braiding	A III 3b
" (" "), " 118,39	"	up-braidinge	"
Midland			
(London MS.), Ps. 118,22	"	upbradeing	"
(Dublin "), " "	"	(reproue)	
(London "), " 118,39	"	reproce	"
(Dublin "), " "	"	(reproue)	"
NPE,1 Tim. 3,7	"	repref	"
Paues (MS.S),1 Tim. 3,7	"	obbrayd	"
WB,EV 2,Ez. 5,15	blasphemia	blasfemye	A III 3c
" ,LV ," "	"	blasfemye	"
" ,EV 1,Ps. 21,7; 30,12	opprobrium	reproof;reproof	"
" , " ," 38,9; 43,14	"	reproof; reproof	"
" , " ," 78,4; 88,42	"	reproof; reproof	"
" , " ," 108,25	"	reproof	"
" , " ,Judith 7,16	"	reproof	"
" , " ,1 Kings (Sam.) 11,2	"	reproof	"
" , " ,2 Esr.(Neh.) 2,17	"	reproof	"
" ,EV 2,Ps. 21,7; 30,12; 43,14	"	repref;repref;repref	"
" , " ," 38,9	"	reprof	"
" , " ," 78,4;88,42;108,25	"	repref;repref;repref	"
" , " ,Judith 7,16	"	repref	"
" , " ,1 Kings (Sam.) 11,2	"	reproue	"
" , " ,2 Esr.(Neh.) 2,17	"	repref	"
" , " ,Bar. 6,71	"	repreue	"
" , " ,Ez. 5,15; 22,4	"	shenship; shenship	"
" , " ,Daniel 3,33	"	shenship	"
" , " ,Joel 2,19	"	shenship	"
" ,LV ,Ps. 21,7; 38,9	"	schenschip; schenschip	"
" , " ," 30,12; 43,14	"	schenship; schenschip	"
" , " ," 78,4; 88,42	"	schenschipe;schenschipe	"
" , " ," 108,25	"	schenschipe	"
" , " ,Judith 7,16	"	schenschip	"
" , " ,1 Kings (Sam.) 11,2	"	schenschip	"
" , " ,2 Esr.(Neh.) 2,17	"	schenship	"
" , " ,Bar. 6,71	"	schenschipe	"
" , " ,Ez. 5,15; 22,4	"	schenschipe;schenschipe	"
" , " ,Daniel 3,33	"	schenschipe	"
" , " ,Joel 2,19	"	schenschipe	"
Surtees (MS.CVD7),Ps. 21,7	"	up-braiding	"
" (" ")," 30,12	"	up-braidinge	"
" (" ")," 38,9	"	up-braiding	"
" (" ")," 43,14	"	up-braiding	"
" (" ")," 78,4	"	up-braidinge	"
" (" ")," 88,42	"	up-braiding	"
" (" ")," 108,25	"	up-braiding	"
Midland			
(London MS.),Ps. 21,7 (21,5)	"	reproceyng	"
(Dublin ")," " (")	"	(reprouyng)	
(London ")," 30,12(30,14)	"	reproce	"
(Dublin ")," " (")	"	(reproue)	
(London ")," 38,9 (38,12)	"	reproce	"
(Dublin ")," " (")	"	(reproue)	

TEXT	LATIN WORD	ENGLISH WORD	SENSE G
(London MS.),Ps. 43,14(43,16)	opprobrium	repruse	A III 3
(Dublin ")," " (")	"	(reproue)	
(London ")," 78,4	"	reproceing	"
(Dublin ")," "	"	(reprouyng)	
(London ")," 88,42(88,40)	"	reproce	"
(Dublin ")," " (")	"	(reproue)	
(London ")," 108,25(108,24)	"	upbraidynge	"
(Dublin ")," " (")	"	(reproue)	
Higd.Trev.,Vol. 3,pp. 374-375	dedecus	schame	B I
Destr.Troy, p. 51,34; 1.1753-4	"	hethyng	"
" " ," 55,18; " 1968	"	spite	"
" " , " 57,4; " 2072-4	"	grem, shame	"
" " , " 81,26; " 3642-3	"	dyshonour (daunger)[9]	"
" " , " 91,13; " 4176	"	shame, shenship [10]	"
" " , " 107,32; " 5038	"	dishonour (spite)[10]	"
" " , " 119,28; " 5617	"	shame	"
Castleford, " 211; l. 25583	"	dishonour, schame	"
WB,EV 1,Isaiah 20,4	ignominia	shenshipe	"
" , " ,2 Par.(Chron.) 32,21	"	shenshipe	"
" , " ,Prov. 14,28	"	shenshipe	"
" , " ,Jer. 51,51; 46,12	"	shenshipe; shenshipe	"
" ,EV 2,Isaiah 20,4	"	shenshipe	"
" , " ,2 Par.(Chron.) 32,21	"	schenschip	"
" , " ,Prov. 14,28	"	shenshipe	"
" , " ,Jer. 46,12; 51,51	"	shenshepe; shenshype	"
" , " ,Ez. 32,24; 32,25	"	yuel fame; yuel fame	"
" ,LV ,Isaiah 20,4	"	schenschipe	"
" , " ,2 Par.(Chron.) 32,21	"	schenship	"
" , " ,Prov. 14,28	"	schenschipe	"
" , " ,Jer. 46,12	"	schenschipe	"
" , " , " 51,51	"	schame	"
" , " ,Ez. 32,24; 32,25	"	schenschipe; schenschipe	"
Higd.Trev., Vol.8,pp. 130-131	"	mescheef	"
" " , " 3," 374-375	"	schame, schendschip	"
WB,EV 1,Ps. 43,16; 88,46	confusio	confusioun; confusioun	"
" , " ," 68,8	"	shenshipe	"
" , " ," 68,20	"	shame	"
" , " ,Judith 14,16	"	confusioun	"
" , " ,Isaiah 54,4; 61,7	"	confucioun; confusioun	"
" ,EV 2,Ps. 43,16; 88,46	"	confusioun; confusion	"
" , " ," 68,8	"	shenshipe	"
" , " ," 68,20	"	confusioun	"
" , " ,Judith 14,16	"	confusioun	"
" , " ,Isaiah 54,4; 61,7	"	confusioun; confusioun	"
" , " ,Ez. 32,30	"	confusioun	"
" , " ,Hebr. 12,2	"	confusioun	"
" ,LV ,Ps. 43,16; 88,46	"	schenschipe; schenschip	"
" , " ," 68,8	"	schame	"
" , " ," 68,20	"	dispysyng	"
" , " ,Judith 14,16	"	confusioun	"
" , " ,Isaiah 54,4; 61,7	"	schenschipe; schenschip	"
" , " ,Ez. 32,30	"	schenschipe	"

TEXT	LATIN WORD	ENGLISH WORD	SENSE GR.
WB,LV,Hebr., 12,2	confusio	confusioun	B I
Surtees (MS.CVD7),Ps. 43,16	"	schenschipe	"
" (" ")," 68,8	"	schenschip	"
" (" ")," 68,20	"	schenschip	"
" (" ")," 88,46	"	schenschip	"
Midland			
(London MS.),Ps. 43,16 (43,17)	"	confusion	"
(" ")," 68,8 (68,10)	"	confucioun	"
(Dublin ")," " (")	"	(confusion)	"
(London ")," 68,20 (68,23)	"	confisioun	"
(Dublin ")," " (")	"	(confusion)	"
(London ")," 88,46 (88,44)	"	confusion	"
NPE,Hebr. 12,2	"	confusyoun	"
Ancr.R.,p.138,5-6;p.161,3-4	"	scheome	"
" ," 138,28 ;" 161,31	"	schendlac	"
Higd.Trev.,Vol. 3,pp. 420-421	infamia	schaundre (sclaundre?) B II	
" " , "," 356-357	"	evel loos	"
" Harl., " "," 420-421	"	trespas	"
WB,EV 1,Sir.Eccl. 23,36	dedecus	vilenie	"
" ,EV 2, " "	"	vilenye	"
" ,LV , " "	"	schenschipe	"
" ,EV 1,Lev. 18,15; 18,17	ignominia	shenscheep;shenschep	"
" , " , " 20,11; 20,17	"	schenschep;shensheep	"
" , " , " 20,19; 20,20	"	sheensheep;sheenscheep	"
" , " ,Prov. 6,33	"	shenshipe	"
" , " ,Isaiah 47,3	"	shenshipe	"
" , " ,Jer. 13,26	"	shenshipe	"
" , " ,Lam. 1,8	"	shenshipe	"
" ,EV 2,Lev. 18,15; 18,17	"	shenshyp; shenship	"
" , " , " 20,11; 20,17	"	shenship; shenship	"
" , " , " 20,19; 20,20	"	shenship; shenship	"
" , " ,Prov. 6,33	"	shenshepe	"
" , " ,Isaiah 47,3	"	shenshipe	"
" , " ,Jer. 13,26	"	shenshepe	"
" , " ,Lam. 1,8	"	shenshipe	"
" , " ,Ez. 16,36; 16,37	"	yuel fame; yuel fame	"
" , " ," 16,39; 16,52	"	yuel fame; yuel fame	"
" , " ," 16,54; 16,58	"	yuel fame; yuel fame	"
" , " ," 23,10; 23,18	"	yuel fame; yuel fame	"
" , " ," 23,29	"	euyl fame	"
" , " ,Os.(Hosea) 2,9; 4,18	"	yuel fame; yuel fame	"
" , " ,Ez. 16,8	"	shame	"
" , " ,Rom. 1,26	"	yuel fame, schenschip	B I
" ,LV ,Lev. 18,15; 18,17	"	schenschip;schenschip	"
" , " , " 20,11; 20,17	"	schenschip;schenschip	"
" , " , " 20,19	"	schenschip	"
" , " , " 20,20	"	filthe	"
" , " ,Prov. 6,33	"	sclaundrith(sclaundre?)	"
" , " ,Isaiah 47,3	"	schame	"
" , " ,Jer. 13,26	"	schenschipe	"

TEXT	LATIN WORD	ENGLISH WORD	SENSE GR.
WB,LV,Lam. 1,8	ignominia	schenschipe	B II
" ," ,Ez. 16,8; 16,36	"	schenschipe; schenschipe	"
" ," ," 16,37; 16,39	"	schenschipe; schenschipe	"
" ," ," 16,52; 16,54	"	schenschipe; schenschipe	"
" ," ," 16,58; 23,10	"	schenschipe; schenschipe	"
" ," ," 23,18; 23,29	"	schenschipe; schenschipe	"
" ," ,Os.(Hosea) 2,9; 4,18	"	schenschipe; schenschipe	"
" ," ,Rom. 1,26	"	schenschipe	"
NPE,Rom. 1,26	"	schame	"
WB,EV 1,Ex. 20,26	turpitudo	fylþe	"
" , " ," 28,42	"	fylþhede	"
" , " ,Lev. 18,6	"	fulþhed	"
" , " ," 18,7	"	fulþhede; fulþhede	"
" , " ," 18,7	"	fulþhede	"
" , " ," 18,8	"	fulþhede; fulþhede	"
" , " ," 18,9	"	fylþhede	"
" , " ," 18,10	"	fulþhede; fulþhede	"
" , " ," 18,11	"	fulþhe	"
" , " ," 18,12	"	fulþe	"
" , " ," 18,13; 18,15	"	fulþhede; fulþhede	"
" , " ," 18,14	"	fylþhede	"
" , " ," 18,16	"	fulþhede; fulþhede	"
" , " ," 18,17	"	filþhede	"
" , " ," 18,18; 20,18	"	fulþhede; fulþhede	"
" , " ," 20,17	"	fulþhede; fulþhede	"
" , " ," 20,19; 20,21	"	fulþhede; fulþhede	"
" , " ,Prov. 6,33	"	filþe	"
" , " ,Sir.Eccl. 26,11	"	filþehed	"
" , " , " 29,28	"	filþehed	"
" , " , " 30,13	"	filþehed	"
" , " ,Isaiah 47,2	"	filþehed	"
" ,EV 2,Ex. 20,26	"	filthe	"
" , " ," 28,42	"	filthehed	"
" , " ,Lev. 18,6	"	filthed	"
" , " ," 18,7	"	filthheed; filthheed	"
" , " ," 18,7	"	filtheheed	"
" , " ," 18,8	"	filthheed; filthheed	"
" , " ," 18,9	"	filthheed	"
" , " ," 18,10	"	filthheed; filthheed	"
" , " ," 18,11	"	filthheed	"
" , " ," 18,12	"	filth	"
" , " ," 18,13	"	filthhed	"
" , " ," 18,14; 18,15	"	filthheed; filthheed	"
" , " ," 18,16	"	filthheed; filthhed	"
" , " ," 18,17	"	filthheed	"
" , " ," 18,18	"	filthhede	"
" , " ," 20,17	"	filthheed; filthheed	"
" , " ," 20,18	"	filtheheed	"
" , " ," 20,19; 20,21	"	filthheed; filthheed	"
" , " ,	"	filthe	"
" , " ,Sir. Eccl.26,11	"	filtheed	"
" , " , " 29,28	"	filthehed	"
" , " , " 30,13	"	filthehed	"
" , " ,Isaiah 47,2	"	filthed	"

TEXT	LATIN WORD	ENGLISH WORD	SENSE GR.
WB,EV 2,Ez. 16,37	turpitudo	filth	A B II
" , " ,Rom. 1,27	"	filthhede	"
" , " ,Ephes. 5,4	"	filthe	"
" , " ,Apc. 16,15	"	filthhed	"
" ,LV ,Ex. 20,26; 28,42	"	filthe; filthe	"
" , " ,Lev. 18,6	"	filthe	"
" , " , " 18,7	"	filthe; filthe; filthe	"
" , " , " 18,8; 18,9	"	filthe; filthe; filthe	"
" , " , " 18,10; 18,11	"	filthe; filthe; filthe	"
" , " , " 18,12-18,14	"	filthe; filthe; filthe	"
" , " , " 18,15; 18,16	"	filthe; filthe; filthe	"
" , " , " 18,17; 18,18	"	filthe; filthe	"
" , " , " 20,17; 20,18	"	filthe; filthe; filthe	"
" , " , " 20,19; 20,21	"	filthe; filthe	"
" , " ,Prov. 6,33	"	filthe	"
" , " ,Sir.Eccl. 26,11	"	filthe	"
" , " , " 29,28	"	filthe	"
" , " , " 30,13	"	filthe	"
" , " ,Isaiah 47,2	"	filthe	"
" , " ,Ez. 16,37	"	filthe	"
" , " ,Rom. 1,27	"	filthehed	"
" , " ,Ephes. 5,4	"	filthe	"
" , " ,Apc. 16,15	"	filthhed	"
Paues (MS. S),Ephes. 5,4	"	fylþe	"
NPE,Rom. 1,27	"	filthe	"
" ,Ephes. 5,4	"	fylthe	"
Higd.Trev.,Vol. 6,pp. 44-45	"	foyle, filþe, synne	"
" Harl., " ", " "	"	synne	"
Ancr.R., p.77,23-25;p.96,16	"	fulde	"
Midland (London MS.), Hymn 15,36 (Athanasia lex)	confusio	confusion	"
WB,EV 2,Ez. 16,7; 16,22	"	confusioun; confusioun	"
" , " ," 16,52	"	yuel fame	"
" , " ," 16,63	"	confusioun	"
" , " ,1 Peter 4,4	"	confusioun	"
" , " ,Apc. 3,18	"	confusioun	"
" ,LV ,Ez. 16,7; 16,22	"	schenschipe; schenschipe	"
" , " ," 16,52	"	schenschipe	"
" , " ," 16,63	"	schame	"
" , " ,1 Peter 4,4	"	confusioun	"
" , " ,Apc. 3,18	"	confusioun	"
Paues (MS.S),1 Peter 4,4	"	confusyoun	"
Ancr.R.,p.77,20-; p.96,15-	"	scheome	"
WB,EV 2,2 Cor. 6,8	infamia	yuel fame	B III
" ,LV ," " "	"	yuel fame	"
Paues (MS.S),2 Cor. 6,8	"	diffamynge	"
NPE,2 Cor. 6,8	"	ylle fame	"
Higd.Trev.,Vol. 4,pp.280-281	"	evel ded	"
Destr.Troy,p.27,15; 1.833	"	harme	"
" " ," 165,22-;1.8119	"	(shame, shenship)	"
" " ," 228,28-;" 11748	"	fame(... lose)	"
" " ," 238,21; " 12209	"	lose(... lost)	"

TEXT	LATIN WORD	ENGLISH WORD	SENSE GR.
Destr.Troy,p. 238,21;1.12211	infamia	(shame)	B III
WB,EV 1,Sir.Eccl. 3,13	dedecus	vilenye	"
" ,EV 2, " "	"	vylenye	"
" ,LV , " "	"	schenschip	"
Higd.Trev.,Vol. 7,pp. 32-33	"	schame	"
" " , " "," 162-163	"	unworschippe,(blamynge)	"
" " , " 8," 154-155	"	vilenye	"
" Harl., " 7," 32-33	"	miserable honoure	"
" " , " "," 162-163	"	trowble	"
Destr.Troy,p. 20,29;1. 581	"	(lure)	
" " , " " : 586	"	accounted a coward	"
" " ," 165,22;" 8119	"	shame, shenship	"
" " ," 221,25;" 11342	"	shame	"
Chaucer,p.58,8-9;1. 1980-81	"	vylenye	"
WB,EV 1,Ps. 82,17	ignominia	shenshipe	"
" , " ,Isaiah 22,18; 23,9	"	shenshipe; shenshipe	"
" , " , " 30,30	"	shenshipe	"
" , " ,Jer. 3,25; 6,14	"	shenshipe; shenshipe	"
" , " " 8,11; 23,40	"	shenshipe; shenshipe	"
" , " ,Prov. 3,35; 13,18	"	shenshipe; shenshipe	"
" , " ," 17,21; 18,3	"	shenshipe; shenshipe	"
" , " ,Ex. 32,25	"	senschip	"
" ,EV 2,Ps. 82,17	"	shenshipe	"
" " ,Ex. 32,25	"	senship	"
" , " ,Isaiah 22,18; 23,9	"	shenshipe; schenshipe	"
" , " , " 30,3	"	shenshepe	"
" , " ,Jer. 3,25; 6,14	"	shenshipe; shenshipe	"
" , " " 8,11; 23,40	"	shenshipe; shenshipe	"
" , " ,Prov. 3,35; 13,18	"	shenshipe; shenshipe	"
" , " ," 17,21; 18,3	"	shenshipe; shenshipe	"
" , " ,Os.(Hosea) 4,7	"	yuel fame	"
" , " ,Micha 1,11	"	yuel fame	"
" , " ,Naum 3,5	"	yuel fame	"
" , " ,Hab. 2,16	"	yuel fame; yuel fame	"
" , " ,1 Cor. 11,14	"	yuel fame, sclaundre	"
" , " ,1 Mcc. 1,42	"	yuel fame	"
" ,LV ,Ps. 82,17	"	schenschipe	"
" , " ,Ex. 32,25	"	schenschip	"
" , " ,Prov. 3,25; 17,21	"	schenschipe; schenschipe	"
" , " , " 13,18	"	schenschip	"
" , " , " 18,3	"	sclaundre	"
" , " ,Isaiah 22,18; 23,9	"	schenschipe; schenschipe	"
" , " , " 30,3	"	schenschipe	"
" , " ,Jer. 3,25; 23,40	"	sclaundir; sclaundir	"
" , " , " 6,14	"	yuel fame	"
" , " , " 8,11	"	schenschipe	"
" , " ,Os.(Hosea) 4,7	"	schenschipe	"
" , " ,Micha 1,11	"	yuel fame	"
" , " ,Naum 3,5	"	yuel fame	"
" , " ,Hab. 2,16	"	yuel fame; yuel fame	"
" , " ,1 Mcc. 1,42	"	yuel fame	"
" , " ,1 Cor. 11,14	"	schenschipe	"
Surtees (MS. CVD7),Ps. 82,17	"	schenschip	"
Midland (London MS.), Ps.82,17	"	wicked los (wicked des)	"

TEXT	LATIN WORD	ENGLISH WORD	SENSE GR.
Paues (MS.S),1 Cor. 11,14	ignominia	schenschyp	B III
NPE,1 Cor. 11,14	"	vylenye	"
Higd.Trev.,Vol. 2,pp.352-353	"	fyle, unworþy (adj.)	"
Ancr.R., p. 30,4;p. 44,24	"	schome, sunne	"
" , " 123,21;p.145,20-21	"	seoruwe	"
" , " 123,12-;p.145,13	"	scheomfule sunne	"
Destr.Troy,p.165,24; 1.8121	"	fame (of filth)	"
WB,EV 1,Ps. 34,26; 39,16	confusio	confusioun; confusioun	"
" , " ," 70,13; 108,29	"	confusioun; confusioun	"
" , " ," 131.18	"	shenshipe	"
" , " ,1 Kings (Sam.) 20,30	"	confusiown; confusiown	"
" , " ,1 Esr.(Ezra) 9,7	"	confusioun	"
" , " ,Judith 8,19	"	confusioun	"
" , " ,Job 8,22	"	confusioun	"
" , " ,Prov. 10,5; 10,14	"	confusioun; confusioun	"
" , " , " 12,4; 18,13	"	confusioun; confusioun	"
" , " ,Sir.Eccl. 3,12; 25,29	"	shenshipe; shenshipe	"
" , " , " 4,25	"	confusiown; confusion	"
" , " , " 5,17; 20,24	"	confusioun; confusioun	"
" , " , " 20,25; 20,28	"	confusioun; confusioun	"
" , " , " 42,1; 22,3	"	confusioun; confusioun	"
" , " , " 29,19	"	confusioun	"
" , " ,Isaiah 30,3; 30,5	"	confusioun; confusioun	"
" , " , " 42,17; 45,16	"	confusioun; confusioun	"
" , " ,Jer. 3,24; 3,25	"	confusioun; confusioun	"
" , " , " 6,15; 7,19	"	confusioun; confusioun	"
" , " , " 8,12; 10,17	"	confusioun; confusioun	"
" , " , " 11,13; 20,18	"	confusioun; confusioun	"
" , " ,Bar. 1,15	"	confusioun	"
" ,EV 2,Ps. 34,26; 39,16	"	confusioun; confusioun	"
" , " ," 70,13; 108,29	"	confusioun; confusion	"
" , " ," 131,18	"	shenshipe	"
" , " ,1 Kings (Sam.) 20,30	"	confusioun; confusyoun	"
" , " ,1.Esr.(Ezra) 9,7	"	confusioun	"
" , " ,Judith 8,19	"	confusioun	"
" , " ,Job 8,22	"	confusioun	"
" , " ,Prov. 10,5; 10,14	"	confusioun; confusioun	"
" , " , " 12,4; 18,13	"	confusioun; confusioun	"
" , " ,Sir.Eccl. 3,12; 25,29	"	shenshipe; shenshipe	"
" , " , " 4,25	"	confusioun; confusioun	"
" , " , " 5,17; 20,24	"	confusioun; confusioun	"
" , " , " 20,25; 20,28	"	confusioun; confusioun	"
" , " , " 22,3; 29,19	"	confusioun; confusioun	"
" , " , " 42,1	"	confusioun	"
" , " ,Isaiah 30,3; 30,5	"	confusioun; confusioun	"
" , " , " 42,17; 45,16	"	confusioun; confusioun	"
" , " ,Jer. 3,24; 3,25	"	confusioun; confusyoun	"
" , " , " 6,15; 7,19	"	confusioun; confusioun	"
" , " , " 8,12; 10,17	"	confusioun; confusioun	"
" , " , " 11,13; 20,18	"	confusion; confusioun	"
" , " ,Bar. 1,15	"	confusioun	"
" , " ,Ez. 7,18; 36,6	"	confusioun; confusioun	"
" , " , " 36,7; 36,15	"	confusioun; confusioun	"
" , " , " 39,26; 44,13	"	confusioun; confusioun	"

TEXT	LATIN WORD	ENGLISH WORD	SENSE GR.
WB,EV 2,Daniel 3,40	confusio	confusioun, (shame)	B III
" , " ,Os.(Hosea) 9,10	"	confusioun	"
" , " ,Abd. 10	"	confusioun	"
" , " ,Micha 7,10	"	confusioun	"
" , " ,Hab. 2,10	"	confusioun	"
" , " ,So.(Zeph.) 3,5; 3,19	"	confusioun;confusioun	"
" , " ,Jude 13	"	confusioun	"
" , " ,Phil. 3,19	"	confusioun	"
" , " ,Luke 21,25	"	confusioun	"
" ,LV ,Ps. 34,26; 131,18	"	schame; schame	"
" , " ," 39,16	"	confusioun	"
" , " ," 70,13; 108,29	"	schenschip; schenschipe	"
" , " ,1 Kings (Sam.), 20,30	"	confusioun; confusioun	"
" , " ,1 Esr.(Ezra) 9,7	"	schenship	"
" , " ,Judith 8,19	"	confusioun	"
" , " ,Job 8,22	"	schenschip	"
" , " ,Prov. 10,5; 10,14	"	confusioun; confusioun	"
" , " , " 12,4	"	confusioun	"
" , " , " 18,13	"	schenschipe	"
" , " ,Sir.Eccl. 3,12	"	confusioun	"
" , " , " 4,25; 5,17	"	schame; schame; schame	"
" , " , " 20,28; 25,29	"	schenschype; schenschipe	"
" , " , " 20,24; 20,25	"	schame; schame	"
" , " , " 22,3; 42,1	"	schame; schame	"
" , " , " 29,19	"	schame	"
" , " ,Isaiah 30,3; 45,16	"	confusioun; confusioun	"
" , " , " 30,5	"	schame	"
" , " , " 42,17	"	schenschipe	"
" , " ,Jer. 3,24; 3,25	"	schenschipe;schenschipe	"
" , " , " 6,15	"	confusioun	"
" , " , " 7,19; 8,12	"	schenschip; schenschipe	"
" , " , " 10,17; 11,13	"	schenschipe;schenschipe	"
" , " , " 20,18	"	schenschipe	"
" , " ,Bar. 1,15	"	schenschipe	"
" , " ,Ez. 7,18; 36,6	"	schenschipe;schenschipe	"
" , " , " 36,7; 36,15	"	schenschipe;schenschipe	"
" , " , " 39,26; 44,13	"	schenschipe;schenschipe	"
" , " ,Daniel 3,40	"	schame	"
" , " ,Os.(Hosea) 9,10	"	confusioun	"
" , " ,Abd. 10	"	confusioun	"
" , " ,Micha 7,10	"	confusioun	"
" , " ,Hab. 2,10	"	confusioun	"
" , " ,So.(Zeph.) 3,5; 3,19	"	confusioun; confusioun	"
" , " ,Jude 13	"	confusioun	"
" , " ,Phil. 3,19	"	confusioun	"
" , " ,Luke 21,25	"	confusioun	"
Surtees (MS.CVD7),Ps. 34,26	"	schenschipe	"
" (" ")," 39,16	"	schenschipe	"
" (" ")," 70,13	"	schenschipe	"
" (" ")," 108,29	"	schendnes	"
" (" ")," 131,18	"	schendnes	"
Midland			
(London MS.),Ps. 34,26(34,29)	"	confusion	"
(" ")," 39,16(39,21)	"	confusion	"
(" ")," 70,13(70,14)	"	confusyon	"

TEXT	LATIN WORD	ENGLISH WORD	SENSE GR.
(London MS.),Ps.108,29 (108,28)	confusio	confusion	B III
(" ")," 131,18 (131,19)	"	confusioun	"
Paues (MS.S),Jude 13	"	confusyoun	"
" (" "),Phil. 3,19	"	confusyoun	"
Higd.Trev.,Vol. 5,pp.244-245	"	schame, schendnes	"
" Harl., " "," "	"	confuscioun	"
Ancr.R.,p. 112,15; p.133,30	"	scheome	"
" ," 123,16; " 145,14	"	schendfulnes	"
" ," 123,18; " 145,17	"	schendlac	"
" ," 123,20; " 145,20	"	schendlac	"
" ," 137,28; " 160,23	"	scheome	"
" ," 138,15; " 161,14	"	scheome	"
Higd.Trev.,Vol. 7,pp.358-359	turpitudo	schame of cowardise	"
" Harl., " "," "	"	(signe of a) cowarde	"
Ancr.R.,p. 123,19-;p. 145,22	"	þet fule	"
Chaucer,p.104,120-2;1. 3699-	"	filþe, synne	"
Destr.Troy,p.165,24; 1.8121	"	filth	"

4. Unclassified Middle English Material

TEXT	LATIN WORD	ENGLISH WORD	SENSE GR.
Higd.Trev.,Vol.1, pp. 94-95	confusio (linguarum)	spreding	-
" " , " ", " 208-209	confusio (turrim)	tour Babel	-
" " , " ", " 344-345	confusio (linguarum)	men speked many languages	-
" " , " 2, " 250-251	confusio (linguae)	schedyng; schedyng	-
" Harl., " 1, " 94-95	confusio (linguarum)	confusion (of tonges)	-
" " , " ", " 208-209	confusio (turrim)	confusion	-
" " , " ", " 344-345	confusio (linguarum)	confusion	-
" " , " 2, " 250-251	confusio (linguae)	confusion; confusion	-
Ancr.R., p.100,32-33; 121,18-19	confusio (vir confusionis)	bimased (mon)	-
" , p.101,13; 121,35	confusio (Ysboseeth)	bimasede (gost)	-
Chaucer,p. 111,96-99; 1. 3960-64	confusio	confusioun	-
" ,p. 129,91; 1. 4570	"	confusioun	-
WB,EV 2,Acts, 19,29	"	confusioun	-
" ,LV , " , "	"	confusioun	-

5. Notes to Classified Middle English Material

[1]In italics, signifying that it is written by alia manus in the MS.,
e.g. or scoorne (p. 189; WB,EV 1,Sir.Eccl. 27,31), or scornyng (p. 191;
WB,EV 2, Os. 7,16), and wrong (p. 192; WB,EV 1,Eccl., 5,7).

[2]Ps. 78,4: subsannatio et inlusio in the "Gallican" text (derisu et
contemptu in the "Roman" text). See p. 191.

[3]Ps. 43,14: subsannationem et derisum in the "Gallican" text (derisu
et contemptu in the "Roman" text). See p. 191.

[4]Destr.Troy, p. 51,33-35; l. 1753-54: ..., nisi tam grauis iniuria,
tam ignominiosa iactura dedecoris meum animum perurgeret.: But þe
harme and hethyng of my kynd suster, þat is set vnder seruage, ...
See pp. 22-24 and 196.

[5]Destr.Troy, p. 56,14-; l. 2032-: ..., minaces iniurias a Thelamone
sibi datas, ...: The tene & the torfor of Telamon after ... See pp. 22-
24 and 197.

[6]Destr.Troy, p. 59,16-; l. 2211- : "Karissime mi domine rex, nunquid
est hominum inhumanum et humana dissidens a natura de illatis iniuriis
passos non appetere ultionem? Et si nos, qui tanta nobilitate uigemus
quorum iniuria minima pudoris est magni (cum personarum qualitas
iniuriarum qualitatem minuat et augmentet), si uindictam appetimus de
iniuriis nobis illatis, non sumus degeneres hominum a natura, cum ...:
Most worshipfull fader, & my fre kyng! Hit is kendly by course & custome
of men, þat any hardlaike has, or a hede shame, ffor to wreke in hor
wrathe of wranges before.   And if we, þat are worthy, & wight men in
Armys, Take harme, other hethyng, or hurtys vnзoldyn, Of any erdyng in
erthe euenyng to vs, Hit were shortly a shame & a shire greme. ffor þe
more he is mighty, þat the mysse tholis, The more the greuaunce is
grete & to gref turnys ... See pp. 22-24 and 197.

[7]Destr.Troy, p. 68,2-3; l. 2768-69: Etsi illa ratio debuit esse
potissima, illatarum scilicet iniuriarum uobis et michi uindictam
appetere, ...: To venge of our velany, of our vile grem, And hardlaike
we hade of hom in þis londe ... /l. 2779: And wreke vs of wrathe &
wranges before. See pp. 22-24 and 197.

[8]Destr.Troy, p. 143,5-6; l. 6944: ..., reducens eis ad memoriam pre-
teritas iniurias eis a Grecis illatas: Haue mynd of þe malis, & the
mykell harme, ... See pp. 22-24 and 197.

[9]Destr.Troy, p. 81,25-26; l. 3642-43: ..., nostra scripta mittemus
vt in huius ulciscendi causa dedecoris nobis potenter assistant.": "...
To helpe vs in hast our harmys to venge, And dyshonour and daunger done
to our rewmes." See pp. 22-24 and 202.

[10]Destr.Troy, p. 107,32-33; l. 5038-39: Quanto uero dedecore, quantis
minis legatum meum affecerint satis patet uobis et michi.: Of the dishonour ye did to my dere legat, And with spite in your speche dispiset
my name, ... See pp. 22-24 and 202.

APPENDIX D. BIBLIOGRAPHY

The bibliography does not include the excerpted Latin, Old English,
and Middle English texts. Those texts are presented with bibliographi-
cal references in Appendix **A**.

Authorized Version (King James Version). The Holy Bible. London &
  New York, Collins' Clear-Type Press. [AV]

AV, see Authorized Version (King James Version).

Baugh, Albert C. (1959). A History of the English Language. 2nd ed.
  London, Routledge & Kegan Paul.

Baugh, Albert C. (ed.) (1967). A Literary History of England. 2nd.
  ed. London, Routledge & Kegan Paul.

Bennett, J.A.W., & Smithers, G.V. (eds.) (1966). Early Middle English
  Verse and Prose. Oxford, Clarendon Press.

Bosworth, J. & Toller, T. Northcote (eds.) (1898-1921). An Anglo-
  Saxon Dictionary. Oxford, Clarendon Press. [BT]

Brockhaus, F.A. (ed.) (1972). Der Sprach-Brockhaus. 8. Aufl. Wies-
  baden, Brockhaus.

BT, see Bosworth & Toller (1898-1921).

Büchner, G. (1968). "Vier altenglische Bezeichnungen für Vergehen und
  Verbrechen (firen, gylt, man, scyld)". Berlin, diss. Freie Universität.

Campbell, A. (1959). Old English Grammar. Oxford, Clarendon Press.
  [OEG]

Campbell, Jackson J. (1951). "The Dialect Vocabulary of the Old English
  Bede". Journal of English and Germanic Philology, pp. 349-372.

COD, see Fowler & Fowler (1976).

Collins, see Hanks, Patrick (1979).

Engnell, Ivan (1962-1963). Svenskt Bibliskt Uppslagsverk. 2:a uppl.
  Stockholm, Esselte.

Fetzlaff, G. (1954). "Bezeichnungen für die sieben Todsünden in der
  altenglischen Prosa". Berlin, diss. Freie Universität.

Forcellini, E. (1858-1875). Totius latinitatis lexicon opera et studio
  Aegidii Forcellini lucubratum ... novo ordine digestum ... cura et
  studio Doct. Vincentii De-Vit. I-VI. Prati. [Forcellini]

Fowler, H.W., & Fowler, F.G. (eds.) (1976). The Concise Oxford Dictionary of Current English. 6th ed. Oxford, Clarendon Press. [COD]

Freudenthal, K.F. (1959). Gloria, temptatio, conversio. Stockholm, Almqvist & Wiksell. (Göteborger germanistische Forschungen 3.)

Förster, Max (1906). "Altenglische Predigtquellen I". Archiv für das
  Studium der neueren Sprachen und Literaturen 116, pp. 301-305.

Förster, Max (1909). "Altenglische Predigtquellen II". Archiv für das
  Studium der neueren Sprachen und Literaturen 122, pp. 246-262.

Georges, K.E. (1951). Ausführliches lateinisch-deutsches Handwörter-
buch. 9. Aufl. I-II. Basel, Schwabe. [Georges]

Hall, John R. Clark, & Meritt, H.D. (1970). A Concise Anglo-Saxon Dictionary. 4th ed. Cambridge, University Press. [HM]

Hanks, Patrick (ed.) 1979). Collins Dictionary of the English Language.
London & Glasgow, Collins. [Collins]

Hellquist, E. (1957). Svensk Etymologisk Ordbok. 3:e uppl. I-II. Lund,
Gleerups.

HM, see Hall & Meritt (1970).

Holthausen, E. (1963). Altenglisches etymologisches Wörterbuch. Heidelberg, Winter.

Jordan, Richard (1905). "Eigentümlichkeiten des anglischen Wortschatzes".
Anglistische Forschungen 17.

Ker, N.R. (1957). Catalogue of Manuscripts Containing Anglo-Saxon. Oxford, Clarendon Press. [Ker]

Kirby, Thomas A., & Woolf, Henry Bosley (1949). Philologica: The Malone
Anniversary Studies. Baltimore, Johns Hopkins Press.

Kjellmer, Göran (1971). Context and Meaning. Stockholm, Almqvist & Wiksell. (Gothenburg Studies in English 22.)

Kjellmer, Göran (1973). Middle English Words for 'People'. Stockholm,
Almqvist & Wiksell. (Gothenburg Studies in English 27.)

Klaeber, Fr. (ed.) (1950). Beowulf. 3rd ed. Lexington, Massachusetts,
Heath.

Knowles, Dom David (1941). The Monastic Order in England. Cambridge,
Cambridge University Press.

Kroesch, Samuel (1929). "Semantic Borrowing in Old English". Studies in
English Philology. Minneapolis, University of Minnesota Press.

Kurath, Hans, & Kuhn, Sherman M. (eds.) (1952 -). Middle English Dictionary. I - . Ann Arbor, Mich., University of Michigan Press. [MED]

Käsmann, H. (1951). "'Tugend und Laster' im Alt- und Mittelenglischen".
Berlin, Freie Universität.

Legouis, Émile (1950). A Short History of English Literature. Oxford,
Clarendon Press.

Lehrer, Adrienne (1974). Semantic Fields and Lexical Structure. Amster-
dam, North-Holland Publishing Company.

Leisi, Ernst (1967). Der Wortinhalt. 3. Aufl. Heidelberg, Quelle &
Meyer.

Leisi, Ernst (1973). Praxis der englischen Semantik. Heidelberg,
Winter.

Lewis, Charlton T., & Short, Charles (eds.) (1969). A Latin Dictionary.
Oxford, Clarendon Press. [Lewis & Short]

MED, see Kurath & Kuhn (1952 -).

Meissner, Paul (1934-1935). "Studien zum Wortschatz Aelfrics". Archiv
für das Studium der neueren Sprachen und Literaturen 165, pp. 11-19;
166, pp. 30-39 und 205-215.

Menner, Robert J. (1948). "Anglian and Saxon Elements in Wulfstan's Vocabulary". Modern Language Notes 63, pp. 1-9.

Merriam-Webster (editorial staff) (1967). Webster's Seventh New Colle-
giate Dictionary. Springfield, Massachusetts, Merriam. [Webster]

Murray, A. H., Bradley, H., Craigie, W.A., & Onions, C.T. (eds.) (1933).
The Oxford English Dictionary, being a corrected re-issue ... of A
New English Dictionary on Historical Principles. Oxford, Clarendon
Press. [OED]

OED, see Murray, Bradley, Craigie, & Onions (1933).

OEG, see Campbell, A (1959).

OLD, see Souter, A, et al. (1968).

Onions, C.T. (ed.) (1966). The Oxford Dictionary of English Etymology.
Oxford, Clarendon Press.

Quirk, Randolph, & Wrenn, C.L. (1969). An Old English Grammar. London,
Methuen.

Reuning, K. (1941). Joy and Freude. Swarthmore, Pa.

Robinson, J. Armitage (1923). The Times of Saint Dunstan. Oxford,
Clarendon Press.

Schabram, Hans (1965). Superbia I. München, Fink.

Severs, J. Burke (ed.) (1967 -). A Manual of the Writings in Middle
English 1050-1500. New Haven, Conn., Connecticut Academy of Arts
and Sciences.

Skeat, W.W. (1910). An Etymological Dictionary of the English Language. Oxford, Clarendon Press.

Souter, A., et al. (eds.) (1968). Oxford Latin Dictionary. Oxford,
Clarendon Press. [OLD]

Svensk Uppslagsbok (1960-1963). 2:a uppl. Malmö, Norden.

Waldron, R.A. (1967). Sense and Sense Development. London, André
Deutsch (Language Library).

Webster, see Merriam-Webster (1967).

Winter, W. (1955). "Āeht, Wela, Gestrēon, Spēd, und Ēad im Alt- und
Mittelenglischen". Berlin, Freie Universität.

APPENDIX E. INDEX

The numbers in brackets indicate the numbers of the relevant words
in Lists OE 1-2 and ME 1-2. Those words which have no numbers in
brackets are not recorded in the Lists. Other numbers refer to pages
in the text (pp. 5-107). **Underlined numbers indicate main references.**

1. Old English Words

āblysung (58)   6
ābylgd   (47)   65
aefwyrd   6, 11
aepsenys (23)   42
āeswicnes (55)
āewisc   6, 11
āewiscnes   74
anddetnes (59)
andracung (on-)   74
anweordnys (24)   65
ār   104
ārscamu   6, 11
ārung   104
ārweordnes   74, 104
ārweordung   74, 104
āscyndnes (22)   79
āswarnung   6, 11
baeligniso (48)   65
besmitenes   34, 36, 57
bi3-swic **(beswic)** (2)   25, 58, 95
bismer-words (1)   8, 10, 11, 25-26, 27-28, 36, 56, 57-58, 60-61,
                           70, 76, 81, 87, 93-94, 97
blǣed   104
canc (5)
cancettan (5)
clǣennes   74
costnung (4)   25, 95
demm (44)   65
dōm   104
dōmweordung   104
dugud   104

duolma (60)   11, 72

dysig   89

dysines (16)   95, 97

earfode (49)   65

ebolsung (14)   10, 41, 60-61, 70, 95

edwīt (12)   6, 8, 44-46, 51-53, 63-64, 65, 68, 70, 88, 90, 92, 94, 98

edwītscipe   6, 11

edwītspraec (12)   42, 46

edwītstaef (12)   6, 46

firenlust (33)   38-39

fōlnes (40)

forescending (22)   79

forwandung (61)   6, 74

fraced (13)   6, 42, 83

fracodlic (13)   83

fracodne (13)

fracodword (13)   82

fūlnes (40)

fȳlþ (40)   78, 96, 97, 100

gānung (10)

gecanc (5)

gedrōefnis (56)   8, 52, 72, 77, 79, 80, 88, 92, 96

gehealdsumnes   74

gemeng (57)   72, 78, 80, 96

gemengnes (57)   72-73, 78, 80, 96

gemengung (57)   72, 78, 80

gescendnes (22)   6, 21, 52, 77, 79, 80, 95

gescendd (22)   77, 79, 80, 92, 96

gewrixle (63)   11, 73

gielping   104

gilp   104

gleng   104

glīu (9)

glīwung (9)

golfetung (25)   58, 95

grama (29)   65, 68, 97

gylt (15)   8, 49, 88, 89

gyltlic (15)   41, 46, 60

hāeman (41)   96

hearm (35)   42, 62, 70, 92, 95, 97, 99

hearmcwide (35)   42, 46, 62, 70, 92, 95, 99

hearmcwidolnes (35) 62, 70, 95, 99

hearmsprāec (35)   62, 99

hisping (3)   65

hlacerung (26)   53, 58, 95

hlcahter (7)   53, 58, 70, 95, 97

hlēorsceamu (6)   72

hlīsa   104

hōltihte (38)   62

hosp (3)   8, 44-46, 52-53, 61, 63-64, 65, 68, 70, 88, 90, 92, 94, 95, 98

hygdignis   74

hyrwing (17)   60, 95

ierre   89-90

lāedo (43)   65

lēas (37)   62

lēasgielp   9

lēasspellung   28, 90

līcettan (36)   62

līcettung (36)   62

lōf   104

māernes   104

māerdo   104

maed   104

netenes (32)

onhrōp   89

onscunung   84

ōretla (30)

orwyrd (28)   6, 79, 81, 82-83, 92

rīceter   104

risne   104

sacu   27

scamu (6)   6, 73, 74, 75, 77-81, 83, 92, 96, 97, 99

scamung (6)   6, 77, 79, 96

scand (22)   6, 8, 65, 68, 81, 84, 88

scandlicnes (22)   6, 78, 80, 88, 96

sceamian (6)   81

scondehlewung (22)

scyld   8, 89

scyndan (22)   77

sīdefulnys   74

swic (2)   25, 58, 95

swicung (2)   25, 58, 95

tǣl (8)   6, 53, 60, <u>62</u>, 70, 83, 88, 95

tǣlhlehter (7)   95

tǣlic (word) (8)   60, 95

tǣlung (8)

tēlnis (8)   <u>62</u>, 70, 95

tēona (27)   62, <u>64-65</u>, 68, 70, <u>81</u>, 83, 88-89, 92, 94-95, 97, 98

tēoncwide (27)   64, 94

tēonful (þing) (27)   64

tēonrēden (27)   64

tēonword (27)

tīr   104

trega (50)   65

tȳnan (45)   65

ðrym(m)   104

ðrymdōm   104

ðryð   104

unār (51)   6, 9, 65, 90

unēðnys (52)   65

ungerisne/-nu (21)   6

ungerisnes (21)

ungewiss (31)   6, 79, 81

unhlīsa (11)   6

unriht (46)   89

unðeaw   89-90

unweorðnes   6, 90

unweorðscipe (24)   6, 9, 89-90

unweorðung (24)   89-90

unwitende (34)   81

unwlite (20)   6, 49

unwlitegian (20)   49

wamm/wemm   6, 11

weorðfulnes   104

weorðlicnes   104

weorðmynd   104

weordnes	104
weordscipe	104
weordung	104
wilnung (62)	72, 73
wīte (42)	65
wītnan (42)	65
wītnung (42)	65
wiþersacung (19)	60-61, 95
wlenc	104
woffung (18)	60, 95
woruldgielp	9
wraecsīd (53)	65
wraeddo (54)	65, 97
wuldor	104
wuldorblaed	104
wuldorfaestlicnes	104
wuldordrymm	104
yfel (14)	81, 82, 84, 89
yfelnes	89
yfelsacung (14)	60-61
yfelsang	61
yrmdu (39)	62

2. Middle English Words

abominacion   101-102, 106

bimased (68)   73

bismer (6)   59

blame (32)   62, 105

blamyng (32)   62, 68, 85, 98, 101, 105

blasfemye (19)   59-60, 70, 98, 101, 105-106

bygile (4)   59

chalenge (49)   62, 70, 101-102, 105-106

chalengyng (49)   62, 70, 105

chiding (42)

confusioun (67)   11, 73, 77-78, 79, 80, 101-102, 105-106

contek (38)

coward (24)   35

cowardise (24)   35

craving (50)   62, 105

damage (57)

deed (17)

defilen (34)

defoul (34)

derf (word) (61)   23-24, 85

derision (13)

desceit (3)   59, 70, 98, 101-102,

dishonour (21)   23-24, 77-78, 85

dispisyng (10)   68, 70, 98, 102, 105

destroyen   (39)

diffamyng (14)

dishese

dispit (9)   68, 70, 98, 102

dispitous (word) (9)

dispitousness (9)

eny thing ... (51)   62, 105

fame (yuel/of filth/
      losen) (14)   23, 50, 67, 78-79, 80, 97-98, 101, 102

filth (45)   36, 78-79, 80, 98, 100

filthhed (45)   78-79, 80, 97, 98, 100

fule (**fyle**/foyle) (34) 36, 100

gram (23)   97

greuans (55)

greuen (55)

gilt (60)

hardlaike (56)

harm (52)   69, 70, 98, 99

harmen (52)

hethyng (5)   59

hokor (7)   105

hurtys (58)

ill   101

illusioun (2)   58-59, 68, 70, 98, 101, 105-106

iniury (35)   68, 70, 98, 102, 105-10

iniuryos (word) (35)

loos (evel/wicked/   23
    losen)

meschif (46)

missiggen (36)

mouwing (27)   58-59, 70, 98

mysse (63)

obbrayd (64)

opprobry (66)   106

outerage (43)

rebuke (12)

redur (62)

repref (8)   44-45, 47, 51-52, 66, 67-69, 70, 98, 102

repreuyng (8)   66, 67-69, 70, 98

reproce (65)   69, 70, 98, 101

reproceing (65)   69, 70, 98, 101

saye ... (37)

scandle   101, 105-106

schedyng (69)   73

schendful (word) (22)

schendfulnes (22)   79, 106

schendlac (22)   79

schendnes (22)   79

sclaundre (16)   79, 101, 105-106

scorn (1)   58-59, 68, 70, 98, 101

scornen (1)

scornyng (1)   58-59, 68, 70, 98, 101

seoruwe (47)

schame (20)   23, 35, 77-78, 79, 80, 83, 98, <u>99</u>

schenschipe (22)   23, 44, 45, 48, 50, 51, <u>66-67</u>, 77, 79, 80,
                                     84-85, 98, <u>100</u>,

snering (28)

spite (9)

spreding (70)   73

strif (31)   68, 70, 98, 102

striuyng (word) (31)

synne (44)   36, 79

tene (59)   97

trespas (18)

trouble (26)

turmenten (33)   68

undermouwing (27)   58-59, 70, 98

undernyming (29)

unright (54)   68

unri3tfulness (54)

unrightwisness (54)   68

unworschippe (25)   85

unworþy (48)

upbraidyng (64)   69-70, 98

vilenye (11)   79

wlating   106

woh/wouh (53)   68, 70, 98, <u>100</u>

wrong (30)   <u>66</u>, 68, 70, 97, 98, <u>100</u>

yuel   84, 97, 101

3. Latin Words

abominatio   27, 84, 101, 106

blasphemia   (7)   10, 31, 41, 43, 46, <u>59-61</u>, 63, 70, 95, 101, 105-106

calumnia   (12)   32, 42, 43, 46, <u>62</u>, 64, 69, 85, 92, 99, 105

cauillatio   27

coinquinatio   34

combustio   34

confusio (16)   11, 33-34, 42, 43, 48, 51, 52, 53, 59, 66-67, <u>71-73</u>,
                      76,81, 83, 84, 96, 105-106

contumelia   (10)   9, 31,42, 43, 47, 64, <u>65</u>, 66, 68, 70, 81-83, 85, 88-
                      90, 92, 94

conuitium   27

crimen   90

dedecus   (8)   9, 31, 42, 43, <u>48-50</u>, 66, 69, 71, 81, 84, 85, 97

dedignatio   90

derisus (4)   30, 43, 45-47, 53-54, 57, 58, 87, 95

execratio   27

exprobratio   27, 64, 90

evangelium   9

gannatura (5)   30

gloria (inanis/   9
      temporalis)

ignominia   (11)   23, 31, 34, 38-39 43, <u>48-50</u>, 51, 66-67, 71-72, 73,
                      74, <u>76</u>, 81-82, 84, 89, 101

improbitas   27, 84, 89

indignatio   9, 27, <u>89-90</u>, 101

infamia   (6)   23, 30, 43, <u>48</u>, 50, 64, 71, 87, 90, 101, 105

injuria   (14)   9, 23-24, 32, 43, 63, <u>64-66</u>, <u>68</u>, 70, 84, 88-90, 92,
                      94, 97, 105-107

inlusio   (1)   30, <u>34</u>, 35-36,43-44,46, 47, 57, 58, 59, 87, 95, 105

inproperium   27, 52, <u>63-64</u>, 66-67

inquinatio   27, 34, 36, 57

inrisio   (2)   30, 43, 45, 47, 105

ira   89

laus humana   9

ludibrium   (3)   30, 41, 43, 57, 83, 85, 87, 95

macula   11, 27, 87

nenias (vanitates)   11, 28

obscenitas   27

opprobrium   (15)   33, 42, 43, 44-47, <u>51-54</u>, <u>63-64</u>, 66-67, 69, 70, 85,
                        89-90, 92, 93, 94, 97, 106

perjurium   27

probrum   27, 64, 90

pudor   11, 27, 71, 72, <u>73-75</u>, 76, 83

reverentia   11, 27, 38, 71-72, <u>74-75</u>, 76

rixa   11, 27

rubor   27

scandalum   27, 84, <u>101</u>, 105-106

scelus   27, 84, 87, <u>89</u>

spurcitia   100

subsannatio   (9)   31, 43, 46-47, 58, 59, 95, 105

turpitudo   (13)   23, 32, 35, 36, 39, 43, <u>48-50</u>, 71, 78, 81, 100

verecundia   11, 27, 71-72, <u>73-75</u>, 76, 83

vituperatio   27, 101